Home Baking
made easy

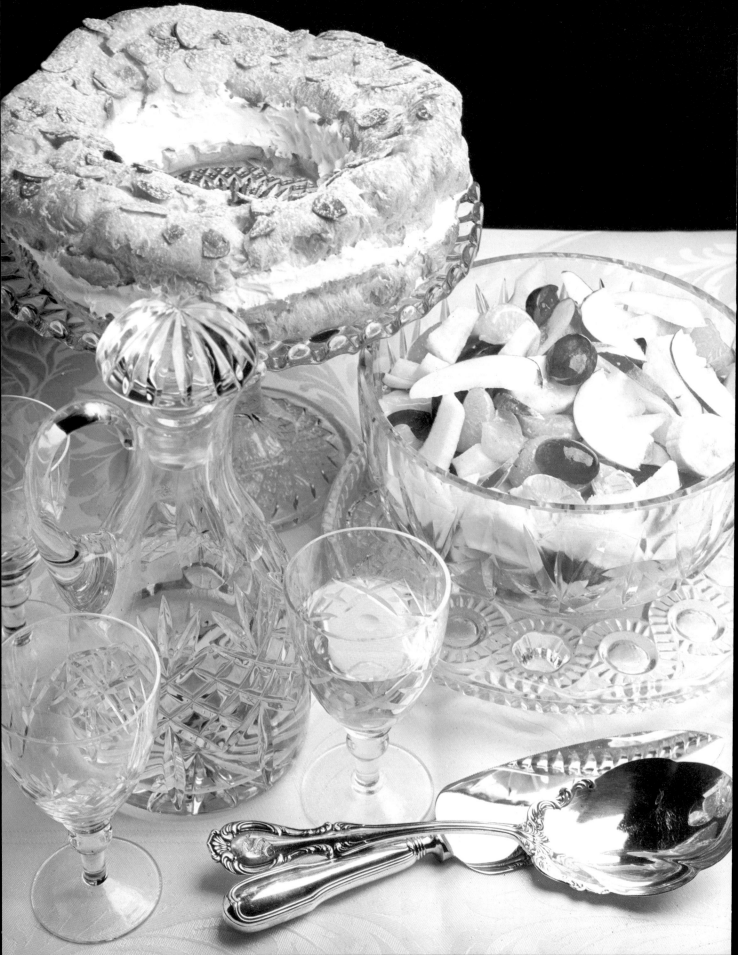

Home Baking
made easy

Marshall Cavendish

Picture Credits

Rex Bamber: 73, 103, 144
Alan Duns: 18, 19/20, 21/2, 24/5,
27, 29, 32/3, 34, 70,
71, 76, 77, 78, 85, 89,
90/1, 114, 148, 159,
162/3, 164/5, 166/7,
169, 176, 178, 179
Gales Honey: 123
Melvin Grey: 35, 37, 38/9, 43, 44/5,
46, 92(cut), 96, 97,
126, 140, 140/1,
146/7 T&B
Antony Kay: 115, 118/9, 120/1, 122,
123
Paul Kemp: 8/9, 11, 15, 16/7, 79,
98, 104, 106/7, 125,
129, 132, 134,135, 137,
142/3
David Levin: 12/3, 30, 31, 36, 40/1,
42, 44/5, 58/9, 60,
62T&B, 63, 66/7, 74,
81, 82, 84, 86/7, 94,
105, 108TL, 108/9 R,
110/111, 112/3, 116/7,
130/1, 138, 142/3, 145,
149, 151, 152/3, 160/1,
170/1, 172/3, 174/5,
182/3, 183, 184
Roger Phillips: 26, 124(cut), 154TL,
154/5, 156/7, 158, 168
Paul Williams: 47, 48/9, 50/1, 54/5,
56, 57, 68/9, 99/100,
102, 180 B & TR, 181

Time symbols: an indication of preparation and cooking time is given for each recipe. This is calculated for beginners new to the techniques involved: experienced cooks need allow less time.

 less than 1 hour

 1-2½ hours

 Over 2½ hours

Published by Marshall Cavendish Books Limited
58 Old Compton Street
London W1V 5PA

First printing 1979
This printing 1986

ISBN 0 85685 704 1

Printed and bound in Hong Kong by Dai Nippon Printing Company

INTRODUCTION

The unforgettable fragrance of freshly baked cakes and biscuits evokes not only nostalgic childhood memories but also regret for their incomparable taste and texture as compared to products packed with preservatives and covered in plastic bought from the supermarket.

Home Baking Made Easy can contribute to the idea of family sharing for everyone can help in some little way, whether it is stirring a rich mixture of fruit and eggs for a Dundee Cake, kneading a basic bread dough or taking up the challenge of making a decorative Battenburg. Special occasions are catered for too, and there are cream-filled profiteroles made with mouth-watering choux pastry and lots of exciting ideas on icing and decorating, together with detailed instructions on how to make your own equipment.

Home Baking Made Easy is colourfully illustrated and each recipe has been carefully organised so that it is easy to follow. It is a valuable addition to any cookery bookshelf and guarantees many delicious treats ahead for friends and family.

CONTENTS

Bake a favourite cake

The creaming method is used for the widest choice of cakes—rich in butter, sugar and eggs with a light, yet lusciously moist, texture. Here we show you how to make some favourite tea-time classics, including a feather-light Victoria sponge and a buttery rich Madeira cake.

R ich cakes contain a higher proportion of fat and sugar than plain cakes. To incorporate these satisfactorily, a different method of preparation is used. The traditional way to make rich cakes is by the creaming method. Equal quantities of fat and sugar are vigorously beaten together with a wooden spoon until light and fluffy. This is known as 'creaming' to distinguish it from beating with a whisk. Eggs are then beaten in and, lastly, the flour is gently folded in.

Many of the same cakes can be made using the quicker and certainly easier, all-in-one baking method, but the extra time spent on the creaming method pays dividends. With the all-in-one method extra

Bake a cake that is as light as air with a deliciously rich flavour.

baking powder is used as the raising agent. With the creaming method, air is beaten in to raise the cake. Thorough creaming is therefore very important. The air expands on heating, forcing the cake to rise.

Cakes made by the creaming method have far better keeping qualities. Moreover, the actual process of creaming produces a far finer texture.

INGREDIENTS
Flour
Self-raising or plain flour, or occasionally a mixture of the two, are used for creamed cakes. The choice depends on the type of cake being made, but it must be a soft flour because this absorbs fat well and gives the cake a deliciously light, soft texture.

Strong flour is not suitable as it gives too coarse a texture to the cake. Use the type of flour specified in recipe and always sieve the flour. Sieving not only aerates the flour, but it also removes any lumps which will cause an unevenly blended mixture.

Baking powder
If plain flour is used, a chemical raising agent (usually baking powder) is used to help the cake rise. The amount needed will depend upon the proportion of eggs to flour. As the number of eggs increases, the amount of chemical raising agent needed will decrease. If the recipe calls for baking powder, it must be accurately measured and sifted with the flour.

Salt
A pinch of salt is added to bring out the flavour of the other ingredients. It should be sifted with the flour.

Fat
Butter is by far the best choice as it gives the richest flavour and a lovely golden colour to the cake. Although expensive, it is well worth using for those cakes which contain little or no additional flavourings.

Hard margarine is less expensive to use but will not give such a good flavour as butter. Hard margarines are best used for cakes which have pronounced flavours such as spices.

Whipped margarines are the most economical of all the fats to use and will give an extremely light result. Unlike butter or hard margarine, whipped margarine contains no water, so approximately one-fifth less is used.

Sugar
Caster sugar should be used as its fine crystals dissolve easily when creamed with the fat. Coarse sugars such as granulated and Demerara are not suitable because they do not dissolve when creamed with the fat and will give the cake a speckled appearance.

Eggs
Eggs make the cake light, give it a good flavour and a moist, soft texture. Eggs should always be medium sized unless the recipe states otherwise, and are used at room temperature. If you store eggs in the refrigerator, you should remove them at least one hour before they are going to be used. Using eggs straight from the refrigerator will increase the danger of the mixture curdling.

Liquids
The eggs in the recipe contain a high proportion of water, so this contributes to the liquid in the cake mixture. The amount of liquid needed in addition will depend on the proportion of fat and sugar used.

In some cases, a small proportion of extra liquid is added to a cake and this may be either milk or water. The liquid must be used at room temperature. Water, rather than milk, is best for Victoria sponge mixtures, as it gives a lighter result.

The liquid added to a rich cake mixture should be just enough to produce a soft dropping consistency. This consistency is one that is moist enough to drop easily from a spoon when the mixture is lifted above the bowl. A dropping consistency, however, is a good deal stiffer than a pouring consistency and should not be confused with it, or a consistency resembling batter.

FLAVOURINGS
Liquid flavourings
Liquid sweeteners, such as honey or golden syrup, may be used in place of up to half the given amount of sugar in a recipe. Liquid sweeteners will give a moister, denser cake, as well as a hint of their own individual flavours.

Flavouring essences are very often used but should be used with extreme caution as their flavour is deceptively strong. Never use them straight from the bottle, but add them drop by drop. Flavouring essences should be added before the eggs.

Powdered flavourings
Ground spices are a convenient and easy way to give a cake a subtle flavour. Cocoa powder is used when a rich chocolate flavour is required. Instant coffee and liquid coffee also make delicious cakes. Unless otherwise stated, the amount of flour will have to be reduced by the same amount as the powdered flavouring.

Always sieve the powdered flavouring with the flour to ensure an even distribution in the mixture. If using self-raising flour, the cocoa is best dissolved in a little hot water. This is then allowed to cool before it is beaten into the creamed fat and sugar mixture. Instant coffee, if powdered, can be sifted with the dry ingredients, but if the coffee is in granules, it should be dissolved first in a little hot water and then added to the creamed fat and sugar.

Powdered additions
Ground rice or cornflour can both be used to give a shorter, melt-in-the-mouth texture to cakes. The same rules apply to these as to powdered flavourings.

GUIDE TO PROPORTIONS FOR CREAMED CAKES
*individual recipes may vary slightly

plain flour	100 g [¼ lb]	175 g [6 oz]	225 g [½ lb]
baking powder	2.5 ml [½ teaspoon]	5 ml [1 teaspoon]	5 ml [1 teaspoon]
salt	large pinch	large pinch	large pinch
fat	100 g [¼ lb]	175 g [6 oz]	225 g [½ lb]
sugar	100 g [¼ lb]	175 g [6 oz]	225 g [½ lb]
eggs	2 medium-sized	3 medium-sized	4 medium-sized
liquid	15–30 ml [1–2 tablespoons]	30 ml [2 tablespoons]	15–45 ml [1–3 tablespoons]*

Flavoured additions
Crystallized fruit makes a delicious chewy addition. Make sure that any thick coating of sugar on the fruit is removed before using or the fruit will sink in the cake mixture. Wash the fruit under hot water, drain and dry completely then toss lightly in flour. Glacé cherries and mixed peel are popular, but finely chopped angelica and stem ginger are also excellent. When using glacé cherries, always halve them because whole cherries are too heavy to be supported by the cake mixture.

Nuts impart their own rich flavour, and give a moist, chewy texture. Always use the nuts as directed in the recipe, and check whether they should be used ground, chopped or whole. When ground nuts are used, a corresponding reduction of the amount of flour is made.

Caraway seeds are the traditional flavouring for seed cake. Use only as directed in the recipe as their flavour is surprisingly strong.

PREPARING CAKE TINS
For success, rich cake making relies on the application of a simple set of rules. One very important rule is that you choose and prepare the baking equipment before you start preparing the cake so that there is no delay between the making and the baking. Choose shallow tins for cakes you intend to eat immediately because a shallow tin bakes a cake quickly. Use deep, round or square tins for fruit cakes or cakes with good keeping qualities.

All cake tins must be lined with greaseproof paper to prevent sticking and burning. To line large square tins, see page 30.

Sandwich tins are usually base lined, not side-lined as others are. However, to give a Victoria sandwich a professional touch, dust the ungreased insides of the tins with equal quantities of sugar and rice flour. This gives the cake an appetizing sugary crust.

OTHER EQUIPMENT
Once the tin(s) are prepared, the next step is to collect together the equipment for making the cake.

The correct proportions for rich cakes are important, so you will need accurate scales and measuring spoons. In addition to these you will also need a sieve and bowl for the dry ingredients and a bowl and whisk for the eggs. Unless you have an electric mixer, you will need a wooden spoon for the creaming of the fat and sugar. Wooden spoons come in all sizes, so choose one that is easy to manage; a large cumbersome spoon will prove difficult and make the creaming process heavy going.

Choose a large mixing bowl for creaming the fat and sugar together, so that these can be vigorously beaten without the mixture overflowing. A rubber spatula is handy for scraping the mixture down the side of the bowl and it is also the best tool for turning the cake mixture into the prepared tin with the minimum of waste. You will need a metal spoon for folding in the flour and a palette or round-bladed knife for levelling the mixture in the tin. Oven gloves and a wire rack are necessary for turning the cake out of the tin once it is baked.

OVEN TEMPERATURES
Always heat the oven to the recommended oven temperature. This means heating the oven 20 minutes before the cake is to be baked, and is usually the first step when baking a cake. If a cake is put into the oven before it has reached the correct temperature the rise will be uneven.

The importance of baking cakes at the temperature given in the recipe is stressed in previous courses. If the oven temperature is too low, the cake will have a heavy texture and will sink in the centre. Too hot an oven will result in a cake that forms a peak and cracks. A very hot oven will cause the sugar to caramelize and produce a hard, tough crust.

Large cakes without fruit should be baked at 180°C [350°F] gas mark 4. Cakes cooked in sandwich tins need the same temperature. The temperature for small cakes will depend on the individual recipe to a certain extent but the average temperature is 190°C [375°F] gas mark 5.

Oven positions
The position in the oven depends on the size and type of cake. When baking two sandwich cakes bake them on the same shelf, close together but not touching. If your oven is heated from the back, place the tins side by side. If it is heated from the sides, position one tin towards the back of the oven and the other towards the front. Always check that there is a gap of at least 2.5 cm [1"] between the sides of the oven and the sides of the tins. If this is not done, the hot air will not be able to circulate freely and the results will be 'half-baked'!

Shelf positions
Large plain cakes should be baked on a shelf in the centre of the oven. Small cakes and sandwich cakes just above the centre of the oven.

MAKING A CREAMED CAKE
Assembling ingredients
Start by assembling all the ingredients listed in the recipe. Then prepare the baking tin(s). Make sure that the oven shelves are positioned correctly and heat the oven to the required temperature.

The ingredients should be used at room temperature and this will make preparation much easier. This means

Having all the ingredients ready before you start baking is the recipe for success when using the creamed method for cakes.

removing items from the refrigerator one hour before you start cake making. Whichever fat you are using remove it from the refrigerator one hour before it is required; rock hard fat is extremely difficult to cream. On the other hand, never try short cuts, such as heating the fat to soften it, because this will only result in an oil which is impossible to cream properly. Use eggs at room temperature. If they are used when very cold, this could have a curdling effect when they are added to the creamed fat and sugar mixture.

Preparing additions

Prepare additional flavouring ingredients before the cake mixture is made. Chop nuts or fruit if required, wash crystallized fruit, or dissolve cocoa powder or coffee granules.

Sifting dry ingredients

Sift the flour, raising agent and any dry flavouring ingredient into a medium-sized bowl ready for use later. The sifting initiates the aerating process, trapping the air as it falls from the sieve into the bowl.

Creaming fat and sugar

Measure the softened fat into the mixing bowl. This is then creamed, which gives the method its name. The aim of this is to work air into the mixture by blending the fat with a wooden spoon. This initial creaming releases the flavour of the butter, which will eventually be distributed throughout the finished cake, and makes sure that the cake is light in texture.

Creaming by hand: stand the bowl containing the fat on a damp cloth, as this prevents the bowl from slipping. Using a wooden spoon, beat the fat against the side of the bowl until it is light in colour and creamy in texture. All lumps of butter must be dispersed. The changing colour of the fat, from its natural colour to a lighter shade, is a visual indication that it is sufficiently creamed and ready for the next stage.

Adding sugar: beat in the measured amount of sugar, all in one go. Using the same vigorous action, cream the ingredients together for 7–10 minutes or until the mixture no longer feels gritty and is light in colour and fluffy in texture. The change in colour, texture and volume is a direct result of air being incorporated. During this creaming period the mixture will increase in bulk.

During the creaming action, it is wise to stop from time to time and scrape the mixture off the spoon and down the sides of the bowl. If this is not done, undissolved sugar crystals will gather around the sides of the bowl. This will result in the baked cake being streaky or speckled in appearance.

Creaming with a mixer: when using a hand-held or table electric mixer, there is no need to beat the fat first. Simply place the fat and sugar in a mixing bowl and beat at the speed recommended by the manufacturer. Using an electric hand-held or table mixer cuts down on the time taken to cream the fat and sugar together. You should turn off the mixer periodically and scrape down the side of the bowl, as you would for the hand method.

Adding liquid flavourings

Flavouring essences, if used, are added at this stage. Beat them into the mixture so that their flavour is evenly distributed throughout the cake. If citrus zest is used, this is added at this stage.

Adding eggs

The next stage is to add the eggs and this requires careful attention. Eggs contain approximately two-thirds water and this must be completely absorbed into the fat and sugar.

Step-by-step to Victoria sponge sandwich

MAKES 18CM [7"] CAKE
175 g [6 oz] self-raising flour
175 g [6 oz] butter or
    margarine
175 g [6 oz] caster sugar
3 medium-sized eggs
30 ml [2 tablespoons] milk
45 ml [3 tablespoons]
    raspberry or strawberry jam
icing or caster sugar to dredge

1 Put shelf above centre and heat oven to 180°C [350°F] gas mark 4. Prepare two 18 cm [7"] sandwich tins.

OR place the fat and sugar in a bowl and cream together with a hand-held electric whisk.

4 Whisk the eggs lightly then beat into the mixture, a little at a time, beating well after each addition.

5 With a rubber spatula scrape the mixture down sides of the bowl and off the spoon. Beat mixture again.

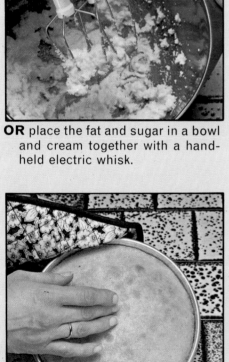

8 Bake for 25–30 minutes. Test by pressing lightly with fingertips. The cakes should be springy but firm.

9 Remove from oven if ready. A well-cooked cake should have slightly shrunk from the sides of the tin. Leave ½ minute to cool.

10 Turn out cakes on to tea-towel. Remove paper and then turn right way up on to wire rack to cool.

2 Sift flour into a bowl and reserve. Put softened butter or margarine in mixing bowl and beat until light.

3 Add sugar to the fat and cream it with a wooden spoon until light in colour and fluffy in texture.

Fold in the flour, one-third at a time, using a figure-of-eight action. Add milk if necessary to make a soft dropping consistency.

7 Divide the mixture equally between the two prepared tins. Level the top with a palette knife.

1 When cold, place one cake on serving plate and spread upper surface with jam.

12 Then dredge surface of remaining sponge liberally with caster or icing sugar. Put this cake on top of the other.

If the amount of sugar used in the recipe is less than 225 g [½ lb] the eggs must be lightly whisked together before they are added, otherwise the eggs can quite happily be added one at a time, directly to the creamed mixture. Whichever way the eggs are added, the mixture must be beaten thoroughly after each addition.

Curdled eggs: if the eggs are added all at once or if they are used directly from the refrigerator, there is the danger that the mixture will curdle. This means that the fat and liquid in the mixture separates. You can see when this happens because, instead of a creamy, smooth texture, the mixture will become lumpy and appear grainy. Curdling is undesirable because a curdled mixture holds less air than a smooth one and therefore produces a heavy cake.

Provided that the eggs are added correctly and used at the right temperature, there is no reason why curdling should occur. If, despite your precautions, the mixture shows signs of curdling, add a little of the sifted flour with the quantity of egg. Curdling can sometimes happen when the last egg is added and in this case, stand the bowl containing the mixture in a bowl of hot water and beat very hard until the mixture assumes its smooth and creamy texture again.

When all the egg has been incorporated, scrape down the spoon and sides of the bowl with a spatula and beat again, very briefly, to ensure even mixing.

Adding the flour

The flour is added to the creamed mixture using a technique known as folding. This is quite different from beating or whisking which is unsuitable for cake mixtures because the brisk action strengthens the gluten in the flour and makes a tough cake. The object of folding one ingredient into another is to blend them together without losing volume. The folding action also aerates the mixture.

Always add the flour to the creamed mixture and never the other way around. Using a metal spoon, add a third of the flour at a time to the creamed mixture. When the flour is added, use a figure-of-eight action to incorporate the flour into the mixture as lightly as possible. Repeat the folding in of the flour, until it has all been incorporated.

Further additions

Further flavouring ingredients such as dried fruit and nuts may be added once the flour is incorporated. Use as light a hand as possible. At this point it may be necessary to add a small amount of liquid in the form of water or milk, to obtain the right consistency. Do this only where the recipe indicates or if by some chance the mixture is exceptionally stiff. It should, at this stage, be of a soft dropping consistency. This is one where the mixture drops easily from the spoon when lifted just above the bowl.

BAKING

Using a spatula, scrape all the mixture down from the side of the bowl and then into the prepared tin(s). Smooth over the surface of the mixture with a palette knife, so that the mixture is level and will rise evenly in the tin. Bake on the shelf stated in the recipe, making sure that the correct oven temperature is reached before putting the tin in the oven.

MAKING SMALL CAKES

Small cakes are ideal for icing and the same rules apply as to larger cakes, though small cakes are not usually filled.

Small cakes are easily made with the basic rich sponge mixture and may be baked in greased 6-, 9- or 12-hole bun tins or foil cases, if you are prepared to pay for convenience, buy paper cases. These need no greasing, but can only be used once.

Do not overfill the paper cases or bun tins. A heaped teaspoon of mixture in each case is quite enough. Nor is it necessary to spread the mixture evenly. It will expand on baking to fill the space

If using paper cases, arrange these first on a baking sheet or tray. A fairly hot oven temperature, 190°C [375°F] gas mark 5, is needed but cakes are baked for only 15–20 minutes just below the centre shelf.

TESTING THE CAKE

Because the temperatures of individual ovens vary, baking times should be used as a guide, so it is always important to be sure that the cake is cooked through. Don't ever be tempted to have a peep at the cake during the course of baking time. Always wait until the end of the minimum baking time to have a look. Opening the door too early, before the cake has time to 'set', causes a sudden rush of cold air to enter the oven. This is a prime cause of cakes dipping in the centre.

To test a plain sponge follow these four golden rules.
- The cake should be evenly browned and well risen.
- The cake should have shrunk away from the sides of the tin.
- There should be no sound of bubbling (of uncooked mixture) when the cake is held to the ear.
- The mixture should feel firm but springy when lightly touched with a fingertip. If any impression of your fingertip remains, the cake will need a little longer baking.

COOLING

Rich cakes should be turned out to cool on a wire rack. Leaving a rich creamed cake in the tin would result in an unpleasant soggy cake.

Turning a cake out of the tin is a simple procedure. First allow the cake to stand in the tin to let it shrink away from the sides. Leave sandwich cakes for approximately half a minute and other types of cakes for 5–10 minutes. Have ready a clean, folded tea-towel and a wire cooling rack.

Next, carefully run a palette knife around the inside of the tin, between the cake and the side of the tin, to ease the cake away. Place the folded tea-towel over the top of the cake and turn the cake tin and tea-towel upside down, holding on to both. Put down the tea-towel with the inverted cake on it, lift off the tin and peel away the lining paper and discard it. Place the wire cooling rack on top of the cake and turn over again, so that the cake is sitting the right way up. Leave until completely cold.

For a large plain rich sponge cake, baked and cooled in a tin with a loose base, there is an even simpler method of removing the cake from the tin. When the cake is cold or cooled sufficiently, stand the cake in the tin on top of a 450 g [1 lb] can. Holding the sides of the cake tin, gently ease the outside ring down from the cake. Lift the cake from the can and remove the base from under the lining paper and peel off all the lining papers. Leave cake on a wire rack until completely cold.

STORING AND FREEZING

Wait until the cake is completely cold for either storing or freezing. Plain, undecorated rich cakes will store successfully for up to 6 days in an airtight tin. Alternatively, they can be wrapped securely in cling film or foil and stored in a cool larder.

Rich spice cakes and those containing flavouring essences should only be frozen for up to two weeks otherwise the flavours of the spices will fade.

Filled sandwich and layered cakes can be frozen for up to two months. Freeze them unwrapped then wrap and pack them into plastic containers to protect the decoration. When ready to serve them, unwrap them immediately after removing frozen from the freezer or the decoration will stick to the wrapper as the cake thaws. Rich cakes usually take 3–4 hours to thaw at room temperature but can be thawed overnight in the refrigerator.

TRADITIONAL MADEIRA CAKE

A madeira is a fairly rich cake with a soft texture. The top is domed, with fine cracks. The decoration is positioned after 30 minutes' cooking time to prevent it sinking. (Don't be tempted to open the oven door beforehand as the cake will not be set and will collapse in the middle.)

Traditionally, madeira cake is served with a glass of madeira sherry— hence its name—but it is equally as good served with a cup of tea.

MAKES 10–12 SLICES
100 g [¼ lb] plain flour
100 g [¼ lb] self-raising flour
pinch of salt
175 g [6 oz] butter
175 g [6 oz] caster sugar
4 medium-sized eggs
5–15 ml [1–3 teaspoons] milk (optional)

For the decoration:
2 thin slices candied citron peel

1 Position oven shelf in the centre. Heat oven to 180°C [350°F] gas mark 4. Grease and fully line a deep round 18 cm [7"] cake tin.

2 Sift the flour into a medium-sized bowl together with the salt. Set aside.

3 Place the butter in a large mixing bowl and beat with a wooden spoon until soft and light.

4 Add the sugar and cream ingredients until light and fluffy. Stop beating occasionally to scrape down sides of bowl with a spatula.

5 Whisk the eggs lightly together and add gradually to creamed mixture, beating after each addition. If any sign of curdling occurs add a little of the sifted flour.

6 When all the egg has been incorporated, scrape down the spoon and the sides of the bowl with spatula and beat again briefly.

7 Gently fold in the sifted flour until completely incorporated. If necessary, add enough milk to give a soft dropping consistency.

8 Place mixture into prepared tin and smooth over the surface with a palette knife. Bake for half an hour.

9 Without removing tin completely from oven, carefully lay the citron peel across the centre of the cake. Return to the oven for a further $1\frac{1}{4}$ hours.

10 Leave cake to cool in the tin for 10 minutes before turning out. Cool.

Variations

●For a rich seed cake, omit the citron peel and add 10 ml [2 teaspoons] caraway seeds to the sifted flour.

●For a cherry cake omit the citron peel, flavour the cake with a few drops of almond essence. Wash and dry 100 g [$\frac{1}{4}$ lb] halved glacé cherries and toss in 15 g [$\frac{1}{2}$ oz] of the measured amount of flour. Add the halved glacé cherries when all the flour has been incorporated by carefully folding them into the mixture.

●Chop 75 g [3 oz] walnuts coarsely and mix them with the sifted flour. Omit the citron peel and add the grated zest of one small lemon to the creamed butter and sugar mixture. Fold the nuts into the mixture with the flour.

●To make a ginger cake, omit the citron peel. Sift 2.5 ml [$\frac{1}{2}$ teaspoon] ground ginger with the flour and add 100 g [$\frac{1}{4}$ lb] drained, rinsed, dried and

From the top: traditional Madeira cake, caraway seed cake and cherry cake—just three of the exciting variations of the delicious Madeira cake.

coarsely chopped stem ginger when all the flour has been folded into the mixture.

●For a melt-in-the-mouth almond cake, omit the citron peel. Use only 175 g [6 oz] flour and add 25 g [1 oz] ground almonds and 25 g [1 oz] ground rice to the sifted flour. Flavour the mixture with 2.5 ml [½ teaspoon] almond essence.

●To make a coconut cake, omit the citron peel and add 100 g [¼ lb] desiccated coconut to the sifted flour.

FROSTED WALNUT LAYER CAKE

This decorative cake is iced with a deliciously soft frosting which spreads easily and should be used as soon as made. Make sure the cake is cool and ready before you prepare the frosting. Use 10 ml [2 teaspoons] instant coffee powder dissolved in 10 ml [2 teaspoons] water if you have no coffee and chicory essence. It is best to decorate the cake on the day you intend to serve it.

MAKES 900 G [2 LB] CAKE
175 g [6 oz] plain flour
5 ml [1 teaspoon] baking
  powder
pinch of salt

175 g [6 oz] butter or
  margarine
175 g [6 oz] soft brown sugar
10 ml [2 teaspoons] coffee and
  chicory essence
3 medium-sized eggs
50 g [2 oz] walnuts
30 ml [2 tablespoons] milk
  (optional)

For the frosting:
1 medium-sized egg white
175 g [6 oz] caster sugar
30 ml [2 tablespoons] cold
  water
pinch of cream of tartar

For the decoration:
walnut halves

1 Position the oven shelf in the centre of the oven. Heat oven to 180°C [350°F] gas mark 4.

2 Grease and fully line a deep 15 cm [6"] round cake tin. Re-grease the lining paper.

3 Sift flour together with the baking powder and salt into a bowl. Reserve.

4 Put the fat in a large mixing bowl and beat until soft and light. Add the sugar and cream the ingredients together until light and

fluffy. Scrape down the spoon and the sides of the bowl with a spatula.

5 Add the coffee and chicory essence, a little at a time, beating well after each addition.

6 Whisk the eggs lightly together and add gradually to creamed mixture, beating well after each addition. If any signs of curdling occur add a little of the sifted flour.

7 Scrape down the spoon and sides of the bowl and beat again briefly. Reserve 4 walnut halves then chop remainder coarsely.

8 Gently fold in the sifted flour until completely incorporated. Fold in chopped walnuts. If necessary, add enough milk to give a soft dropping consistency.

9 Put mixture into the prepared tin and smooth over the surface with a palette knife. Bake for 1–1¼ hours until well risen and evenly browned.

10 Allow cake to cool in tin for 5 minutes before turning out. Allow cake to cool completely on a wire rack.

11 Cut the cold cake horizontally into three equal layers, using a long sharp knife, then place the bottom layer on a wire rack.

12 To start making the frosting, put all the frosting ingredients in a large bowl and beat lightly together with a table mixer or hand-held electric whisk until mixed together.

13 Place the bowl over a pan of hot, but not boiling, water. Beat for 7–10 minutes if using a hand whisk, or 2–3 minutes if using a hand-held electric whisk, until the frosting stands in soft peaks.

14 Spread a scant quarter of the frosting over the bottom layer of cake, then place the middle layer on top. Spread a further scant quarter of the frosting over the centre layer and top with the remaining layer of cake.

15 Quickly spread the remaining frosting on to the top of the cake, using a small palette knife, and spread down the side.

16 Swirl the frosting decoratively with the palette knife. Decorate the top with walnut halves.

Frosting variations
● For a coffee frosting, add 5 ml [1 teaspoon] coffee and chicory essence to the mixture while it is being beaten but before it is placed over the pan of hot water to thicken.
● For caramel frosting, use Demerara instead of caster sugar.
● For lemon frosting, add 5 ml [1 teaspoon] lemon juice before beating over a pan of hot water and before the mixture thickens.
● For orange frosting, add a few drops of orange essence and a few drops of edible orange food colouring before beating over a pan of hot water and before the mixture thickens.

BUTTERFLY CAKES
Of all the small sponge cakes there are to make, butterfly cakes are perhaps the best known and the most popular with the younger members of the family.

MAKES ABOUT 15 CAKES
100 g [$\frac{1}{4}$ lb] self-raising flour
2 medium-sized eggs
100 g [$\frac{1}{4}$ lb] butter or margarine
100 g [$\frac{1}{4}$ lb] caster sugar

For the butter-cream icing:
50 g [2 oz] butter, softened
100 g [$\frac{1}{4}$ lb] icing sugar
few drops of pink food colouring

1 Heat oven to 190°C [375°F] gas mark 5. Place 15 paper baking cases on a baking sheet.

2 Sift the flour into a bowl and reserve. Place the eggs in a small bowl and whisk together lightly.

3 Place the fat into a bowl and beat until light and creamy. Add the sugar and beat until light and fluffy.

4 Beat in the eggs a little at a time, beating well after each addition. Fold in the flour using a metal spoon.

5 Divide the cake mixture between the paper baking cases, put approximately 1 heaped teaspoon of the mixture in each paper case.

6 Bake just below the centre of the oven for 15 minutes, until cakes are golden brown.

7 Transfer cakes to a cooling rack to cool. Meanwhile make butter-cream icing by creaming the butter with the sifted icing sugar. Colour with a few drops of colouring.

8 When the cakes are completely cold, cut a thin slice, horizontally from the top of each cake, cut each slice in half and place the halved 'tops', cut side facing down, on a cooling rack.

9 Sift a little plain icing sugar to just coat the tops of the cakes. Put a generous swirl of butter-icing on to the centre of each cake with a teaspoon or pipe on icing.

10 Replace two halves of cake cut from the top on to each cake, to represent butterfly wings. Press them gently into the butter-icing so that they are secure.

11 Repeat with the remaining cake tops. Put any remaining icing between the two 'butterfly wings' or pipe decoratively.

Bake a clever cake

Make a birthday or family anniversary into something memorable with a cake that is designed to catch the eye and appeal to the imagination. Novelty cakes come in all shapes and sizes and they are surprisingly simple to make, as is shown here.

It is great fun to make a cake that is out of the ordinary, when the occasion demands it. With a bit of imagination you can produce a wonderfully decorative centrepiece for the party table. Do remember that a simple decoration is often the most effective, or there is a danger that the results will be garish instead of entertaining.

Details given show you how to cut cakes into different shapes, using a cardboard template. They can then be decorated to carry out a theme and various ideas are illustrated, so that you can follow these, then develop your own themes.

Cake boards

Novelty cakes look their most attractive when served on a cake board. These are thick square or round boards covered with a hard wearing silver foil, available from large stationers and department stores. They are sold in a variety of sizes so choose one that matches your cake tin; the board should be about 2.5 cm [1"] bigger all round than the decorated cake.

Alternative bases for decorated cakes are plain, clean wooden boards covered with silver foil or a cake stand or plate.

CUTTING DECORATIVE SHAPES

A fancy-shaped cake tin will automatically give you a decorative shape—a prettily iced cake, which has been baked in a ring or fluted cake tin is elegant enough to serve as a dinner party dessert. Heart-shaped and numeral tins are available from

most large stores. However, if you do not want the expense of a special tin, a knife can easily be used to produce some amazingly decorative cakes starting with a plain square or round shape.

Whichever tin you choose, remember that it is essential that it is correctly prepared. If the cake sticks when it is turned out, its appearance will be spoilt so do be scrupulous and line the tin with greaseproof paper. You must also use the correct size tin for the amount of cake mix. For example, a mixture made from 100 g [¼ lb] flour will fill two 18 cm [7"] sandwich tins or one deep round 15 cm [6"] tin.

Large shaped cakes

Simple designs can be cut from larger cakes baked in deep or sandwich tins. The rich sponge mixture given on pages 12–13, is the most suitable; this may be plain, coloured or flavoured as you wish. Select a suitable size for the number of servings you require.

Choose your design with regard to the cake tins you own. The simplest shape to cut from a round cake is a heart, but a star shape, horseshoe or butterfly is not difficult. The simplest shape to cut from a square is an octagon but you may want to try cutting out a number. First trace your design on to a thin sheet of cardboard. This should correspond exactly with the dimensions of the cake tin, so that the minimum amount of cake is cut away.

The cake must be completely cold before you start. Place it on a wooden board or work surface. You will need a medium-sized and a small sharp knife. If you are working with a cake that has been baked in a deep tin, first cut it into layers. If you are using sandwich cakes place the layers side by side on the work surface or wooden board.

Put the cardboard template on top of each layer of cake and cut around it

Handy hints

●Butter-cream icing will keep for up to three weeks in the refrigerator stored in a covered container. Make up a quantity of plain icing and flavour as required.
●To coat small cakes with glacé icing, secure each in turn on a fine skewer and quickly dip in the icing. Place on a wire rack, with a plate underneath to catch any drips, and leave to set.
●To thicken up icing, beat in a little sifted icing sugar; to thin icing down, add a few drops of warmed water.

Cakes can be shaped after baking by cutting round a paper template. Use a round or square cake according to your chosen design.

to form the cake shape. Hold the knife vertically at the side of the template and use a sawing motion to cut as this gives an even neat cake edge. The trimmings need not be wasted as they can be used for trifles and puddings (if they last that long).

IDEAS FOR NOVELTY CAKES

These super novelty cake ideas will make a talking point for a party and make it memorable.
●To make a surprise marshmallow cake, bake a rich sponge cake in a lined 20 cm [8"] deep cake tin. The moment you take the cake from the oven, cover the entire surface of the cake with pink and white marshmallows, split horizontally, packing them tightly together, cut side down. The heat from the cake melts the sweets and they merge together and stick to the surface of the cake. (The lining paper prevents the marshmallows from slipping off the top before they stick.) Leave the cake to cool in the tin. Turn out and remove lining paper carefully. When cold, cut cake into two layers and sandwich together with vanilla butter-cream icing.
●For a Christmas star, first slice a 23 cm [9"] deep round cake into three equal layers. Make a star-shaped template from thin cardboard. Place the cake on a wooden board or working surface and using the template, carefully cut round the design. Sandwich each cake layer together with vanilla-flavoured butter-cream icing. Brush the top and sides of the cake with melted apricot jam. Coat cake completely with white glacé icing. When set transfer the cake carefully to a cake board or plate. Pipe shells or stars of vanilla-flavoured butter-cream icing around the top outer edge of the cake. Top each shell or star with a silver ball. Pipe a border of butter-cream icing shells or stars round the base of the cake to finish.
●To make a parcel cake; first cut a 20–23 cm [8–9"] deep square cake into two layers. Sandwich together with butter-cream icing flavoured to your taste. Brush the top and sides of the cake with a melted jam to glaze, coat cake with glacé icing. When set, fill a medium-sized nylon piping bag fitted with a plain tube with sufficient butter icing to pipe a name and address on the top of the cake. Next, pipe lines of butter-cream icing to represent the

string. Pipe on a stamp, if you like, in the top right hand corner, using your own design.

● Make a maypole birthday cake, using a Victoria sandwich cake (see pages 12–13). Sandwich together with apricot jam, then brush the top and side with melted apricot jam. Colour enough glacé icing with a few drops of pink food colouring to cover cake. Coat cake with glacé icing, while icing is still soft, decorate the outer edge of the top of the cake with crystallized rose or violet petals. Place a striped straw in the centre of the cake, secure some narrow ribbons to the top with a tiny spot of glue. These should spiral down to the bottom of the cake.

● To make a festive fruit gateau, first cut a deep round 20 cm [8″] cake into two layers. Put the layers on a wooden board and cut a circle from the centre of the top layer of cake using a 4 cm [1½″] cutter and reserve. Sprinkle sherry over the bottom layer of cake to soak in and place on a serving plate. Place the top 'ring' of cake on top of the bottom layer. Brush the surface and sides with sieved and melted raspberry jam. Coat cake with pale pink glacé icing, leaving the centre 'hollow' plain. To serve, pipe thick whipped cream which has been flavoured with sherry into the centre hollow and top with fresh raspberries. Sift a little icing sugar over the circle cut from top layer of cake. Place at an angle on top of raspberries.

● For a drum cake, bake two chocolate sandwich cakes in 20 cm [8″] tins. When cold, sandwich cakes together with chocolate-flavoured buttercream icing to make a tall drum shape. Check the surface is level and trim any projecting edges. Coat cake completely with white glacé icing. Leave until set. Next, fill a medium-sized piping bag fitted with a plain tube. Half fill with chocolate glacé icing. Pipe diagonal lines of icing from the top to the base of the cake all around the sides. Leave to set, then pipe similar lines, slanting in the opposite direction, to make a diamond pattern around the side of the cake. Pin a narrow band of red paper or satin ribbon around the bottom of the cake. Then pin a second band around the top, so that it stands just above the surface of the cake. For the drumsticks, place two ball-shaped lollipops at angles to each other on top of the 'drum'.

BATTENBURG VILLA

When time is short and a special cake is needed for a child's birthday, use ready-made cakes and sweets. This one can be assembled in under an hour.

If you have more time on your hands, use home-made Battenburg cakes following recipe given on page 36. You will need a 23 cm [9″] square silver cake board for this cake.

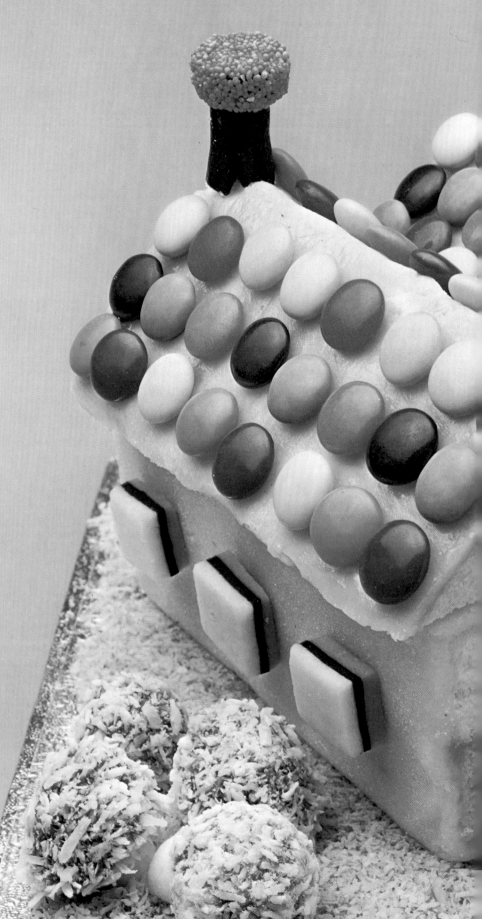

SERVES 20

25 g [1 oz] desiccated coconut
few drops green food
    colouring
60 ml [4 tablespoons] apricot
    jam
3 Battenburg cakes
3 small tubes sugar-coated
    sweets
small, mixed liquorice sweets
small packet of coconut
    mushroom sweets

1 Put the coconut in a small bowl and add a few drops of green food colouring. Mix together with a fork to colour coconut evenly.

2 Put the jam and 30 ml [2 tablespoons] water in a small saucepan over a low heat. Stir until the jam has melted.

3 Using a pastry brush, coat the cake board with half the melted jam. Sprinkle green coconut over board to represent grass.

4 Brush one side of one Battenburg cake with apricot jam and press a second cake alongside it. Put the two cakes in centre of board.

5 Cut the remaining Battenburg cake into 2 triangular wedges by cutting from one corner through to the opposite corner.

6 Put the two triangles of cake, cut side down, on a wooden board. Cut a 12 mm [½"] strip from the long side of each cake triangle, to enable the triangles to fit together neatly.

7 Using half of remaining jam, brush over the top of the two Battenburg cakes on the board. Place the remaining two wedges with the triangle pointing upwards and the cut sides lying together, on top of the whole cakes to represent the roof.

8 Brush the roof with jam and cover with sugar-coated sweets, to represent 'roof tiles'.

9 Use the remaining jam to stick on the liquorice sweets to represent windows, doors and chimney, as shown in the picture. Position the coconut mushroom sweets in the 'garden' of the house.

Assemble this cake, which will delight any child, using bought cakes and sweets, in less time than it takes to blow up the party balloons.

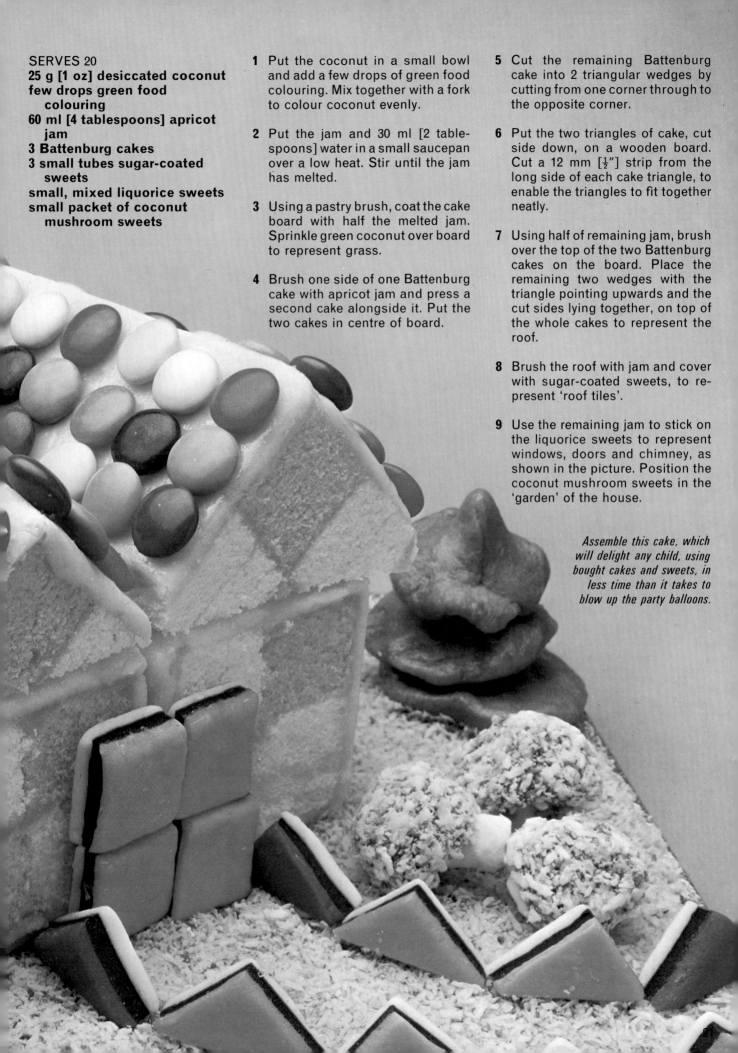

SPORT'S SPECIAL

◪◪◪ This car cake will be the pride and joy of any child when birthday time comes around. The cake is made from a rich sponge mixture, marbled inside and uses only one sandwich tin. The art comes in the stylish assembly. You will need a 25 cm [10"] square silver cake board.

SERVES ABOUT 10
175 g [6 oz] self-raising flour
3 medium-sized eggs
175 g [6 oz] butter or margarine
175 g [6 oz] caster sugar
25 g [1 oz] cocoa powder

For the butter-cream icing:
225 g [½ lb] icing sugar
22.5 ml [1½ tablespoons] cocoa
100 g [¼ lb] butter, softened

For the glacé icing:
100 g [¼ lb] icing sugar
30 ml [2 tablespoons] warm water

For the decoration:
15 ml [1 tablespoon] apricot jam

45 ml [3 tablespoons]
  Demerara sugar
two 25 cm [10"] strips liquorice
50 g [2 oz] marzipan
25 g [1 oz] icing sugar
small box mixed liquorice
  sweets
4 small plain chocolate-coated
  biscuits

1 Heat oven to 180°C [350°F] gas mark 4, and prepare a 20 cm [8"] round sandwich tin by lining with greaseproof paper.

2 Sift flour into a bowl and reserve. Place the eggs in a small bowl and whisk lightly, then reserve.

3 Place the fat in a mixing bowl and beat until light and creamy. Add the sugar and beat until light and fluffy.

4 Beat in the eggs, a little at a time, beating well after each addition. Fold in the flour using a metal spoon.

5 Place one half of the mixture in a

Make this simply sensational sport's special, then watch the children race to eat the wheels and all spare parts.

separate bowl. Sift the cocoa powder on to this and fold it in.

6 Place alternate spoonfuls of the cocoa and plain mixtures into the prepared tin.

7 Smooth the top of the mixture with a round-bladed knife or palette knife. Bake for 25–30 minutes until cake is cooked.

8 Turn cake on to a tea-towel and then transfer on to a wire rack to cool.

9 Start preparing the icings. To make the butter-cream icing, sift the icing sugar and cocoa into a mixing bowl. Beat in the softened butter until light and fluffy.

10 Cover with a damp cloth and reserve.

11 Make the glacé icing by mixing the sugar with the water. Cover the bowl with a damp cloth.

12 Make a medium-sized paper piping bag, as directed on page 40. Snip off tip from piping bag and slip in a small plain icing tube.

13 To prepare cake board, place the jam in a small saucepan with 15 ml [1 tablespoon] water. Place over a low heat and stir until the jam has melted.

14 Use a palette knife or pastry brush to coat the surface of the cake board with the melted jam.

15 Sprinkle the jam-coated board with Demerara sugar to resemble a road surface. Place two parallel lines of liquorice strips, diagonally on the board to mark the edges of the 'road'.

16 Put the cake on a wooden board and cut it into two equal pieces to make two semicircles.

17 Use 30 ml [2 tablespoons] of chocolate butter-cream icing to sandwich the two cakes together. Stand the semicircles, cut side down, on a board.

18 Using a small sharp knife, cut a small, rounded triangle-shaped wedge from each end of the cake to form the outline of a car. One end

should resemble a car bonnet and the other a car boot. Reserve the cake wedges.

19 Cut the tip of the triangle from each of the reserved wedges of cake. Space these apart like the front and back axles and place them on the prepared board, so that the 'car' can rest on them. Place the 'car' in position on top, facing down the liquorice road.

20 Use a small palette or round-bladed knife to cover the entire surface of the cake with the reserved butter-cream icing. Smooth the surface.

21 Fill a piping bag with glacé icing. Roll out the marzipan thinly on a board lightly dusted with sifted icing sugar.

22 Use a small blob of glacé icing to stick a round liquorice sweet in the centre of each biscuit. Pipe lines of glacé icing radiating from the sweet in the centre of each biscuit to represent the wheels.

23 Place the 'wheels' in position against the side of the car, at each corner, sticking them to the wedges under the car with a small blob of glacé icing.

24 Use a sharp knife to cut out ten small squares from the marzipan for the car 'windows'. Cut out two thin strips for the front and back 'bumpers'.

25 From the remaining marzipan, cut out a small oblong for the 'number plate'.

26 Pipe a number or child's initials on the 'number plate', and reserve.

27 Put two windows on the top front and back of the car. Place three windows along each side of the car. Place a liquorice sweet on the bonnet at the front of the car and two square ones at the back.

28 Place the number plate above the front bumper. Use the remaining glacé icing to outline the windows and to pipe two windscreen wipers (one on each front window).

29 Place the candle holders and candles along the top of the car.

MARZIPAN FESTIVAL CAKE

◩◩◩ *The corn motif makes this splendid cake ideal for a harvest festival tea, but it would do beautifully for many other festive occasions. It tastes every bit as good as it looks. If you are nervous about making the fruit from marzipan, they are available ready made from confectioners and grocers. Buy only 450 g [1 lb] marzipan to cover the cake.*

SERVES 12
For the cake:
350 g [¾ lb] self-raising flour
6 medium-sized eggs
350 g [¾ lb] butter or margarine
350 g [¾ lb] caster sugar
zest and juice of 2 medium-
**   sized lemons**

For the decoration:
60 ml [4 tablespoons] apricot
**   jam**
about 25 g [1 oz] icing sugar
700 g [1½ lb] marzipan
few drops of orange, green,
**   red, purple (or blue) food**
**   colourings**
angelica
8 whole cloves

1 Prepare a 23 cm [9"] deep tin by lining with greaseproof. Make cake following the instructions for a cake made by the creaming method given on pages 12–13. Bake the cake at 160°C [325°F] gas mark 3 for 1 hour 40 minutes.

2 Allow the cake to cool completely on a wire rack. Place apricot jam and 30 ml [2 tablespoons] water in a small saucepan, reserve.

3 Lightly sprinkle a board or work surface with sifted icing sugar. Work the marzipan between your hands until soft and malleable.

4 Place 225 g [½ lb] marzipan in a polythene bag and reserve. Roll out 175 g [6 oz] of the remaining marzipan to a 23 cm [9"] circle. The easiest way to do this is to roll out a slightly greater weight and then to cut round a 23 cm [9"] plate. Reserve the circle.

5 Use a clean piece of string to measure around the circumference of the cake. Cut the string where it meets so you know the exact length of marzipan needed to surround the cake.

6 Measure the depth of the cake with a ruler by placing the ruler vertically against the side of the cake.

7 Roll out the remaining two-thirds of marzipan (about 275 g [10 oz] with the trimmings) to the length of the piece of string and to the depth of the cake. Trim the marzipan if this is necessary.

8 Put saucepan containing the apricot jam over a low heat and stir the jam until it has melted.

9 Brush the side of cake with apricot jam, reserving enough to coat the top.

10 Hold the top and bottom surfaces of the cake between the palms of your hands and lower the cake on to one end of the long piece of marzipan.

11 Roll the cake along the marzipan strip with a firm but not heavy hand, to secure the marzipan on to the side of the cake. Pat the join to secure it.

12 Place the cake on a 25 cm [10"] round plate or board. Brush the reserved apricot jam over the top of the cake and cover with reserved circle of marzipan.

13 Press marzipan circle down lightly but securely. Trim any unsightly edges at the top or bottom of the cake if necessary with a very sharp knife so that the edges are even.

14 Remove the reserved marzipan from polythene bag and work this between the hands to soften.

15 To make ears of corn to trim the outside of the cake, first cut a scant quarter of the marzipan (reserving the remainder). Divide this quarter of marzipan into 8 equal-sized pieces.

16 Working on one piece at a time, roll each one into a sausage shape, about 5 cm [2"] long. Use the tip of a sharp knife to cut along each side of the shape at 6 mm [¼"] intervals to resemble the ears of the stalk of corn.

17 Repeat with the remaining pieces of marzipan, reserve the ears of corn.

Don't wait for harvest festival to come around before trying this cake.

18 Divide the remaining marzipan into five equal portions ready to make different types of fruit.

19 To make oranges, colour one portion with a few drops of orange food colouring, divide marzipan into 4 pieces and roll each piece into a ball.

20 Roll each ball lightly against the finest side of a grater so that the ball resembles orange skin. Stick a clove into each ball for the stalk.

21 To make the apples, colour one portion of marzipan with a few drops of green food colouring, divide into 4 pieces.

22 Roll each piece of marzipan into a ball shape and stick a clove into each to resemble the stalk. Cut small pieces of angelica to resemble the leaves and stick two small angelica leaves by the side of each stalk.

23 To make the bananas first divide one portion of marzipan into 5 pieces. Roll each piece into a sausage shape about 5 cm [2"] long, slightly tapering at each end.

24 Blend a drop or so each of orange and green food colouring together to make a brown colour. Then use a fine paint brush to paint lines along each banana shape and a little dab at the top end of each banana.

25 To make cherries, colour one portion of marzipan with red food colouring in sufficient quantities to make the marzipan red.

26 Divide the red marzipan into 4 pieces. Roll each piece into a small ball and stick a 5 cm [2"] thin piece of angelica into each ball for the stalk.

27 To make grapes, first colour the last piece of marzipan with a few drops of purple food colouring (use red and blue mixed if purple is not available).

28 Divide the purple marzipan into about 2 dozen pieces of varying sizes and roll each piece into a ball.

29 Press balls together to form a small bunch of grapes.

30 Arrange 'ears' of corn around top outer edge of cake. Arrange the 'fruit' just off the centre of the cake, as shown in picture.

Homely family cakes

Plain cakes made without eggs are ideal for family teas—those occasions when you would like to provide something more than toast but don't feel justified in lashing out on anything very rich or fancy.

Plain cakes are at their very best shortly after they have come out of the oven so there is no need to resist the temptation to cut into them while they are still warm and smelling deliciously inviting. Cut plain cakes into thick slices and spread them with plenty of creamy butter (plain cakes are also called tea-breads, probably for this reason) or, for a real treat, serve them with cream.

Plain cakes are made by the rubbing-in method. This is the same method used for making shortcrust pastry (see pages 135–139), and is a very simple procedure.

The proportion of fat to flour is half or less and no eggs are used so the results are economical, but certainly not dull, since the basic mixture can be adapted in innumerable ways.

The most important things to remember are to weigh your ingredients carefully and to handle the mixture lightly. These are the keys to success because they ensure the cake rises properly and has that characteristic open, light texture of a well-made plain cake.

In cakes made without eggs the raising agents used are chemical. These produce a gas, carbon diox-

With its crunchy topping of flaked almonds, old-fashioned honey tea-bread shows just how eye-catching a plain cake made without eggs can be!

ide, which expands on heating, so 'lifting' the cake. Air also expands on heating and, although it is not the main raising agent in rubbed-in cakes, the amount incorporated during the rubbing-in operation is valuable. So be sure to rub in lightly and evenly, and do all subsequent mixing lightly too—or you will expel the air again.

BASIC INGREDIENTS
Flour

The texture of a good plain cake is described as 'tender'. This 'tender' texture can only be achieved by the use of a 'soft' flour, that is, one which does not contain a high proportion of gluten. (Gluten is the elastic substance which develops and strengthens on beating, a property required for making bread but not for cakes.) On the domestic market it is seldom possible to buy a special, very low gluten flour (except for people on gluten-free diets) but plain white flour is perfectly suitable. If you want to give your cakes an even 'shorter' texture you can make a soft flour effectively at home by substituting cornflour for part of the flour in the ratio of one part cornflour to seven parts plain white flour. For example, where a recipe specifies 225 g [½ lb] plain white flour, use 200 g [7 oz] plain white flour and 25 g [1 oz] cornflour.

Never use strong white flour, brown flour or wholewheat because they would give the cake a dense, heavy texture. And never use self-raising flour. Recipes vary in the amount and type of raising agent needed; self-raising flour contains a standard quantity and type of raising agent which might not be what is wanted.

Raising agents

As soon as the raising agents are mixed together in the presence of a liquid they begin to produce carbon dioxide. When they are heated the reaction speeds up and the gas bubbles expand, forcing the cake to rise. The mixture must therefore be baked as soon as it has been prepared so that it does not lose the raising effect of the gas bubbles. The process continues slowly and steadily for some time which is why recipes give long cooking times even for quite small cakes.

Always measure carefully: an excess of raising agent will either give an uneven, coarse texture, or it will overstretch the gluten, causing the cake to collapse. Too much bicarbonate of soda will give a bitter taste. But, if there is insufficient raising agent not enough gas will be produced to aerate the mixture and the cake will be unappetizing.

Bicarbonate of soda can be used alone but it is usually used in conjunction with another acid substance, such as cream of tartar, sour milk, vinegar or black treacle, to produce a stronger reaction.

Baking powder: the commercial variety is a blend of two parts bicarbonate of soda to one part cream of tartar, with the addition of ground rice to help preserve the mixture. It is much better, and more economical, to make your own baking powder at home as and when you need it. Simply combine two parts bicarbonate of soda to one part cream of tartar and leave out the ground rice.

Salt

A little salt is always added to bring out the flavour of the other ingredients.

Fat

The fat in a cake has several vital roles to play. It helps to tenderize or soften the gluten and starch in the flour, so contributing to that 'melt-in-the-mouth' texture. It traps the air bubbles which make the cake light and it helps to keep the cake moist during storage.

Whichever fat you choose it should be at room temperature so that it can easily be rubbed in. If the fat is too hard or too soft the mixing will be uneven and the cake tough.

Butter gives the best flavour but it is expensive. Also, it tends to become too soft and oily in warm conditions, or if handled too much.

Margarine: hard margarines are excellent, particularly those which contain some butter. They are less expensive than butter and remain firmer during use. Whipped margarines are not suitable because they are too soft.

Lard should only be used in mixtures containing ingredients with strong distinctive flavours, such as spices. Lard is a 'pure' fat so you will need less of it than butter or margarine (reduce the quantity of fat given in the recipe by about a quarter, so where a recipe gives 100 g [¼ lb] butter use 80 g [3¼ oz] lard). As lard does not 'hold' air very well, the cakes will not have a really light, open texture.

Sugar

Sugar helps to improve the flavour, texture, appearance and keeping qualities of the cake. As with fat, sugar softens the gluten and gives a more tender cake. Used in the right proportions, sugar helps the cake to rise, but too much sugar softens the gluten so much that it is unable to support the risen shape and the cake will sink. Fat and sugar are usually present in equal amounts. If the sugar exceeds the fat the cake will be more tender and spongy. If the fat exceeds the sugar it will have a richer but closer texture.

Caster sugar is best as the many small, sharp-edged crystals grate readily on the fat, aiding the rubbing-in process. Also, it dissolves easily during cooking.

Granulated sugar can be used but it will not mix in as efficiently because the crystals are rather coarse, and it will give the cake a speckled appearance.

Soft brown sugar is sometimes used to add distinctive flavour and colour. Demerara sugar is not suitable because it is too coarse.

Liquid

Milk is usually used to bind the rubbed-in ingredients together. For a basic recipe using 225 g [½ lb] flour, 150 ml [¼ pt] milk is sufficient to bind the mixture to the right consistency. If additional liquid flavouring or fruit is used the milk is usually reduced to keep the balance of liquid to dry ingredients in correct proportion.

ADDITIONAL INGREDIENTS

Dry flavourings: when cakes are flavoured with certain powders, such as chocolate, an adjustment must be made to the amount of flour used, usually gram for gram (ounce for ounce), otherwise the cake will be dry and tough. Ground spices are used in such small quantities that this is not necessary. On the other hand, when fruit or nuts are added, the mixture must contain slightly less liquid than normal to make it stiffer so that it can support the weight of the additions.

Dried fruit: dried peaches, bananas, pears and figs can be used as well as the conventional currants, sultanas and raisins. Nearly all dried fruit purchased nowadays is cleaned and can virtually be used straight from the packet. Just take a quick glance to make sure that there are no stalks. Dried fruit is rich in fructose (natural fruit sugar). This high sugar content means you can reduce the amount of sugar specified in a recipe.

Fresh and canned fruit can be used and give cakes a lovely moist con-

sistency. Prepare fresh fruit in the usual way for cooking, chopping it quite small. Always drain canned fruit well before using. Thick fruit purées add moisture and flavour.

Crystallized fruit can be added for extra sweetness, flavour and texture. Glacé cherries must be washed well in hot water to remove the heavy syrup coating or else they will sink. Drain them, then dry and chop finely: they are rather heavy and the cake structure will not be able to keep them suspended if they are too large. Ready-prepared candied peel is easily available—just check that there are no large pieces.

Nuts: all nuts should be shelled and chopped before using. For a slightly stronger nutty flavour, toast the nuts by spreading them in a single, even layer on a grill pan or shallow dish and grill under a moderately high heat. Turn the nuts frequently to ensure an even colour. They can also be browned in a moderate oven (180°C [350°F] gas mark 4) provided that an eye is kept on them.

Liquid flavourings add extra colour as well as special flavours. When adding liquids you will have to adjust the proportions of the other ingredients accordingly. Too wet a mixture will give a close-textured, flat cake and any fruit present will sink to the bottom of the cake.

Honey, syrups and jam lend their own particular sweet flavour and can be used to replace some of the sugar. They will produce a closer-crumbed, moist cake with a better storing quality.

CHOOSING AND PREPARING BAKING TINS

Because the mixture must be cooked as soon as it has been prepared,

Drained canned fruit can be used to give plain cakes a lovely moist consistency.

always choose and prepare the baking tin before you start making the cake itself.

Square or rectangular tins are generally used because plain cakes or tea-breads are usually sliced and buttered in the same way as bread.

Two types of rectangular tin can be used. Those with sloping sides and a base which is smaller than the top of the tin are called loaf tins. Sizes vary enormously and are not standardized. Don't worry if the measurements of your tin vary slightly from those recommended in the recipe: the precise size of the tin is not vital when making plain cakes without eggs.

You can also use a straight-sided rectangular tin, although these can be rather hard to obtain.

Square cake tins have straight sides. They are available in standard sizes. Some have a loose-bottomed base, which makes turning out the cooked cake easier, and some have a non-stick surface.

A round cake tin can be used instead of a square one. But remember that a square tin holds about the same amount of mixture as a round tin which is 2.5 cm [1"] larger in diameter than the length of one side of the square tin. So if the recipe calls for a 20 cm [8"] deep square tin you can use a 23 cm [9"] deep round tin instead.

Greasing and lining the baking tin

The base and sides of your tin must always be greased before the cake mixture is poured in. (It is advisable to do this even when using a non-stick tin.)

If the recipe contains honey, treacle, syrup or jam you should also line and re-grease the tin. It is extremely difficult to fully line a loaf tin because it has sloping sides. Usually, therefore, just the bottom of the tin is lined. If you are using a square tin it is worth taking the trouble to line the sides as well as the base.

Step-by-step lining a square tin

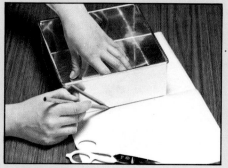

1 Place tin on lining paper and outline the size of the base in pencil. Cut out base lining with scissors, just inside pencil mark.

2 Cut a strip for each side of the tin. Make each strip 6 cm [2½"] deeper and 2.5 cm [1"] longer than the sides of the tin.

3 Make a 1.2 cm [½"] fold along one of the long edges of each strip. Crease firmly. Snip diagonally to fold at 1.2 cm [½"] intervals.

4 Grease sides and base of tin. Position strips with snipped edge on base. Position base lining paper. Grease again.

For perfect results always grease, line and re-grease your baking tins. Particular details for square tins are shown here.

OVEN TEMPERATURES

The cake assumes its final shape while it is in the oven so just as much attention must be paid to the baking of the cake as to its making. Turn the oven to the recommended temperature before you start making the cake mixture so that the right temperature will be reached by the time you need it.

It is extremely important to bake at the recommended temperature and shelf position because the heat not only expands the gas produced by the raising agents, but will also caramelize the surface sugar, giving a soft brown crust.

If the temperature is too high the cake will begin to cook and assume its final shape (the cooking term is to 'set') before it has risen. Setting starts from the sides and gradually moves towards the centre. If this occurs too quickly it produces a cake with a cracked peak in the centre and any fruit contained in the cake will sink. It also means that when the outside of the cake is ready the inside is still raw and, by the time the inside is cooked, the outside will be burnt.

If you bake at too low a temperature the raising agents will work but there will be insufficient heat to set the cake in its risen shape so that it will collapse and sink in the middle. Also a hard, sugary crust will form in the sunken shape.

As a general rule, the plainer or smaller the cake the hotter the oven should be. For larger or richer cakes the temperature will be reduced. Small cakes are baked in the hottest part of the oven, usually the top. Larger cakes, which require longer, slower cooking, are baked on the middle or lower shelves.

EQUIPMENT AND PREPARATION

When you have prepared the tin and heated the oven you can make the cake. For this you will need: measuring equipment, large mixing bowl, fine-meshed sieve, palette knife for cutting in the fat, metal spoon for folding in the milk and any additional ingredients, and a rubber spatula for scraping the prepared mixture into the bowl. Don't forget that you will also need oven gloves. (Those which have a magnet attached and can be fastened to the oven door save a frantic search for a glove at the vital moment when the cake is ready.) You also need a thin metal skewer for testing the cake and a wire rack or tray on which to cool the cake.

THE BASIC METHOD

Being organized is a great help towards good results so do all the weighing, measuring and any necessary preparation of additional ingredients such as fruit before you start to make the cake.

Always sieve the flour together with the salt, powdered raising agents and any powdered flavourings such as spices, if used, into the mixing bowl. Sieving aerates the ingredients and ensures their even distribution.

Add the fat, which should be at room temperature, to the bowl and use a palette knife to cut it into the flour. When all the pieces of fat are pea sized and coated with flour, use your hands to rub the fat into the flour until the mixture resembles even-sized breadcrumbs. Remember that light stroking movements will give the best results. Lift the mixture high and let it trickle through your fingertips and fall back into the bowl.

Use a metal spoon to stir in the sugar. Make a hollow in the centre of the mixture, pour in the milk and add additional ingredients if used. Fold these ingredients into the rubbed-in mixture with a metal spoon. Use light, gentle movements to keep the mixture as airy as possible. On no account stir the mixture. Take the spoon right down to the bottom of the bowl, bring it up around the side of the bowl and then back to the centre, folding the mixture over (hence the technical term 'folding'). Repeat this action until the ingredients are just blended, and then stop: further folding would reduce the air content.

Scrape the mixture into the prepared tin with a rubber-bladed spatula. Plain cake mixtures are stiff and will not flow and adopt an even surface of their own accord. So use the spatula or the palette knife to

Making plain cakes without eggs

1 Heat oven to recommended temperature. Sieve flour, salt, powdered raising agents and any powdered flavourings.

2 Cut fat into flour until the pieces are pea sized and coated with flour. Rub in until mixture resembles even-sized breadcrumbs.

3 Stir in sugar. Make a hollow in the middle of the mixture, pour in milk and add any additional ingredients, if used.

4 To fold in the ingredients, use the spoon in a sweeping movement. Cut down to the bottom of bowl and bring spoon up round sides.

5 Fold again from the centre, turning the mixture over carefully. Do not use a stirring action. Stop when ingredients are incorporated.

6 Scrape mixture into prepared tin and smooth the top. Make a slight hollow in the surface for large cakes. Bake.

7 At the end of baking time test by inserting a thin metal skewer into the middle of the cake. When ready it should come out clean.

8 Leave the cooked cake to stand in the tin to allow it to shrink away from the sides. Then run a palette knife around inside of rim.

9 Put a clean, dry tea-towel over the rack to avoid marking the surface of the cake. Turn the cake out and leave to cool.

smooth the top, making sure that the mixture is packed into the corners and sides of the tin before baking. If you are making a large cake, make a small hollow in the centre of the surface so that the cake will have an even surface when cooked.

At the end of baking time test that the cake is cooked by inserting a thin metal skewer into the middle of the cake—the skewer should come out clean.

Leave the cooked cake to stand in its tin for 3 minutes after it has come out of the oven to allow it to shrink slightly from the sides of the tin and to make turning out easier.

Run the palette knife around the inside rim of the tin to make sure that the cake is loose, then turn out on to a wire rack to cool.

SERVING SUGGESTIONS
Plain cakes made by the rubbing-in method are traditionally served undecorated, simply cut into slices and

spread with butter. This is particularly good if the cake is eaten while still slightly warm.

But there is no reason why you should not spend a little extra time to transform a plain cake into a more appealing 'special' treat. Allow the cake to become cold before decorating.

● Spread flavoured glacé icing thinly over the surface of the cooked cake. Edge the iced surface with crystallized violets, slices of crystallized fruit or whole nuts, or scatter slivers of stem ginger or chopped nuts over the surface.

STORING

Because of their crumbly, dry texture these cakes are best eaten really fresh and still warm from the oven. Should you be able to resist the temptation of eating it all at a sitting, a plain cake can be wrapped in greaseproof paper or kitchen foil and stored in an airtight tin or plastic box with a well-fitting lid for a maximum of 3 days.

These cakes should never be frozen because they become too dry.

Handy hints

As an alternative to plain butter to spread on plain cake (or even on hot toast) make flavoured butter. Be sure the butter is at room temperature before you start.

● Mash 50 g [2 oz] butter with the zest and juice of half an orange.

● Mix 2.5 ml [½ teaspoon] cinnamon powder with 15 ml [1 tablespoon] caster sugar. Mash it into 50 g [2 oz] butter.

● Plain cakes made without eggs are traditionally served undecorated, so here is a trick to avoid marking the surface of the cake with the criss-cross pattern of the cooling rack: put a clean, dry tea towel over the rack before turning out the cake.

DATE AND WALNUT CAKE

⧗ *Don't be deterred by the use of vinegar in this cake—it is added as a raising agent and not for flavouring purposes. You will not be able to detect its taste at all. The vinegar is added separately and last of all to prevent the possibility of it curdling with the milk. Use kitchen scissors to prepare the dates and dip the blades in hot water to make the job even easier. The cake is baked at a lower temperature than is usual for plain cakes because the treacle, sugar and dates make it quite rich.*

MAKES 900 G [1¾ lb] CAKE
125 g [¼ lb] pressed dates
50 g [2 oz] walnuts
225 g [½ lb] plain flour
5 ml [1 teaspoon] bicarbonate of soda
pinch of salt
125 g [¼ lb] butter or margarine
150 ml [¼ pt] milk
25 g [1 oz] black treacle
75 g [3 oz] caster sugar
30 ml [2 tablespoons] vinegar

Plain cakes are a family treat, eaten warm with butter. Date and walnut cake is moist because it contains treacle.

1 Position the shelf in the centre and heat the oven to 160°C [325°F] gas mark 3.

2 Grease and line a 15 cm [6"] square tin and grease the lining.

3 Finely chop the dates and then chop the walnuts.

4 Sieve the flour together with the bicarbonate of soda and salt into a large mixing bowl.

5 Add the fat and use a palette knife to cut it into the flour until the pieces are pea sized and well coated with flour.

6 Rub the fat into the flour with your fingertips until the mixture resembles even-sized breadcrumbs.

7 Make a hollow in the centre of the mixture. Pour in the milk and add the treacle, sugar, dates and walnuts.

8 Using a metal spoon, fold the ingredients into the mixture until lightly blended. Add the vinegar then blend again Do not stir.

9 Bake the cake for 1¼-1½ hours.

10 Use a skewer to test that the cake is cooked.

11 Remove the cooked cake from the oven and allow to cool in the tin for 3 minutes.

12 Turn the cake on to a wire rack.

13 Remove the lining paper from the cake and serve warm or cold.

Variations
In place of the dates and walnuts use either of the following:
● For a currant and sultana cake use 75 g [3 oz] currants and 75 g [3 oz] sultanas plus 5 ml [1 teaspoon] mixed spice.
● To make a pineapple and ginger cake, use 125 g [¼ lb] canned pineapple, well drained and chopped, and 25 g [1 oz] chopped stem ginger. Decorate the cake with ginger-flavoured glacé icing.

DORSET APPLE CAKE
The juice which runs from the fruit during cooking makes this cake deliciously moist. Prepare the apples before you begin the cake.

This cake is particularly good if cut into wedges, while still slightly warm, and spread with cinnamon butter.

MAKES 700 G [1½ LB] CAKE
125 g [¼ lb] cooking apples
half a lemon
225 g [½ lb] plain flour
10 ml [2 teaspoons] bicarbonate of soda
5 ml [1 teaspoon] cream of tartar
pinch of salt
125 g [¼ lb] butter or margarine
125 g [¼ lb] caster sugar
150 ml [¼ pt] milk

1 Heat the oven to 180°C [350°F] gas mark 4.

2 Grease and line a 17.5 cm [8"] sandwich tin. Grease again.

3 Grate the lemon zest.

4 Peel, core and chop the apples. Sprinkle with a few drops of lemon juice to prevent discolouration.

5 Sieve flour, bicarbonate of soda, cream of tartar and salt into a bowl.

6 Add the fat and cut it into pea-sized pieces with a palette knife. Use your fingers to rub the fat into the flour until the mixture resembles even-sized breadcrumbs.

7 Lightly stir in the caster sugar.

8 Make a hollow in the centre of the mixture and pour in the milk. Add prepared apples and lemon zest.

9 Fold in the ingredients with a metal spoon until just blended, using light movements.

10 Scrape the mixture into the prepared tin and smooth over the top.

11 Bake the cake for 45 minutes.

12 Allow the cooked cake to stand in the tin for 3 minutes then loosen and turn the cake on to a wire rack and leave to cool.

Variations
● Any fresh fruit may be substituted for the apples. Use an appropriate spice in place of the lemon zest.
● Use 125 g [¼ lb] canned fruit, well-drained and chopped. For an extra special touch, replace 15 ml [1 tablespoon] milk with 15 ml [1 tablespoon] brandy, sherry or fruit-flavoured liqueur.

HONEY TEA-BREAD
Here is an old-fashioned favourite with the sweet flavour of honey and a hint of spices. Long slow cooking allows flavours to develop to the full.

MAKES 700 G [1½ LB] CAKE
90 g [3½ oz] butter or margarine
225 g [½ lb] plain flour
2.5 ml [½ teaspoon] ground cinnamon
2.5 ml [½ teaspoon] mixed spice
5 ml [1 teaspoon] baking powder
pinch of salt
50 g [2 oz] soft brown sugar
150 ml [¼ pt] milk
100 g [¼ lb] clear honey
75 g [3 oz] finely chopped mixed peel
flaked almonds to decorate (optional)

1 Place a shelf in the middle of the oven and heat to 160°C [325°F] gas mark 3.

2 Grease and line the base of a 20 × 10 cm [8 × 4"] loaf tin and grease again.

3 Assemble all the utensils and weigh the ingredients.

*Alsace cake has a
rich prune topping to contrast
with the plain cake mixture underneath.*

4 Sieve the flour, spices, baking powder and salt into a mixing bowl.

5 Using a round-bladed knife, cut the fat into the flour. Then rub it in with your fingertips until the mixture resembles even-sized breadcrumbs.

6 Make a hollow in the centre and lightly and evenly fold in the sugar, milk, honey and mixed peel. Do not over stir.

7 Scrape the mixture into the prepared tin and smooth the surface.

8 Scatter the flaked almonds over the top if liked.

9 Bake the cake for 1¾-2 hours. Use a skewer to test whether the cake is cooked after 1¾ hours.

10 Remove from the oven and leave in the tin for 3 minutes before turning out on to a wire rack.

11 Serve either warm or cold.

Variation
●For banana honey cake, a deliciously moist variation, simply replace the mixed peel with 125 g [¼ lb] mashed bananas.

ALSACE CAKE
This unusual cake has a spiced prune topping. Use canned prunes or substitute dried prunes, soaked and cooked. The ingredients for the topping are prepared before the cake is made so that there is the minimum of delay in getting it into the oven. The cake mixture itself is plain so a slightly higher than usual oven temperature is used.

MAKES 1KG [2½ LB] CAKE
For the topping:
425 g [15½ oz] canned prunes
1.5 ml [¼ teaspoon] ground cinnamon
50 g [2 oz] walnuts
25 g [1 oz] butter

For the cake:
225 g [½ lb] plain flour
5 ml [1 teaspoon] baking powder
2.5 ml [½ teaspoon] salt
225 g [½ lb] caster sugar
100 g [¼ oz] butter or margarine
90 ml [6 tablespoons] milk

1 Place a shelf in the centre of the oven and heat to 190°C [375°F] gas mark 5.

2 Grease and line a 19 cm [7½"] square tin and grease again.

3 Drain, stone and chop the prunes and set aside.

4 Chop the walnuts.

5 For the topping, melt the butter gently in a small heavy-based saucepan. Remove from the heat and stir in the cinnamon and walnuts. Set aside.

6 Sieve flour, baking powder and salt into a bowl.

7 Using a round-bladed knife, cut the fat into the flour and then rub in with your fingertips.

8 Make a hollow in the centre of the mixture, add the sugar and milk and mix to a light and even consistency.

9 Scrape into the prepared tin and smooth the surface.

10 Lightly press the prunes on top of the mixture, arranging them decoratively.

11 Spoon the butter mixture over the prunes. If the butter has begun to set, reheat it gently until runny.

12 Bake the cake for 40-45 minutes.

13 Use a skewer to test that the cake is cooked.

14 Allow the cooked cake to cool slightly before turning out on to a wire rack.

15 Remove the lining paper while the cake is still warm, cut into slices and serve immediately.

Variation
●For an apricot and almond cake, replace the prunes and walnuts. Pour boiling water over 125 g [¼ lb] dried apricots and soak for two hours in a small saucepan. Bring the soaking liquid to the boil and simmer for 15 minutes, then drain. Replace the cinnamon with mixed spice and top the cake with apricots and flaked almonds.

Fancy that cake

Celebrations merit something extra—a special and beautifully decorated cake is often just the answer. Here we show you how to make cakes with some exciting coloured interiors and how to ice and decorate cakes for amazing and professional-looking visual effects.

Some of the nicest cakes are those that are the simplest to make. They are then decorated to make them into something special. The Victoria sponge made by the creaming method (see on pages 12–13) is the perfect base for a wide variety of fancy cakes. Rich sponge is ideal for icing; its light, spongy texture combines well with sweet, rich fillings and icings. Perhaps the most important factor of all is that it stores well. It can therefore be made in advance— leaving you plenty of time for the decorating.

Here we show you just what can be done to make eye-catching cakes. The Victoria sponge mixture can be used in two ways. The sponge itself can be multi-coloured. For marbled cakes prepared mixture is divided and the portions coloured (and flavoured) differently. The different coloured sponges are then baked in a single tin.

Alternatively, the different coloured cake mixtures can be baked separately and then the cooled sponges are cut and assembled together in a formal pattern—usually some form of chequers. When completed, the cake is iced or coated, so that the colours inside come as a surprise when the cake is cut.

The secret of multi-coloured cakes is hidden inside. The decorative effect you are aiming for will only be visible once the slice of cake is on an individual tea plate.

Another, perhaps more spectacular, way of decorating a cake is to ice the exterior. Here we show you the professional way to go about icing; how to handle the equipment; how to do feather icing; how to decorate the sides of a cake as well as the top. We also help you with a selection of decorative patterns, so that you, too, can make a cake beautiful enough to win first prize at any baking show.

Step-by-step to making a Battenburg cake

SERVES 10
225 g [½ lb] self-raising
    flour
4 large eggs

225 g [½ lb] butter or
    margarine
225 g [½ lb] caster sugar
few drops vanilla extract

few drops red food colouring
apricot jam
225 g [½ lb] marzipan
caster suger

1 Heat oven to 190°C [375°F] gas mark 5. Grease and line a 28 × 18 cm [11 × 7"] swiss roll tin, drawing the greaseproof into a pleat, lengthways. Re-grease.

2 Sift the flour into a bowl. Whisk eggs together lightly in a small bowl. Place the butter or margarine in a mixing bowl and beat until light and creamy.

3 Add the sugar and cream it with the fat until light and fluffy. Beat in a few drops of vanilla extract. Beat in the eggs, a little at a time.

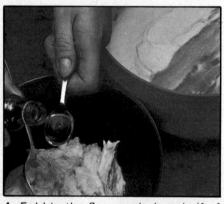

4 Fold in the flour and place half of the mixture in a separate bowl. Add a few drops of pink food colouring and beat well. Place mixture down one side of tin.

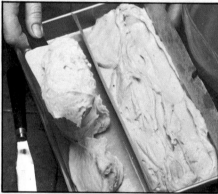

5 Place plain cake mixture down other side of prepared tin. Smooth both mixtures. Bake just above centre of oven for 45–50 minutes until golden brown.

6 Turn cakes on to a wire rack to cool. Cut each cake in half lengthways. Trim the cakes so that they are all exactly the same size.

7 Spread the sides of the cakes with the jam and stick them together, alternating the colours. Press together. Spread outside of cake with jam.

8 Sprinkle the board liberally with caster sugar and roll out marzipan to an oblong 30 × 25 cm [12 × 10"]. Spread with jam. Place the cake length on the marzipan.

9 Wrap the marzipan around the cake, seal the join and trim the edges. Pinch the top edges together to form a pattern and criss-cross the top with a sharp knife.

MULTI-COLOURED CAKES

Multi-coloured cakes are those in which the sponge itself is coloured. The rich sponge mixture can be made into several traditional and well-loved cakes, such as Battenburg or marbled cakes. Though these sponges of two or more colours may appear complicated, they are extremely easy to make at home.

The different colours of the sponge are achieved by food colourings. The sponge may also be coloured by dry flavourings, such as a cocoa powder, which both colours and flavours it at the same time.

Chequered cakes

These traditional cakes are made from rich sponge mixture which is divided in two. One portion is usually left plain and the other is coloured and sometimes flavoured. The best known of these cakes is Battenburg. The sponges are baked in a single tin, which is cleverly divided lengthways by a strip of greaseproof paper (known as a wall), which separates the two mixtures. To make a Battenburg you will need a 28 × 18 cm [11 × 7″] swiss roll tin.

After baking, the cold sponge is cut lengthways and reassembled with jam so that, when cut, the individual slices will be chequered. The outside of the cake is encased with marzipan for a Battenburg.

Marbled cake

This cake acquired its name because the sponge has the effect of marble with different colours running through it in a random pattern. The principle is the same as that of the rainbow pudding.

The sponge mix is divided and the portions of the mixture are then coloured. With the pudding, the suet mixture is coloured in various hues, but each tastes identical. The marbled cake is more sophisticated, because each colour usually has a different flavour. The choice is yours, but some obvious colour and flavour combinations are orange colour with orange zest, yellow with lemon zest, plain with vanilla, pink with raspberry or strawberry, green with almond or pistachio, coffee and chocolate powders will give a dark sponge. You can also try more sophisticated ideas; a touch of orange in a sponge coloured and flavoured with chocolate is excellent. Additions can also be made sparingly to one of the sponge mixtures, for example walnuts to coffee sponge. Follow the ideas and proportions for additions given on page 10. A recipe for a marbled cake is given here as guidance. You can then experiment with your own colours and flavours.

Marbled cakes are simplicity itself to make. After the sponge has been divided and coloured, the different sponge mixtures are put together in the same tin. A skewer is then swirled through to give a marbled effect.

WALNUT AND CHOCOLATE MARBLE CAKE

⊠⊠⊠ *The secret of this cake is revealed when the cake is cut to show the interesting 'marble look' of the two different coloured cake mixtures. It is a beautifully moist cake that the children especially will be unable to resist.*

MAKES 10–12 SLICES
225 g [½ lb] self-raising flour
pinch of salt
50 g [2 oz] cocoa powder
175 g [6 oz] butter or margarine
175 g [6 oz] caster sugar
4 medium-sized eggs
50 g [2 oz] chopped walnut

For the decoration:
225 g [½ lb] chocolate butter-cream icing
60 ml [4 tablespoons] chocolate vermicelli
8 walnut halves

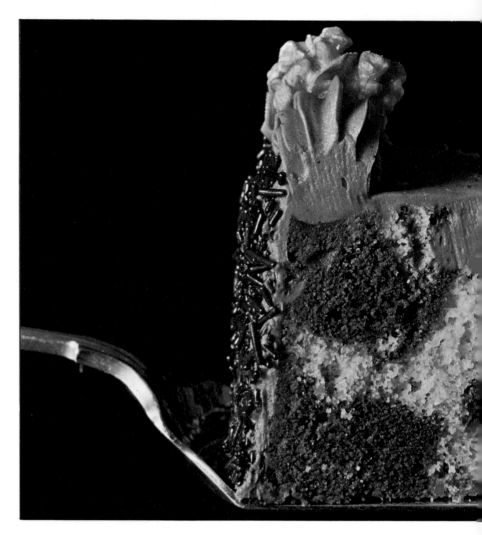

1 Position oven shelf in the centre. Heat the oven to 180°C [350°F] gas mark 4. Grease, fully line and regrease a deep, 18 cm [7"] round cake tin.

2 Sift the flour and salt into a bowl and reserve. Sift the cocoa powder into a second bowl and mix it to a thick paste with a little hot water. Put this aside to cool.

3 Place the butter or margarine in a mixing bowl and beat with a wooden spoon until soft and light. Add the sugar and cream together until light and fluffy.

4 Whisk the eggs lightly together and add gradually to the creamed mixture, beating well after each addition.

5 Gently fold in the sieved flour until completely incorporated. Transfer half of the mixture into another bowl.

6 Add the walnuts to one part of the cake mixture. Stir in until completely incorporated.

7 Add the chocolate paste to the other half of the cake mixture and beat together, until the paste is evenly distributed throughout the mixture.

8 Place the two mixtures in the prepared tin in alternate heaped teaspoons until both mixtures are used up.

9 Smooth over the surface with a palette knife. Swirl through the mixture with a skewer, briefly and with a light hand.

10 Bake for 45–50 minutes until cake is cooked. Leave the cake to cool in the tin for 10 minutes before turning out. Cool.

11 Place a generous third of the chocolate butter icing in a piping bag or pump fitted with a shell or star nozzle.

12 Spread the sides of the cake with half remaining icing to completely cover. Smooth with a palette knife.

13 Sprinkle the chocolate vermicelli on to a large piece of greaseproof paper.

14 Hold the top and bottom of the cake between the palms of your hands and carefully roll the iced side of the cake in the vermicelli to coat evenly.

15 Place the cake on a serving plate. Carefully spread the remaining icing from the bowl smoothly over the top of the cake.

16 Pipe a border of shells or stars around the top outer edge of the cake. Decorate the shells or stars with the walnut halves.

PREPARING A CAKE FOR ICING

An extra bit of care in preparing the cake before you fill and decorate it makes all the difference between an adequate result and a simply splendid one. It is worth taking the trouble to make sure the cake is in good condition before you start.

Use cold sponge

The first rule is to make sure that the cake is completely cold. Any icing applied to a warm cake will certainly melt. Bear in mind that it is not

ICING EQUIPMENT

With the correct basic equipment, piping decorative shapes is not as complicated as it at first appears. Piping icing also requires patience and know-how about the various kinds of equipment that you can use. These include an icing pump, the piping bags, which may be bought, or disposable ones made of grease-proof paper at home, plus a selection of tubes and nozzles.

Icing pump

An icing pump resembles a hyperdermic syringe and more often than not is called a piping syringe. Pumps are available in plastic and metal and consist of a cylinder with a detachable plunger at one end. This descends into the tube, forcing out the icing in the cylinder through a detachable nozzle or tube, situated at the opposite end to the plunger. An icing pump can be a little awkward to handle if you are a beginner because it takes a bit of getting used to.

Investing in an icing pump means you are buying a set which usually includes the syringe with plunger, the nozzles and tubes. It should be stressed that the icing pump is best used with a thick icing such as a butter icing or crème au beurre. If you tried to use a thin glacé icing in an icing pump, it would run through.

Piping bag

The alternative to the pump is a forcing bag which, as the name suggests, is a bag through which icing is forced. The bag looks like an

advisable to decorate a cake which is only just cold, because it tends to be too soft to handle. Purists insist that the cake should be at least 12 hours old, but this is a matter of convenience. If you want to, save time by making the cake one day, storing it overnight as directed on page 14, then decorate it the next day.

Level the surface

The second rule is that the surface of the cake for icing must be level. It is both difficult to ice a cake with a peaked surface and also looks unsightly and spoils the effect after you have gone to trouble in the baking.

Even if you have followed all the rules for baking that should produce a level surface, but still find the cake peaks, then do not be put off. There are ways to deal with this. For large cakes, place the cake on a level surface. Slice the 'peak' from the surface of the cake horizontally with a long-bladed sharp knife, using a sawing motion. Brush away any loose cake crumbs, using a pastry brush. Repeat if there is still a peak, until the cake is level.

Cakes baked in sandwich tins do not, however, require the same treatment if the surfaces are slightly uneven. Simply turn them upside down. If, on the other hand, they are very peaked, then follow the same procedure as for the larger cakes. Always brush away the loose crumbs caused by slicing the cake, otherwise they will make the icing lumpy.

Fillings

Unless you are making a particularly buttery cake, you will need to add extra flavour and moistness to a large basic cake with a filling. If you do not own sandwich tins in which to bake the cake, it may be made in a deep round or square tin. The cake is then sliced horizontally with a sharp knife for filling. Fillings are spread on to layers to sandwich a cake, they add both moisture and a contrast of texture and flavour. Butter icing, crème au beurre or a fresh thick cream can all be used, flavoured to taste or to complement the icing. There are a host of fillings to be made from basic crème au beurre which is simple and quick to make.

elongated triangle and may be made from nylon, cotton, plastic or greaseproof paper with an opening at the point of the triangle. The chosen icing nozzle is slipped into the bag when empty and sticks out of the opening so that icing will pass through it. A bag can be filled with any consistency of icing.

For beginners at icing, an icing bag is a good investment as it is easier to use. The icing bags on sale come in varying sizes, with appropriate nozzle sizes. There are several important points to consider, to save you time and money when purchasing. If you intend to pipe a little but often, then it is best to learn how to make greaseproof paper piping bags and invest in a medium or large commercial piping bag for bigger jobs.

Greaseproof piping bag
The main difference between a bought piping bag and a greaseproof paper one (which is equally as good and less expensive) is that a paper piping bag takes slightly less icing and can only be used once, for one batch of icing. The bag is made, the nozzle selected and fitted and the icing is inserted inside ready to use. But once that batch of icing is used, it is inadvisable to undo the bag and try to refill it.

If you are using different coloured icings for one cake, you can make several greaseproof paper piping bags. It is essential to make them all before you start, making sure that you have the correct size of nozzle or tube in each. Bought piping bags or pumps can easily be washed and

dried if more than one colour icing is being used. This can, however, be a time consuming process, but can be speeded up when you have a selection of bags or pumps to hand.

The nozzles
Strictly speaking a nozzle is a metal or plastic tube through which the icing passes from the bag (or pump) on to the cake. A nozzle is cone shaped, with a pattern cut from the pointed end of the cone. When the icing is being forced through this decorative point, it produces a pattern—a star, a leaf, a shell or whatever—depending on the nozzle you have chosen, for the particular decoration you need.

If the cone gives a plain thread of icing then it is called a tube, but it depends on the manufacturer as to

Making a greaseproof paper piping bag

1 Cut a 25 cm [10"] square from greaseproof paper. Fold this across diagonally, to make two triangles.

2 With base line facing away bring left-hand corner of the base up to meet the top of the triangle, so that the left-hand corner twists to meet the top of the triangle.

3 Holding the two points at the top together, bring up the right-hand corner to wrap it around the back so that the right corner meets top of the triangle to form a cone.

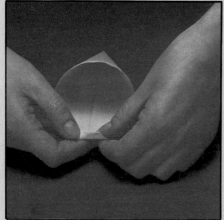

4 Fold the three corners (now all at the top) towards the inside of the cone. This prevents the bag from springing open.

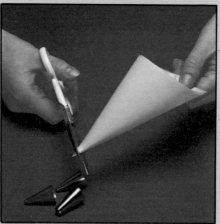

5 Cut off the point of the piping bag to fit the size of the chosen nozzle or tube. Slip this into the bag to point out the bottom.

6 Holding the bag in one hand at an angle, fill it no more than half full with a teaspoon. Fold the top of the bag down to secure for use.

what brand name it bears. Plain tubes are used for straight lines, trellis or writing and dots of icing.

If you are using a greaseproof paper piping bag to pipe threads of icing, there is no need to use a tube. Simply snip off the pointed end of the bag. How much you cut off from the tip of the bag will determine the size of the thread of icing. Always cut away a little less than you think you need, so as to be on the safe side. If the hole is not big enough, you can always cut off more.

Whether you invest in metal or plastic nozzles or tubes they should be kept scrupulously clean. If any icing is allowed to remain in the cone, it will harden (after a period of time) and block the cone the next time you use it. If the same nozzle or tube is going to be used to pipe different coloured icings consecutively, then it is essential that the cone is absolutely clean, so that the different colours are not allowed to mingle.

Simple piping techniques
Piping pumps and piping bags are virtually used in the same way and the same nozzles and designs may be used with either.
Using a piping bag
Before you start, make sure that there is no way that the icing can escape from the top of the bag while you are pressing it out through the other end. If the bag is made from greaseproof, fold down the top securely until it reaches the icing. With other piping bags, twist the folded top until you reach the icing.

Hold the filled piping bag in your right hand, so that the bag rests in the palm of the hand and your thumb is pressed on to the top of the bag securing the twist or fold that you have previously made. Bring your fingers round the bag so that you are holding it firmly. Your left hand is free to direct the bag if the pattern requires.
Using an icing pump
The body of the pump is held in the right hand with the nozzle or tube facing the surface to be iced and the left hand is used to depress the pump, thus forcing out the icing.

PIPING ICING
Piped icing can look as good as it tastes. Butter icing, crème au beurre

Assembling an icing pump

1 Screw chosen nozzle or tube into the collar and screw the collar into the end of the icing pump.

2 Fill the icing pump two-thirds full with icing. Hold icing pump with the left hand.

3 Hold the plunger in the right hand and insert into top of icing pump. Secure it in place.

Assembling and filling a nylon piping bag

1 Slip chosen nozzle or tube into bag to project through the hole. Fold back outside of top of piping bag.

2 Place assembled bag inside a tall jar with the folded rim of the bag resting on the rim of the glass.

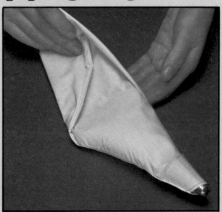

3 Half fill the bag with icing. Fold over icing bag to reach icing and twist, forcing out any trapped air.

Piping lines

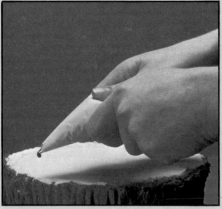

1 Hold the bag or pump fitted with a plain tube at a 45° angle to the surface to be iced, about 12 mm [½"] above it.

2 Press out the icing carefully, lifting the pump or bag up slightly, so that the icing falls on to the cake.

3 Continue pressing the icing until the line is complete. To end the line, lower the tube to touch the cake.

Piping feather icing

1 Pour glacé icing on to top of cake and spread over evenly with a round-bladed or palette knife.

2 Pipe parallel lines of contrasting colour across the iced surface, approximately 12 mm [½"] apart.

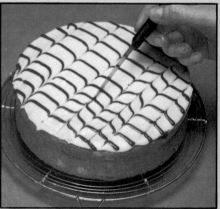

3 Quickly draw the point of a knife or a fine skewer through the piped lines in alternating directions.

Piping a trellis

1 Cover the surface of the cake with straight parallel lines.

2 Pipe a 'ladder' of parallel lines at right angles on top of previously piped lines.

and glacé icing are all suitable for piping and they complement the texture of the butter sponge. Plain or flavoured icings can be used.

Very rarely will you come across a recipe or see a cake where an icing of any description is piped straight on to a bare sponge. Generally speaking, each kind of icing is piped on to a cake which is already covered with icing of the same type. Thus, butter icing is usually piped on to butter icing and glacé icing on to glacé icing. However, butter icing can be piped on to a base of glacé icing as long as the icing underneath has had time to set and so hold the piping on top of it.

The icing you choose to pipe should first and foremost be free from any lumps of undissolved sugar

or flavouring (if used), as a lump will block the nozzle or tube. The second requirement is that the icing should be thick and firm if it needs to keep its shape on the cake. Glacé icing is usually of a coating consistency but by using less liquid it can be made semi-thick so that it will hold its shape if piped. When dry, glacé icing will set.

Quantities* of butter-cream icing for 18 cm (7") sandwich cake

*amount of icing sugar used, not total weight

For filling	75 g [3 oz]
For a topping	75 g [3 oz]
To coat the sides	175 g [6 oz]
To coat the sides and topping or fill	225 g [½ lb]

FEATHER ICING

This very pretty way of using glacé icing really is a lot less complicated than it appears. Quantities vary from 100 g [¼ lb] to 225 g [½ lb] icing depending on cake size.

Feather icing is only applied to the top of a cake and uses one batch of glacé icing, with a portion reserved (usually a third) which is coloured or flavoured to produce the decoration known as 'feathering'. This method of icing is unusual because it is the only occasion where the piped decoration is added while the base icing (or covering) of glacé icing is still soft.

Start by making a medium-sized paper bag and fitting it with a small plain tube.

Make a quantity of icing depending on the size of the cake used. Once the icing is made, transfer a scant third of it to a separate bowl. At this

point cover both bowls with a damp clean cloth to prevent the icing from drying and forming a crust. Colour the scant third of icing with a few drops of edible food colouring to contrast with, or complement, the colour of the icing over the cake. The cake covering may be plain and the decoration coloured or vice versa, or both may be coloured.

Fill the piping bag with the scant third of icing ready to use. Then, pour the remaining icing over the top of the cake and quickly spread over the surface to completely and evenly cover it. Quickly pipe parallel lines across the surface of the icing, approximately 12 mm [½"] apart.

Draw the point of a knife or a fine skewer through the piped lines making alternate strokes in opposite directions. Wipe the blade of the knife or the tip of the skewer clean in between each stroke.

DECORATING THE SIDE OF A CAKE

Many professional-looking effects are surprisingly easy to achieve at home. In this course we shall concentrate on the simplest ways to tackle the decorating of the side of a cake. More sophisticated methods are included in a later course.

The first rule is that the sides of the cake must always be done before the top is decorated.

Decorating with icings

The easiest way to decorate the side of a cake is to totally cover it with a thick icing such as a butter icing or crème au beurre. Glacé icing can be used, but this is more difficult. Glacé icing is best used where the entire cake is to be covered so that the icing runs from the top of the cake and down the sides. Glacé icing may be spread on to the side of the cake, but the procedure is a messy one because it tends to dry out quickly and the appearance is not very sophisticated.

Simple ways with thick icing

● Use a round-bladed knife or a small palette knife and spread the entire surface of the side of the cake with a layer of icing. Using the knife, place the straight side of the blade against the side of the icing (but not touching the cake) and draw it completely around the cake to attain a smooth surface.
● Spread the entire surface of the side of the cake with icing. Smooth the icing with a round-bladed knife or palette knife. Take a fork and, starting at the base of the cake, draw the prongs of the fork up the side of the cake. Continue to work from the base to the top of the cake until you meet your first marking.
● This 'forking' can be done imaginatively by waving the line being drawn with the fork.

Additional decorations

While a simple covering of a thin or thick icing suits the great majority of cakes, others look exciting when covered with additional decorations, for example coconut, nuts and chocolate.

To stick the decorations to the side of the cake, the side must either be brushed with a thin coating of sieved apricot jam glaze or an icing. Choose the decoration to complement the filling and topping, and make sure that the decorations you choose are of a suitable size and will easily adhere to the cake sides. Bear in mind the size and shape of the cake and keep decorations in proportion.

For a professional touch choose any of the following. Chocolate vermicelli, chopped nuts and desiccated coconut are the most popular choice of decoration. Nuts can also be used plain, flaked, nibbed or toasted. Finely crushed praline, caramel or biscuits or grated chocolate are also excellent.

The amount you need will depend on the size of the cake and, to a certain extent, how thick you want the decoration to be. As an approximate guide, 30–45 ml [2–3 tablespoons] is sufficient to cover the side of an 18 cm [7"] round or square cake.

Step-by-step to decorating the side of a cake

1 Brush the side of the cake only with apricot jam glaze, or coat with butter-cream icing.

2 Sprinkle the decoration of you choice on to a large sheet o greaseproof paper.

3 Hold the cake firmly with the palm of one hand on the base and the other on the top.

4 Roll the cake evenly in the de coration to coat. For a square cake press each side in turn.

Piping shells

Piping stars

1 Hold pump or bag fitted with a 'shell' or 'star' nozzle at a 45° angle to the surface to be iced.

2 Hold the nozzle close to the cake and press out a blob of icing on to the surface of the cake.

1 Use a 'star' or 'rosette' nozzle. Hold the bag or pump vertically, close to the cake surface.

3 Pull the nozzle down and away sharply to taper the end of the blob.

4 Pipe the next 'shell' directly on to the end of the tapered shell.

2 Using short squeezes of the bag or plunges of a pump, press out icing. Lift off quickly.

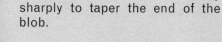

SUPER DECORATED CAKES

Here are some suggestions for dressing up a simple Victoria sandwich cake. Quantities given are for an 18 cm [7″] cake. Instructions for making and flavouring the cake are given on pages 12–13. The chart tells you the quantities of butter icing needed. You will notice that when this is used to coat the sides and fill or top the cake the amount is slightly reduced. This means that it is spread a little thinner—otherwise the results would be too sickly. If decoration is to be piped, allow an extra 50 g [2 oz] icing. Butter-cream icing or crème au beurre may be used in the following cakes.

●For a special chocolate cake, bake a chocolate flavoured sandwich. When cold, sandwich together with 30–45 ml [2–3 tablespoons] black cherry jam or preserve. Coat the sides with butter icing and roll in chocolate vermicelli to coat. Ice the top of the cake smooth with chocolate butter icing. To decorate, pipe 6–8 whirls of butter icing around the edge of the cake and top each with a piece of glacé cherry. Alternatively, cover the top with a layer of chocolate caraque

and then dust with a small quantity of icing sugar.

●For praline cake, sandwich, then spread the sides of the cake with lemon butter icing. Roll the side of the cake in a mixture of finely crushed praline and toasted, chopped almonds (which have been mixed together). Spread the top of the cake smooth with lemon butter icing and decorate with a border of piped shells. Sprinkle some more of the praline and nut mixture over the surface.

●Make this dinner party special. Bake a ginger flavoured cake. When cold, sandwich with a ginger flavoured crème au beurre. Use a little syrup from a jar of stem ginger to flavour this. Coat the top and side of the cake with more of the same crème au beurre, and smooth with a palette knife. Just before serving fill 6–8 bought brandy snaps with cream and arrange them decoratively over the top of the cake, so that they fan out from the centre. Top each with ginger.

●Make a fancy mocha cake. Sandwich, then coat the side of a chocolate cake with coffee butter icing. Coat the side in toasted,

chopped hazelnuts. Spread the top of the cake with more of the same butter icing, then decorate with stars or shells of icing around the outside edge of the top of the cake. Place a triangle of chocolate on top of each whirl, so that the point faces inwards, towards the centre of the cake.

●For a congratulation cake, sandwich, then brush the side of a coffee flavoured cake with apricot jam. Roll the side of the cake with toasted desiccated coconut and spread the top with 100 g [¼ lb] white glacé icing. Leave to set, then pipe your greeting with brown, coffee glacé icing.

●Make an orange liqueur gateau. Sprinkle each layer of cake with 45 ml [3 tablespoons] Grand Marnier. Sandwich the cake layers together with 30–45 ml [2–3 tablespoons] lightly whipped cream, which has been flavoured with orange zest. Spread the side of the cake with orange butter icing and roll in finely crushed biscuit crumbs. Spread the top of the cake with 100 g [¼ lb] orange flavoured glacé icing and allow to set. Pipe whirls of butter icing around the edge of the cake and decorate each with a slice of crystalized orange.

Bake a special cake

When you want a cake for a special occasion the traditional choice is a rich fruit cake. Packed with dried fruit, spices and other good things, these cakes keep well, taste good and are the perfect base for Christmas, Easter and birthday decorations.

Making your own wedding or Christmas cake or a cake for a special celebration might seem rather daunting but once you can make the basic rich fruit cake on which all these are based, you will find the rest easy. To make the basic cake see pages 47–53. Once mastered, pages 57–69 will show you how to make the almond paste to cover the cake, how to make traditional royal icing and how to design, assemble and ice a variety of cakes for those special days.

Rich fruit cakes are all based on the creaming method (see instructions on pages 8–14). These cakes are high in butter, sugar and eggs and are made extra delicious by the addition of dried fruit, chopped peel, nuts and spices. These cakes have excellent keeping qualities and if stored correctly will remain moist for several months. Some cakes (notably

Christmas and wedding cakes which have spirit added at intervals after baking) actually improve with keeping.

It is true that rich fruit cakes can crack or sink but this only happens if you fail to line the tin correctly, use the wrong size tin or bake at the wrong temperature. The guides to quantities and temperatures that you will find here will ensure that you use the right tin every time so success is (almost) guaranteed!

INGREDIENTS

It is the quantity of fat and sugar in relation to flour which determines the richness of a cake. It is not, as is often thought, the amount of fruit used. The proportions of fat to sugar for rich fruit cake are basically the same as for creaming cakes (see page 8), but more of each is used. In some recipes, proportions may vary slightly. If there is more fat than sugar, the cake will be richer than if equal quantities were used. If there is more sugar, the cake will have a spongy texture. In this course you will find a chart giving amounts of ingredients for making rich fruit cakes of varying sizes. For fruity cakes, a little more flour than fat or sugar is used because of the high fruit and egg content.

Flour

Usually plain white flour is used for rich fruit cakes. The amount of flour used is almost always the same as the amount of butter or fat and sugar, except for very rich traditional cakes (see chart).

Raising agent

To help the cake rise, a raising agent is sometimes but not always added with the flour. For a very rich fruit cake with a dense texture, such as a wedding or Christmas cake, a raising agent is often omitted entirely.

The usual raising agent is bicarbonate of soda for a dark cake or baking powder for a light cake. Quantities depend on the amount of other ingredients in the cake.

Fat

There is no doubt that butter gives the finest flavour to rich cakes and it is well worth using if the cake is for something like a wedding or christening. A combination of butter and hard margarine gives good results or you can use hard margarine alone. The amount of fat is usually the same as the amount of flour, except in very fruity cakes where it is about 25–100 g [1–4 oz] less.

Have the fat soft but not oily when you come to use it. This makes creaming easier and gives lighter results.

Sugar

Caster or soft brown sugar are the sweet choices for rich fruit cakes. Soft brown sugar gives darker results. Treacle, golden syrup or marmalade may be used in place of some of the sugar but it is best to find a recipe and follow carefully if you want to do this. The quantity of sugar is always the same as the quantity of butter or fat and flour, except in very rich cakes where quantities are as given in the chart on pages 52–53.

Eggs

Eggs add moisture, flavour and colour to the cake and also help to give a good, soft texture. They also help the cake to rise. Large eggs are usually used for rich cakes.

Liquids

Sometimes a little extra liquid is added both to give flavour and to produce the steam which helps the cake to rise. For very rich traditional cakes, brandy, rum or sherry are used. The amount depends on the recipe. Cakes with spirits added in this way keep well. Other liquids which can be added are milk, orange juice, cold strained tea or beer.

Fruit

Fruit adds colour, flavour, texture and sweetness to rich cakes. It also contributes to their keeping qualities. Only dried and crystallized or glacé fruits are used. Canned or fresh fruit is too soft and contains too much liquid to make a satisfactory cake.

As a guide, you can add between 225 g and 1.4 kg [$\frac{1}{2}$–3 lb] fruit to every 450 g [1 lb] flour. The richer the cake, the higher the proportion of fruit.

You can use just one kind of fruit or several different kinds. Currants, raisins, sultanas, candied peel and glacé cherries, the traditional cake fruit, are all good choices. Prunes and dates are excellent in dark cakes. Less usual, but well worth trying in light fruit cakes are dried pears, apricots and peaches.

Always use good quality fruit. It should look plump and juicy. Most cake fruit is ready washed these days so there is no need to go to all the trouble of washing and drying. Avoiding washing is a good thing because wet fruit tends to sink. All dried fruit should be tossed in a little of the flour used for making the cake to give an "insurance" against sinking.

Most dried fruit is sold stoned but you may still find some large raisins sold unstoned. Removing the stones

from these is done by rolling the fruit between your fingers.

Glacé fruit must, of course, be washed and well dried before being included in rich cakes. The sugar which coats glacé fruit can make the fruit sink to the bottom and spoil the cake. Glacé cherries, pineapple, apricots and greengages are all good, particularly in light fruit cakes. Candied peel can be bought readyshredded in packets but for superior flavour it is best if you can buy peel in what old fashioned grocers call 'caps'. These are large pieces of peel (often half the fruit from which the peel was taken) which are filled with sugar in the centre. Before using, scoop out the sugar then mince or shred the peel to roughly the same size as the ready-cut kind.

Angelica can be used in light fruit cakes. It should be soaked in warm water to remove the sugar, patted dry then chopped into small pieces. Crystallized ginger, although not a fruit, can be included in the fruit content for rich cakes. Treat in the same way as angelica.

Nuts

Chopped nuts are often used in fruit cakes or can be used whole on top of traditional cakes such as Dundee cake. Almonds, hazelnuts and wal-nuts are the usual choice. The nuts should always be of the skinned variety as the skin can taste rather bitter in a cake. Like fruit, nuts should be tossed in flour.

Spices

Spices are an essential ingredient in dark rich cakes, both to give flavour and to aid in preserving the cake. The spices should always be powdered. Nutmeg, cinnamon, ginger, mixed spice and allspice are best for cakes. Always follow recipe instructions carefully when adding spice as too much can overpower the cake.

Fruit zest

Grated orange or lemon zest are favourites to include in light and some dark fruit cakes.

MAKING THE CAKE

Making a rich fruit cake demands a fair degree of organization from the cook. It goes without saying that with so many ingredients, everything should be measured out first and be ready to use before you start mixing the cake. Follow the plan given here and all will go smoothly.

Preparing the tin

Fruit cakes are baked in deep round, square or 'novelty' tins. These must be fully lined and greased, as shown on page 30. It is advisable to put a double layer of greaseproof paper on the bottom of the cake with grease between the layers.

Large rich fruit cakes which need long slow baking must have extra protection to prevent the edges burning before the middle is cooked. This can be given by tying a double thickness of strong brown paper around the outside of the tin. The tin is then baked sitting on several layers of brown paper or newspaper so that the bottom is protected.

Heating the oven

As with all cakes, the oven must be heated well in advance so it is at exactly the right temperature when you put the cake in. Usually the larger and richer the cake, the lower the oven heat needs to be. This means that some wedding cakes may need several hours baking. Always follow the temperatures given in recipes. Don't increase it thinking that it seems too low.

Preparing the fruit and nut

Next prepare the dried fruit and chop nuts. Ordinary cake fruit will need no preparation but glacé cherries must be washed, dried and halved. Other glacé fruit should be treated in a similar way. Full details are given in the section on fruit. Toss fruit and

nuts in a little of the flour used for the cake. When you have measured out all your ingredients, you can start on the cake.

Creaming

The making of a rich fruit cake starts with creaming the fat and sugar together, exactly as described on pages 10–11 where full details of making cakes by the creaming method are given.

Adding eggs and flour

It is when the eggs and flour are added that the making of rich fruit cakes differs from the making of creamed cakes. The eggs are beaten with any other liquid (such as spirits) and added alternately with the sieved flour, spices and any raising agent used. As there are usually quite a lot of eggs in a rich fruit cake, this method is a good idea because it reduces the risk of curdling.

Adding the fruit

The dried fruit is beaten into the mixture after all the eggs, liquid and flour have been incorporated. Mix the fruit in well so that it is evenly distributed throughout the mixture.

Filling the tin

The mixture should be of a soft dropping consistency when the time comes to put it in the tin. Turn the prepared mixture into your tin and level the top in the usual way. If you are making a cake requiring prolonged baking, it is a good idea to wet your fingers and smooth the top. The film of moisture prevents the cake drying out during cooking. Hollow the centre of the cake slightly to prevent peaking. If the cake contains a high proportion of fruit and is to be iced, make the hollow deeper than usual to ensure a good level surface.

Toppings

Fruit cakes which are not required for icing can have fruit or nut toppings added before baking. These are applied to the cake after you have put it in the tin, levelled the surface and made the anti-peak hollow in the middle.
● For traditional Dundee cake, arrange blanched almonds in concentric circles on top of the cake.
● For crunchy-topped cake, scatter the surface of the cake with flaked almonds.
● For a caramel topping, roughly crush sugar cubes and scatter over the top of the cake.
● For fruit and nut topping, sprinkle the cake with chopped glacé fruit and roughly chopped brazil nuts.

BAKING

Bake the cake as directed in the recipe. When the top begins to colour, protect the surface with a piece of foil or greaseproof paper. Foil is easier to manage because it can be moulded to the edge of the tin. The foil can be removed just before the end of cooking to complete browning. Always test that the cake really is cooked at the end of the cooking time recommended. Ovens can vary in temperature according to the variences of the power supply, so it isn't always safe to think that the time for baking a cake in a recipe is guaranteed. There is a couple of simple tests to check that cakes of this type are cooked.

Testing

To test the cake, gently insert a skewer in the centre. If the skewer comes out clean, the cake is cooked. A second test is to remove the cake from the oven and hold it to your ear. If the cake is still 'singing', then it is not cooked.

Cooling

When the cake is cooked, remove from the oven and leave to cool in the tin. This helps to keep the crust soft and avoids the danger of the cake cracking or breaking when turned out. When the cake is cool enough to handle easily (after about 30 minutes), turn out on to a wire rack and leave until completely cold.

SLICING FRUIT CAKES

Traditionally, fruit cakes are not cut into wedges but are sliced across. These slices are then cut into pieces of the desired size. This gives flat rather than triangular pieces of cake.

STORING

Light fruit cakes can be eaten the day after they are made, but very rich cakes such as a wedding cake, need time to allow the flavour to mature. These are best kept for 2–3 months. To store these cakes, leave the lining paper attached and allow the cake to become completely cold. Wrap the cake in kitchen foil and store in an airtight tin or snap-top container.

A good way to enrich the cake during this time is to add alcohol. To do this, prick the surface of the cake and brush with a little brandy, rum or sherry every week until the cake is needed for icing.

Dundee cake is one of the most famous of all rich cakes and provides a good example of how these cakes are made. This mixture is rich enough to use for a wedding cake or christening cake if you add a little sherry or brandy after cooking as described in the section on storage.

MAKES 8–10 SLICES
50 g [2 oz] candied peel
50 g [2 oz] glacé cherries
100 g [¼ lb] blanched almonds
275 g [10 oz] butter or margarine
275 g [10 oz] soft brown sugar
275 g [10 oz] plain flour
5 ml [1 teaspoon] mixed spice
grated zest of 1 lemon
4 large eggs
100 g [¼ lb] currants
100 g [¼ lb] raisins
100 g [¼ lb] sultanas

4 Chop half of the almonds. Split the other half lengthwise and set aside. Toss fruit and chopped nuts in a little of the flour.

8 Transfer the mixture to the prepared tin. Level the top. Make a hollow in the centre to prevent peaking during cooking.

Step-by-step to Dundee cake

Line a 20 cm [8"] round or 18 cm [7"] square cake tin with greaseproof paper. Tie a double thickness of brown paper round the tin.

2 Heat the oven to 160°C [325°F], gas mark 3. Scrape sugar from candied peel caps and chop the peel roughly.

3 Wash syrup from glacé cherries using warm water. Dry well. Halve the cherries using a sharp knife, Set aside.

5 Put fat and sugar in a large bowl and cream with a wooden spoon or an electric whisk until light and fluffy.

6 Sift the flour and spice. Add lemon zest. Beat eggs. Add a little of the egg to the creamed mixture.

7 Continue adding egg and flour alternately until it has all been used. Beat in all the fruit and chopped nuts.

9 Arrange the halved nuts in concentric circles. Put a thick piece of newspaper on a baking tray and put the cake tin on it.

10 Bake for 2½–3 hours. When the cake is coloured, cover with foil. At the end of cooking time test with skewer.

11 Cool the cake in the tin, then turn on to wire cooling rack. Leave to cool completely before storing.

Size of tin	15 cm [6"] round	15 cm [6"] square 18 cm [7"] round	18 cm [7"] square 20 cm [8"] round	20 cm [8"] square 23 cm [9"] round
Currants	225 g [½ lb]	350 g [¾ lb]	450 g [1 lb]	625 g [1 lb 6 oz]
Sultanas	90 g [3½ oz]	140 g [4½ oz]	200 g [7 oz]	225 g [½ lb]
Raisins	90 g [3½ oz]	140 g [4½ oz]	200 g [7 oz]	225 g [½ lb]
Glacé cherries	50 g [2 oz]	75 g [3 oz]	150 g [5 oz]	175 g [6 oz]
Chopped candied mixed peel	25 g [1 oz]	50 g [2 oz]	75 g [3 oz]	100 g [¼ lb]
Chopped blanched almonds	25 g [1 oz]	50 g [2 oz]	75 g [3 oz]	100 g [¼ lb]
Plain flour	175 g [6 oz]	215 g [7½ oz]	350 g [¾ lb]	400 g [14 oz]
Salt	pinch	pinch	pinch	pinch
Mixed spice	1.25 ml [¼ teaspoon]	2.5 ml [½ teaspoon]	2.5 ml [½ teaspoon]	5 ml [1 teaspoon]
Cinnamon	1.25 ml [¼ teaspoon]	2.5 ml [½ teaspoon]	2.5 ml [½ teaspoon]	5 ml [1 teaspoon]
Fat (butter or margarine)	150 g [5 oz]	175 g [6 oz]	275 g [10 oz]	350 g [12 oz]
Soft brown sugar	150 g [5 oz]	175 g [6 oz]	275 g [10 oz]	350 g [12 oz]
Eggs	2½ large	3 large	5 large	6 large
Brandy or rum	15 ml [1 tablespoon]	15 ml [1 tablespoon]	15–30 ml [1–2 table-spoons]	30 ml [2 tablespoons]
Oven temperature*	150°C [300°F] gas mark 2	150°C [300°F] gas mark 2	150°C [300°F] gas mark 2	150°C [300°F] gas mark 2
Approximate cooking time	2½–3 hours	3 hours	3½ hours	4 hours
Weight of cooked cake	1.15 kg [2½ lb]	1.45 kg [3¼ lb]	2.2 kg [4¾ lb]	2.7 kg [6 lb]

Grated lemon or orange zest is often included, see recipes, or use according to taste.

AND CORRESPONDING SIZED FRUIT CAKES

(in almond paste and royal icing)

23 cm [9"] square / 25 cm [10"] round	25 cm [10"] square / 28 cm [11"] round	28 cm [11"] square / 30 cm [12"] round	30 cm [12"] square
800 g [1¾ lb]	1.15 kg [2½ lb]	1.5 kg [3 lb 2 oz]	1.7 kg [3¾ lb]
375 g [13 oz]	400 g [14 oz]	525 g [1 lb 3 oz]	625 g [1 lb 6 oz]
375 g [13 oz]	400 g [14 oz]	525 g [1 lb 3 oz]	625 g [1 lb 6 oz]
250 g [9 oz]	275 g [10 oz]	350 g [¾ lb]	425 g [15 oz]
150 g [5 oz]	200 g [7 oz]	250 g [9 oz]	275 g [10 oz]
150 g [5 oz]	200 g [7 oz]	250 g [9 oz]	275 g [10 oz]
600 g [1 lb 5 oz]	700 g [1½ lb]	825 g [1 lb 13 oz]	1 kg [2 lb 3 oz]
pinch	pinch	pinch	pinch
5 ml [1 teaspoon]	10 ml [2 teaspoons]	12.5 ml [2½ teaspoons]	12.5 ml [2½ teaspoons]
5 ml [1 teaspoon]	10 ml [2 teaspoons]	12.5 ml [2½ teaspoons]	12.5 ml [2½ teaspoons]
500 g [1 lb 2 oz]	600 g [1 lb 5 oz]	800 g [1¾ lb]	950 g [2 lb 2 oz]
500 g [1 lb 2 oz]	600 g [1 lb 5 oz]	800 g [1¾ lb]	950 g [2 lb 2 oz]
9 large	11 large	14 large	17 large
30–45 ml [2–3 tablespoons]	45 ml [3 tablespoons]	60 ml [4 tablespoons]	90 ml [6 tablespoons]
150°C [300°F] gas mark 2	150°C [300°F] gas mark 2	150°C [300°F] gas mark 2	150°C [300°F] gas mark 2
6 hours	7 hours	8 hours	8½ hours
4 kg [9 lb]	5.2 kg [11½ lb]	6.7 kg [14¾ lb]	7.7 kg [17 lb]

*For cakes 25 cm [10"] and over reduce oven temperature to 130°C [250°F] gas mark ½ after ⅔ cooking time.

GENOA CAKE

⊠⊠⊠ *This is a moist, light fruit cake with a deliciously lemony flavour. It is suitable for a cut and come again cake rather than for a special cake to be iced. In Genoa cake, the quantity of flour is greater than the quantity of fat or sugar to give a slightly softer cake.*

MAKES 8–10 SLICES
100 g [¼ lb] glacé cherries
50 g [2 oz] candied peel
40 g [1½ oz] blanched almonds
175 g [6 oz] caster sugar
175 g [6 oz] butter or
** margarine**
3 large eggs
15 ml [1 tablespoon] milk
225 g [½ lb] plain flour
5 ml [1 teaspoon] baking
** powder**
grated zest of 1 lemon
50 g [2 oz] flaked almonds
** or chopped walnuts to**
** decorate (optional)**

1 Grease and line a 20 cm [8"] round or 18 cm [7"] square cake tin. Tie a double thickness of brown paper around the outside.

2 Wash the glacé cherries and dry well. Halve. Scoop sugar out of candied peel caps and chop the peel roughly. Chop the almonds. Toss nuts and fruit in a little of the flour used for the cake.

3 Put the fat and sugar in a large bowl and cream with an electric whisk until light and fluffy.

4 Beat the eggs with the milk. Sift flour and baking powder together. Add lemon zest.

5 Add eggs and flour to the creamed mixture alternately, beating well after each addition.

6 Beat in the fruit and nuts. Transfer mixture to the cake tin. Level the top and make a hollow in the centre.

7 Scatter with chopped nuts. Put a thick piece of newspaper on a baking tray. Place the cake on the tray and bake for 3–3¾ hours until a skewer inserted at centre of cake comes out clean.

8 Allow to cool in tin. Turn out on to a wire rack until completely cold.

WHITE FRUIT CAKE

⊠⊠⊠ *The cake is not literally white but is pale in colour as opposed to dark which is the usual shade for rich cakes. The top of this cake is decorated in the continental way with glacé fruits and nuts, beautifully glazed. On the continent, this cake is used as a Christmas cake. For extra light results, this cake is made with a combination of self raising and plain flour with a little cornflour added to give a softer texture.*

MAKES 12–15 SLICES
100 g [¼ lb] plain flour
100 g [¼ lb] self raising
** flour**
50 g [2 oz] cornflour
100 g [¼ lb] glacé pineapple
175 g [6 oz] glacé cherries
100 g [¼ lb] mixed glacé
** fruit**
50 g [2 oz] crystallized
** ginger**
50 g [2 oz] mixed candied
** peel**
50 g [2 oz] angelica
50 g [2 oz] blanched almonds
50 g [2 oz] walnuts
225 g [½ lb] butter or
** margarine**
150 g [5 oz] caster sugar
4 large eggs
15 ml [1 tablespoon] lemon
** juice**
45 ml [3 tablespoons] milk

To decorate:
22 shelled brazil nuts
22 pieces glacé pineapple
16 halves glacé cherry
10 blanched almonds
3 walnuts
45 ml [3 tablespoons] clear
** honey**

1 Line a 20 cm [8"] round cake tin. Tie a double thickness of brown paper around the outside of the tin to prevent over-browning.

2 Heat the oven to 160°C [325°F] gas mark 3. Sift flours and cornflour together.

3 Wash the glacé fruit and pat dry. Scrape sugar out of candied peel caps and chop roughly. Soak angelica and ginger in warm water for about 2 minutes. Pat dry and chop. Chop the nuts.

4 Mix the fruit and nuts together. Toss in a little of the flour.

5 Put the fat and sugar in a large bowl. Cream together using a wooden spoon or electric whisk until light and fluffy.

6 Beat the eggs with the lemon juice and milk. Beat eggs and flour into creamed mixture alternately.

7 Beat in the fruit and nuts. Turn into the prepared tin. Level the top and make a hollow in the centre.

8 Put a thick piece of newspaper on a baking tray. Bake in the centre of the oven for 2½ hours or until a skewer inserted in the cake comes out clean. Cover the cake with foil as it begins to colour.

9 Cool in the tin for 15 minutes. Turn on to a wire cooling rack and leave until completely cold.

10 Brush the top of the cake with clear honey. Arrange the brazil nuts around the edge. Reserve remainder.

11 Next make a circle of pineapple, then cherries and continue until the top of the cake is covered.

12 Heat the honey in a small heavy-based pan. When liquid, brush liberally over the decoration on the top of the cake. Leave to set for at least 1 day before cutting.

ECONOMICAL CHRISTMAS CAKE

This cake is rather cheaper to make than the usual rich fruit cake prepared for Christmas. You will find details on icing a Christmas cake on pages 57–67.

MAKES 10–12 SLICES
225 g [½ lb] margarine
225 g [½ lb] soft brown sugar
275 g [10 oz] plain flour
2.5 ml [½ teaspoon] bicarbonate of soda
5 ml [1 teaspoon] mixed spice
pinch of nutmeg
grated zest of ½ lemon
225 g [½ lb] sultanas
100 g [¼ lb] currants
225 g [½ lb] raisins
4 large eggs
a few drops of vanilla extract
a few drops of almond extract
15 ml [1 tablespoon] marmalade

1 Line a 20 cm [8″] round tin. Tie a double thickness of brown paper around the sides.

2 Heat the oven to 150°C [300°F] gas mark 2. Put margarine and sugar in a bowl.

3 Cream margarine and sugar until light and fluffy using either a wooden spoon or an electric whisk.

4 Sift the flour, bicarbonate of soda and the spices. Toss fruit in a little of the flour. Stir in the lemon zest. Beat the eggs with the extracts. Beat marmalade into egg mixture.

5 Add flour and eggs to the creamed mixture alternately. When all have been added, beat in the fruit until it is evenly distributed.

6 Turn the mixture into the prepared tin. Level the top and make a hollow in the centre.

7 Put a thick piece of newspaper on a baking tray. Place the cake on the tray. Bake towards the bottom of the oven for 4 hours.

8 When the cake begins to colour, cover with foil. Remove just before the end of cooking.

9 Cool in the tin. Turn out on to a wire rack. Leave until cold then wrap in foil to store.

Something to celebrate

The focal point of any wedding reception, christening or engagement party, or Christmas tea, is inevitably the cake. Packed with luscious fruit and beautifully decorated, a home-made celebration cake is a real tribute to your skills as a cook. Pages 47–56 show you how to make the basic cake and here you will discover how it can be beautifully, yet simply, iced to grace any party table.

Traditional iced fruit cakes have always been an important part of any family celebration. Unfortunately, although most cooks can manage the baking of the cake without too much difficulty, they fall down when it comes to the icing. Icing traditional cakes is nothing to be afraid of, especially if you follow the advice given in this course and learn to walk with the simpler forms

of decoration before you go off at a headlong gallop with elaborate piping and intricate designs.

Celebration cakes are always based on a rich fruit cake mixture. Full details on making a variety of suitable cakes are given on pages 47–56. To turn an ordinary fruit cake into something special, you must first

coat it with almond paste and then cover it with white royal icing—a special stiff icing that sets very hard and gives a good, glossy finish.

BASIC EQUIPMENT

Although you can improvise, if you are making a very special cake, it is well worth having the right equipment for the job.

Turntable
This is essential for really smooth, flat icing as it enables you to move the cake around evenly as you work.

Cake board
A cake board is traditional and necessary for royal iced cakes as they are awkward to transfer to a serving plate after icing. Cake boards can be bought or you can cover a board with silver paper or foil.

Palette knife
A palette knife is essential to spread the icing evenly.

Plain edged scraper
A piece of card or plastic will do for this. The scraper is simply a straight edge which can be used to smooth the sides of the cake.

Icing ruler
An icing ruler helps to keep the top of the cake smooth and if you buy a good one, can be useful in many other ways. Good icing rulers have letter and shape stencils for run out designs and are marked in centimetres or inches so you can plan the spacing of your design.

ALMOND PASTE

The first thing to do towards decorating your celebration cake is to prepare the almond paste.

Ingredients
The quantity of ingredients depends on the size you want your cake to be. Quantities of almond paste for completely covering cakes of various sizes are given in the chart. The weight of paste made is twice the weight of ground almonds used.

Almonds
The most obvious ingredient of almond paste is, of course, ground almonds. It is the flavour of these almonds which makes the paste contrast so pleasantly with the sweet icing. When making almond paste, the quantity of almonds is the same as the quantity of sugar. The quantity of almonds is also always half the amount of the weight of paste you are making. Therefore if a recipe calls for 450 g [1 lb] of almond paste, it would be made with 225 g [½ lb] ground almonds.

Sugar
For really smooth almond paste,

Step-by-step to almond paste

MAKES 450 G [1 LB]
100 g [¼ lb] icing sugar
100 g [¼ lb] caster sugar
225 g [½ lb] ground almonds
5 ml [1 teaspoon] lemon juice
few drops of almond essence
1 small egg, beaten

1   Sift the sugars and the ground almonds into a bowl. Make a well in the centre.

2   Add the lemon juice, almond essence and some of the egg. Mix well. If there is not enough liquid, add more egg.

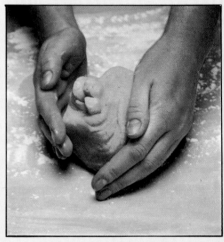

3   Mix to a smooth paste. Turn out on to a board sprinkled lightly with icing sugar. Knead for 3 minutes.

always use equal quantities of caster and icing sugar. The quantity of sugar is always the same as the quantity of ground almonds.

Flavourings
To give the paste a good flavour, a little lemon juice and almond essence are always added to the paste. For 450 g [1 lb] paste, add 5 ml [1 teaspoon] lemon juice and a few drops of almond essence.

Eggs
To bind the almonds and sugar together and make a smooth, workable paste, beaten egg is used. Generally speaking, you will need one medium-sized egg for each 225 g [½ lb] ground almonds and 225 g [½ lb] mixed caster and icing sugar, but a whole egg may not be necessary.

MAKING THE PASTE
Making almond paste is a fairly simple business. It should not be made too far in advance of the time that it is to be used, otherwise the surface may dry out and crack. Follow these principles for a smooth paste which is easy to use.

Sifting almonds and sugar
Sift the ground almonds and sugar together to ensure that they are evenly mixed and that no coarse particles get into the mixture, as these would spoil the smooth appearance of the paste.

Adding the liquid
Beat the egg and all the liquid together. This will ensure that the

Step-by-step to almond paste decorations

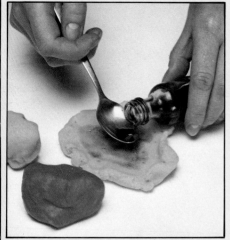

1 To colour almond paste, work edible food colouring into it. Deep colours look best.

2 For holly leaves, draw a leaf on to card. Use as a template to cut shapes. Mark veins with a knife.

OR cut out small rounds using a plain cutter. Cut away the edges with a smaller cutter.

3 For holly berries, roll small balls of almond paste coloured red with food colouring.

4 For candles, colour paste red. Cut one large candle shape or smaller ones. Use yellow almond paste for flames.

5 For bells, draw bell shapes on to card. Assemble small bells in bunches. Large bells can be used alone.

flavourings are evenly distributed throughout the mixture. Make a well in the centre of the sifted almonds and sugar, add the liquid and mix well together.

Kneading

To make the almond paste smooth and free from cracks, it must be kneaded. To do this, turn the paste on to a board which you have scattered with a little sifted icing sugar. This will prevent the paste sticking to the board and as the icing sugar is smooth it will not add coarse granules. Knead the paste by hand as you would bread dough (see on pages 130–132) for about 3 minutes or until it is completely smooth and free from cracks.

USING THE PASTE

Before you can apply almond paste to a cake, you must prepare the cake and make an apricot glaze to stick the paste on to the cake.

Preparing the cake

Needless to say, you must have a level surface to which you apply the almond paste. If the top of the cake has peaked slightly, cut it level and then turn the cake over so that the flat bottom becomes the top to which you apply the almond paste. Applying almond paste to a cut, crumby surface can be rather difficult. By turning the cake over, you play safe.

Preparing the glaze

Almond paste will not stick to your cake by magic. To make it stick, a glaze made from melted apricot jam is used. You do not need very much glaze—about 45 ml [3 tablespoons] is usually sufficient. If more is needed, you can always sieve in a little more jam and re-heat. If less is needed, the unused glaze can be left to set and poured back into the jam jar.

To make the glaze, sieve the jam into a small, heavy-based pan. Add a squeeze of lemon juice and melt over low heat. Other jams can be used but apricot is the traditional choice.

Measuring the paste

Applying almond paste to a cake defeats many cooks because they do not measure the paste properly. It is most important that you measure the

Step-by-step to using almond paste

1 Using a piece of string, measure outside edge of cake. With another piece, measure depth.

2 Cut the top of the cake level if necessary. Turn it over.

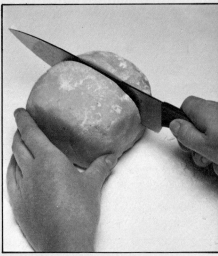

3 Cut off two thirds of the paste.

4 Roll it to a rectangle half the length of the string and twice the depth of the cake. Halve lengthways.

5 Brush each strip with sieved, melted apricot jam.

6 Roll the cake on the strips so that sides are covered. Neaten joins.

7 Roll out remaining third of the paste to fit the top of the cake. Brush cake top with melted jam.

8 Brush a rolling pin with icing sugar. Roll gently over the paste on top of the cake.

9 Run a straight-sided jam jar around the edges of the cake. This will help the paste to adhere.

QUANTITIES OF ALMOND PASTE AND ROYAL ICING

Tin size:								
round	15 cm [6"]	18 cm [7"]	20 cm [8"]	23 cm [9"]	25 cm [10"]	28 cm [11"]	30 cm [12"]	—
square	—	15 cm [6"]	18 cm [7"]	20 cm [8"]	23 cm [9"]	25 cm [10"]	28 cm [11"]	30 cm [12"]
Almond paste	350 g [¾ lb]	450 g [1 lb]	550 g [1¼ lb]	800 g [1¾ lb]	900 g [2 lb]	1 kg [2¼ lb]	1.1 kg [2½ lb]	1.4 kg [3 lb]
Royal icing	450 g [1 lb]	550 g [1¼ lb]	700 g [1½ lb]	900 g [2 lb]	1 kg [2¼ lb]	1.1 kg [2½ lb]	1.4 kg [3 lb]	1.6 kg [3½ lb]

paste to fit the cake, following the simple method shown in the step-by-step instructions.

Decorations

If you do not want to royal ice a cake, quite effective decorations can be made using coloured almond paste. The paste is coloured using edible food colourings and can be used to make holly leaves, berries, flowers, fruit (see pages 24–25 for fruit decorations), Christmas bells, lettering or any other decoration of your choice.

Before you colour the paste, draw out the design you want to use for the cake on a piece of paper. Mark in the colours you will be using.

To colour the paste divide the paste into appropriate amounts and colour, as desired by adding a little food colouring and working in with your fingers.

ROYAL ICING

For traditional celebration cakes, royal icing is always used to cover the almond paste and to decorate the cake. Royal icing sets very hard so it will hold quite a complicated decoration or piping effectively.

Ingredients for icing

Royal icing is simply made from icing sugar and egg whites. A little lemon juice is added for flavour and glycerine is included to give the icing a sheen. The proportions for royal icing are 225 g [½ lb] icing sugar to every egg white and 15 ml [1 tablespoon] lemon juice plus 10 ml [2 teaspoons] glycerine to every 4 egg whites. In this way, you will be able to make an icing which is stiff, glossy and easy to work with. The chart shows how much icing is needed for cakes of various sizes. The weight of icing given in the chart is based on the weight of icing sugar used in the recipe.

Making the icing

Making the icing is quite simple but it does involve a lot of beating. If wished, an electric whisk can be used for this.

First of all you must sift the icing sugar. Icing sugar can be very lumpy and this would spoil the appearance of the icing.

The egg whites should be whisked until they are just frothy—not until they are approaching the consistency of meringue. This makes the whites easy to mix with the icing sugar. To make good royal icing, the icing sugar must be beaten into the egg whites a little at a time. Ideally, you should beat in only 5 ml [1 teaspoon] at a time until half the icing sugar has been used. At this point, you can add the lemon juice. The remaining icing sugar is then incorporated in same way. When all the sugar has been used, the glycerine may be added.

Storing

Royal icing must be kept for 24 hours before it can be used. This allows it to stiffen to the correct texture for icing the cake. Store the icing in a covered container.

USING ROYAL ICING

Royal icing can of course be used for intricate piping but it is best to wait until you are used to working with it before you attempt this.

Here you will see how to rough ice a cake, how to flat ice it and how to do some simple piping.

Preparing to ice

Before you ice any cake, it is important to anchor it to your cake board. This will hold the cake firm as you move your turntable around. To do this, put a blob of icing on the centre of the board and place the cake on it.

For flat icing, it is rather more important to have a turntable as it is difficult to achieve a good, smooth finish without one. You must start icing the cake at least two weeks before it is required as the icing must be allowed to set firmly between coats and must be rock hard on the day you start piping. The piping itself should set too, so the further in advance you start, the better.

Rough icing

The easiest point at which to begin working with royal icing is to rough ice a cake. This method involves covering the cake in icing then roughing it up so that it stands in peaks. This idea is particularly good for Christmas cakes as it gives a frosty effect.

Spreading the icing

Put all the icing on top of the cake. Do not worry that this looks like an awful lot, it spreads over quite thinly. Using a palette knife or an icing ruler, spread the icing over the cake, working backwards and forwards. This will burst any air bubbles in the icing which could spoil the appearance of the cake. When the bubbles have broken, spread the icing to the edges of the top of the cake and then spread it around the sides. It does not matter if the icing is not perfectly smooth as you will be roughing up the surface anyway.

Roughing

When you have spread all the icing and the top and sides of the cake are all covered, use the blade of a round-bladed knife to rough up the icing in peaks. Leave to set for at least a week before cutting the cake. The peaks may be topped with silver cake balls when wet for extra sparkle.

Step-by-step to royal icing

MAKES 900 G [2 LB] ROYAL
ICING
900 g [2 lb] icing sugar
4 large egg whites
15 ml [1 tablespoon] lemon
   juice
10 ml [2 teaspoons] glycerine

1 Sift the icing sugar twice. This will ensure that the icing is lump free.

2 Place the egg whites in a large bowl. Whisk until frothy but not until stiff.

3 Beat the icing sugar into the egg whites using 15 ml [1 tablespoon] at a time.

4 When half the sugar has been added, beat in the lemon juice. Add remaining sugar as before.

5 Beat in the glycerine. Cover with a damp cloth and leave 24 hours.

Step-by-step to rough icing

1 Put a blob of icing on the centre of your cake board and place the cake on this.

2 Put all icing on cake. Work back and forth to remove bubbles, then spread over the top and sides.

3 Using the blade of a knife or the handle of a teaspoon, rough the icing up in peaks.

Step-by-step to flat icing

1 Put a blob of icing on a cake board. Place the cake on this and then put board on a turntable.

2 Put half the icing on top of the cake. Keep the rest covered. Work icing over the cake.

3 Using an icing ruler and working towards you, pull smoothly across the top of the cake.

4 Remove any excess icing from the sides of the cake. Add a little more to top and smooth again.

5 Leave the top of the cake to set for at least 24 hours before starting on sides.

6 To ice the sides, spread icing around the cake. Hold a flat scraper or palette knife against cake.

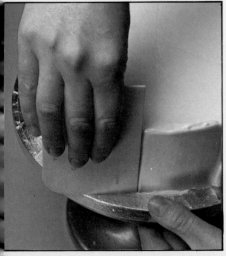

7 Revolve the turntable so the scraper smooths the icing. Lift off just before end.

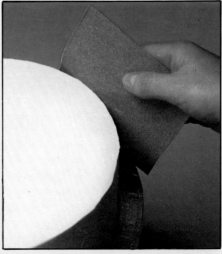

8 Leave the sides to set for 24 hours. Smooth rough edges with emery board or sandpaper.

9 If wished, cover the cake again in the same way using thinned down icing.

Flat icing

Flat icing provides a smooth foundation for intricately piped designs. It is quite difficult to do but must be mastered if you are determined to become a good cake icer.

Starting to ice

During the process of flat icing a cake, keep the bowl of icing covered. This is important if it is your first attempt at flat icing as the icing can harden while you are painstakingly trying to get the surface flat.

It is wiser to apply the top and sides of the cake on separate days as there is less danger of spoiling one while you are trying to get the other flat.

Starting with the top is easiest. Put your cake board on the icing turntable then put about half of the total quantity of icing on top of the cake. Using your palette knife or icing ruler, spread icing over the surface, working backwards and forwards. This will get rid of any air bubbles trapped in the icing. Scrape away any surplus icing that has run down the sides.

Now with your icing ruler at an angle of 30 degrees draw it steadily towards you so that it scrapes across the icing and leaves a smooth, ridge-free surface. Repeat this operation if the cake is not perfectly smooth first time, turning the cake through 90 degrees and adding a little more icing if necessary.

You will find that some surplus icing has run down the sides of the cake. You must remove this before the top of the cake sets or it will harden on the sides and be impossible to remove later. To remove this icing, simply scrape gently away with the blade of a palette knife, taking care not to break into the side of the cake and get crumbs in it. Return the surplus icing to the bowl. Leave the top of the cake overnight to dry.

Coating the sides

Coating the sides of the cake with flat icing is quite a tricky operation but is made much simpler if you have a turntable. First cover the sides of the cake with icing as described for the top, working it back and forth. When the air bubbles have gone hold a plain-edged scraper or a palette knife in one hand to the edge of the cake. With the other hand, revolve the turntable just a little more than a complete revolution. Lift the scraper away so that the minimum mark is left behind. You will probably find that there is some surplus icing on the bottom and at the top edge of the cake. This can be gently removed with a palette knife.

Second coat

To give your cake a really smooth, professional finish, follow the pât-issiers and give a second coat of thin icing. This should be applied about 48 hours after the first coating.

First of all, remove any rough icing at the top edge of the cake by sanding down with an emery board. This will give a really smooth edge. Make up royal icing in the usual way but add an extra egg white to the quantity for the cake you are making so that you have

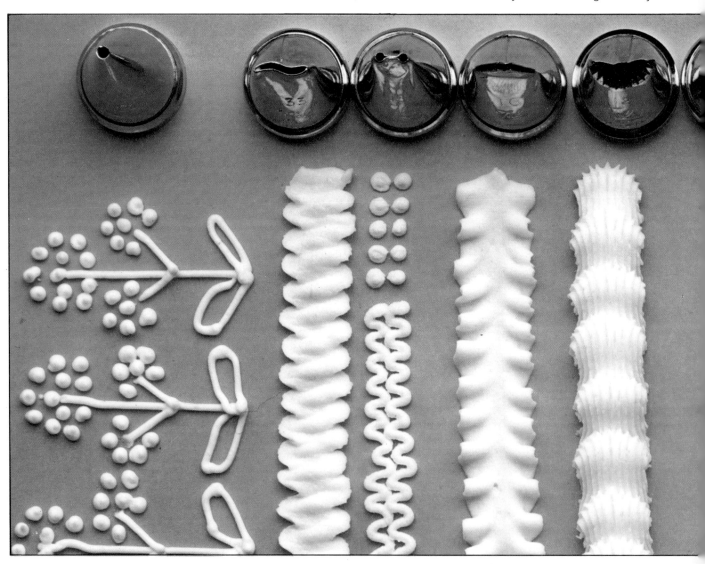

a thin icing. Apply to the top and sides of the cake as before. Wipe any surplus icing away from the edges of the cake board and leave the cake to set for 48 hours.

PIPING

Piping with royal icing may seem rather daunting but with practice, you will find that it is a technique which comes easily to you.

Equipment

To pipe with royal icing, you will need an icing bag (bought or home-made see information on pages 39–41) and a selection of nozzles. Nozzles for royal icing are small and nearly always made of metal to give a clean edge.

Initially, the list of nozzles suggested here is quite adequate. The illustration shows you what kind of nozzles are available and the designs they will produce.

Plain or writing nozzles are useful for piping lines, plain dots and for writing names. They come in various sizes—it is best to have a couple of these nozzles, one to produce thin lines and writing, one for thicker lines.

Star nozzles will make rosettes, zig-zags and ropes. If possible, get two different sizes.

Shell nozzles produce shell borders for the top and bottom edges of your cake. You only need one of these initially.

Planning the design

Before you start icing a cake, it is wise to plan a design. Draw the design out on a piece of greaseproof paper the same size as the top of the cake. Lay over the cake and using a pin, prick through the paper into the icing so that you can see exactly where the design will fall on the cake.

If you are having a design in more than one colour, you will need more than one bag for the icing. Divide the icing up before you start and colour using edible food colourings. Generally speaking, pastel colours look best.

How to pipe

The basics of good piping are explained on pages 35–45.

As you know how to fill and hold the bag, the actual piping should not be too difficult.

Lines

Lines can be used straight—to decorate one half of a cake while the other half is left plain, or can be used to make a trellis. They can also be made wavy or squiggly if wished. Lines are usually used on top of the cake, not on the sides. See page 42 for details of piping lines.

For wavy lines, move the nozzle to and fro.

For squiggles, to fill up an area of

There is a wide range of nozzles available for creating different shapes when piping royal icing.

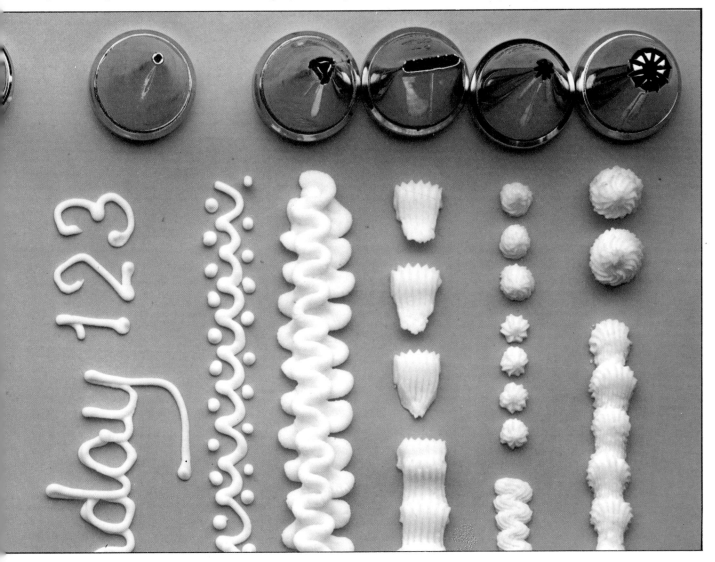

Step-by-step to simple piping

1 Prepare cake with almond paste. Cover with royal icing and leave to set until hard before piping.

2 Plan your design on greaseproof paper. Put the paper on the cake. Prick design through with a pin.

3 To pipe lines, use a writing or plain nozzle. Squeeze out just enough icing to stick to the cake. Raise the nozzle from the cake.

6 For squiggles, mark off the area of cake you want to fill. Use a plain pipe as above but move around with a squiggling motion.

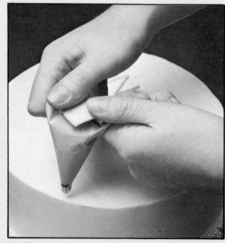

7 For stars, use a star nozzle. Hold the nozzle almost upright to the cake. Pipe out a little icing. Push nozzle down then pull up.

8 For a star border, pipe a series of stars in this way. The tops can be decorated with silver cake balls if wished.

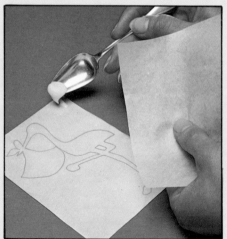

11 For run out designs, first draw simple design on card. Cover with non stick paper. Anchor in place with dots of icing.

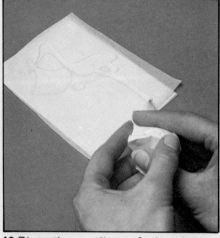

12 Pipe the outline of the design using a writing nozzle. Thin the icing with egg white so it will flow.

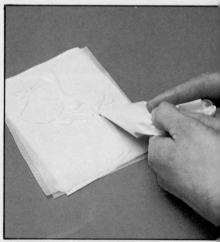

13 Put the icing into a greaseproof paper forcing bag. Cut off the tip. Flood outline of design with icing.

4 Direct the sagging line of icing in the direction you want it to go. Keep the pressure even or the line will be wobbly.

5 For writing, prick out the name using a pin. Follow the letters as directed for piping a line. Block or plain letters are easiest.

9 For shells, use a shell nozzle. Hold at an angle of 45 degrees to the cake. With the nozzle almost on the cake, pipe out a head of icing.

10 Gradually release the pressure. Pull away the nozzle so that the icing curves in a shell shape. Use for borders.

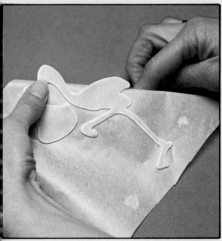

14 Leave the design to dry for several days. Gently lift off the card. Very carefully, peel away the non stick paper.

15 Stick the run out to the cake using thin royal icing. Thick icing raises it from the cake too much and look clumsy.

cake with a different colour, for instance, wave the nozzle about so that you get 'worm tracks'.

Writing names needs practice and it is best to try them out on a piece of greaseproof paper first. Before you start to pipe a name, work it out on a piece of greaseproof paper the same size as the top of the cake so that you know it will fit. Prick the design through on to the cake as described for planning a design. Using a plain or writing nozzle, carefully follow the pin pricks, using a similar technique for piping lines. For a beginner, it is easier to work in plain block capitals. You can get on to more complicated writing later.

Stars

Stars can be used to make a border around the top of the cake and where it joins the cake board. They can also be used to pipe patterns such as stars on the top of the cake. See page 45 for details of piping shells.

Shells

Shells are good for borders around the top of the cake and where it meets the cake board at the bottom. Generally speaking, this is the only way in which shells are used. See page 45 for details of piping shells.

Run out design

Run out designs are piped on to card and then transferred on to the cake when dry. They are a good idea for Christmas cakes as you can make bells, candles, holly leaves and other festive shapes.

To pipe a run out, first draw your shape on card. Try and keep it fairly simple with clean lines. Cut a piece of non-stick paper to cover the card and glue in place with a spot of icing at each corner. Using a writing nozzle, trace the outline of the design. Now thin the icing down with beaten egg white so that it will flow rather than being stiff as royal icing usually is. Pour the icing into a small paper forcing bag without a nozzle (see page 40). Cut the tip off the bag and flood the icing into the outline. It will run smoothly into place.

Leave the shape to set for at least three days then carefully remove the silicone paper from the card. Peel the paper off the back of the shape and stick it to the top of the cake with icing.

Run out designs can be piped straight on to the cake but this is something which requires great skill as mistakes cannot be rectified very easily once they are on the cake.

ICING IDEAS

Given here are some simple ideas for celebration cakes.

●For snowy Christmas cake, flat ice the top and sides. When set, spread some extra royal icing over the sides of the cake. Roughen up with a knife and leave to set. Decorate the top of the cake by colouring a little almond paste green and a very small quantity red. Cut a holly leaf out of card and use as a template to cut out a dozen leaves. Roll the red paste into little balls to make berries. Stick to the top of the cake with a little royal icing, arranged in a circle.

●For a simple christening cake, flat ice the cake. Pipe a shell border around the bottom where it joins the board. Using pale colours, pipe straight lines across half of the cake. Using the same colour, pipe the name of the baby on the other half. Using a small writing nozzle, pipe some dots in the shape of rosettes and then pipe large dots all round the edge of the cake to neaten the top and the ends of the straight lines. Add a bought christening cake decoration if there is room and tie a lace ribbon around the cake.

Once you have learned how to flat ice a cake, it is a simple step to producing professional results like these. The cake at the back is Simnel cake, with almond paste and a little glacé icing.

●For an 18th or 21st birthday cake, flat ice the cake. Cut out an 18 or 21 template and make a run out design in your chosen colour. Pipe a shell border around the bottom and top edge of the cake. Stick the run out in place. Add some bought cake decorations and ribbons.

●For poinsettia cake for Christmas, cover cake with almond paste. Colour equal quantities of almond paste red and green. Using a seed catalogue or an actual plant as a guide, draw a poinsettia flower and a few leaves and use as a template. Mark the leaves with veins using a sharp knife. Stick on the cake.

●For merry Christmas cake, cover with marzipan. Make a template for the words 'Merry Christmas', cut out in coloured marzipan and stick on the cake.

●For Christmas star cake, flat ice your cake. Pipe a star border in a different colour around the top and bottom edges. Top the stars with silver cake balls on the bottom edge.

Make a template of a star. The points should reach the edge of the cake. Pipe out the edges using the same colour as for the star borders. Fill in the middle of the star with piped stars.

●For very easy Christmas cake, flat ice the top and rough ice the sides. Pipe a shell border around the top edge. Decorate the middle with a large ribbon bow.

●For Christmas ribbon cake, flat ice a round cake. Ice a border of dots around the bottom, piping two dots together and then one on top so that you get a triangle effect. Pipe the same border around the top edge with the single dot at the bottom and the two dots close to the edge of the cake.

Using a pin, divide the cake surface in two, leaving a space of about 10 cm [4"] between the lines. Pipe a small shell border along these two pricked out lines. Fill the space between the edge of the cake and the shell line with straight lines.

Take a piece of broad Christmas ribbon and cut a fish tail at one end. Cut to the diameter of the cake. Lay across the cake in the un-iced strip. Secure with dots of royal icing. Pin a Christmas decoration in the middle. Pin matching ribbon around the side of the cake.

SIMNEL CAKE

◨◨◨ *This is an unusual fruit cake with a layer of almond paste on top and another inside the cake. It is the traditional cake for Simnel or Mothering Sunday (the fourth Sunday in Lent) but it is often made for Easter Sunday also. The almond paste balls represent the apostles—minus of course Judas Iscariot.*

MAKES ONE 1.1 KG [2½LB] CAKE
225 g [8 oz] butter
225 g [8 oz] caster sugar
4 eggs
225 g [8 oz] seedless raisins
**225 g [8 oz] mixed currants
and sultanas**
100 g [4 oz] mixed peel
**225 g [8 oz] plain flour,
sifted**
2.5 ml [½ teaspoon] salt
**10 ml [2 teaspoons] mixed
spice**
60 ml [4 tablespoons] brandy
700 g [1½ lb] almond paste
a little apricot glaze
a little glacé icing
bought decorations

1 Line an 18 cm [7"] round cake tin with a double layer of greaseproof paper and grease it well.

2 Cream the butter and sugar together in a basin until light.

3 Lightly beat the eggs and beat into the creamed mixture gradually.

4 Mix together the fruit, flour, salt and spice and fold into the cake mixture.

5 Add the brandy and mix to a soft dropping consistency. Check consistency with a spoon.

6 Take one third of the almond paste and roll out to 18 cm [17"] round.

7 Place half the cake mixture into the prepared tin. Level the surface.

8 Lightly press the round of almond paste on top of the cake mixture. Add remaining mixture.

9 Bake in the centre of a warm oven at 150°C [300°F] gas mark 2 for 2½–3 hours.

10 Leave to cool in the tin before turning out on to a wire rack. Leave until cold.

11 Take half of the remaining almond paste and roll out to fit the top.

12 Brush cake with apricot glaze and press paste into place. Flute the edges.

13 Roll the remaining almond paste into eleven balls and arrange round the top edge of the cake.

14 Place under a hot grill to brown the balls. Ice and decorate later.

Homely high teas

For a really traditional Devon tea you can't beat warm, freshly baked scones split open and served with fruity jam and lots of clotted or whipped cream. Follow the clear step-by-step pictures and instructions. Make different shapes and flavours and find out how to use scone mix as a tasty topping for sweet and savoury dishes.

Traditional scones make a delicious tea-time treat, but the basic mixture is more versatile than just this. You can make lots of savoury and other flavoured variations, and different shapes too. The dough can also be used as a topping (called a cobbler) for both sweet and savoury dishes.

Because the dough is so quick and easy to make, it is the ideal stand-by in emergencies. If you run out of bread, simply prepare a batch of scones—they only take about 10 minutes to make and 12-15 minutes to bake. And there is no need to wait

until the scones are cold as they are best eaten warm. Simply ease them open with your fingers (do not use a knife as this spoils the lovely crumbly texture) and serve thickly spread with butter. When unexpected guests appear and you need to bulk out a dish with store-cupboard items, a cobbler is a quick and satisfactory answer.

EQUIPMENT
Scones are made by the rubbing-in

method. In addition to the usual equipment needed for making and rolling out, you will need pastry cutters to cut out the scones and baking trays or sheets on which to bake them.

Pastry cutters
These come in a variety of shapes, but plain round cutters are traditionally used for scones. They are sold in sets comprising a range of sizes. The 5 cm [2"] diameter cutter is most frequently used for scones.

Cutters made from stainless steel

are best. They do not rust and will not break as easily as the plastic type.

If you do not have a pastry cutter, you can use the rim of a thin drinking glass or a china cup instead.

Baking trays and sheets
The difference between a baking tray and a baking sheet is that the tray has four raised sides, whereas the sheet only has one.

Both trays and sheets are made from metal and are available with and without a non-stick finish.

It does not matter whether you use a tray or a sheet, but don't be tempted to make do with a pottery container. Metal is a good conductor of heat and this is important for the scones to be properly cooked. The oven temperatures used in the recipe section are based on using a tray—you won't get the same results if you place your scones on a ceramic baking dish.

Check that you have enough trays for the number of scones you are making. If you are using a 5 cm [2"] cutter you will get about 12 scones from 225 g [½ lb] dough and you need to space the scones on the tray. A 30 cm [12"] tray will fit nine scones comfortably so, if you are making more, use two trays or use a larger tray, if you have one.

A point to remember when using large trays is that there should be a gap of about 5 cm [2"] between the sides of the tray and the sides of the oven. If there isn't, the hot air cannot circulate freely—it hits the tray and is deflected downwards, resulting in scones that are overcooked on the bottom and undercooked on the top.

You only need to grease the baking tray if the scones contain cheese or a liquid sweetener, such as syrup.

BASIC INGREDIENTS
Flour
You can use either self-raising or plain flour. If plain flour is used you will have to use a raising agent as well. Brown flour can be used and is excellent for savoury scones.

Raising agent
A raising agent is added only if plain flour is used. This can be either baking powder or a combination of bicarbonate of soda and cream of tartar.

Always measure carefully. Too much raising agent will give your scones a dry or acid after-taste. If not enough raising agent is used the scones will not rise well and will have a hard, heavy texture.

Fat
The proportion of fat to flour is 1:4. So, if you are using 225 g [½ lb] flour, you will need to use 50 g [2 oz] fat. The fat is rubbed into the flour so it should be cold but not rock hard. Whipped margarines are not suitable as they are too soft.

Butter and margarine are both excellent: both give a good colour but butter has the edge over margarine for flavour. Lard is not suitable as it gives poor flavour and appearance.

Salt
Salt is always added to enhance the flavour of both sweet and savoury scones. Sift 2.5 ml [½ teaspoon] salt with every 225 g [½ lb] flour.

Liquid
You need to add enough liquid to bind the dry ingredients together to the right consistency. The dough should be soft but not sticky.

Fresh milk gives an excellent soft scone but, for richer results, use sour milk, natural yoghurt or buttermilk. If you're feeling extravagant, try sour cream or thick or thin fresh cream for a really fabulous flavour and texture. Water is not suitable as it gives a poor, rather tasteless scone.

If you use an acid liquid such as soured milk or cream, buttermilk or yoghurt, you must reduce the amount of cream of tartar used at the same time, as shown in the chart. The reason is that these liquids react with the bicarbonate of soda in the mix to release carbon dioxide gas which causes the dough to rise. A compensating cut is therefore made in the cream of tartar, the raising agent used with bicarbonate of soda.

GETTING ORGANIZED
One of the keys to successful scones is to make and bake the dough as quickly as possible. This is because the raising agent begins to work as soon as it comes into contact with a liquid, so the sooner you can pop the scones into the oven the lighter they will be.

The right temperature
Always heat the oven to the recommended temperature: if the oven is too cool the scones will be tough and pale. If scones are baked in too hot an oven they become hard and over-brown. Recipes usually specify a very hot oven—that is, 220°C [425°F] gas mark 7 or 230°C [450°F] gas mark 8. Scones which contain sugar and fruit are baked at the lower temperature to prevent the sugar from caramelizing.

Next, organize your equipment and lay out your baking tray (greased if necessary) ready for use. Then collect and measure your ingredients and do any necessary preparation, such as grating cheese or chopping nuts. You can now begin to make the scones.

MAKING THE DOUGH
Sieve white flour (and raising agents if plain flour is being used) together with the salt (and any powdered flavourings if used). This ensures the ingredients are evenly distributed and aerated and helps keep them cool. Perfectionists even recommend sieving twice! Wholewheat flour is not sieved as this separates out the bran. Just stir the salt into the flour.

Cut in the fat with a round-bladed knife until the pieces are walnut-sized and well coated with flour. Rub the fat into the flour until the mixture resembles even-sized breadcrumbs, then use the metal spoon to stir in any additional dry ingredients if used.

Adding the liquid is one of the most crucial stages in scone-making. You need to add enough liquid to give a soft, but not sticky, dough. If too little liquid is used, the scones won't rise well and will have a heavy texture. When too much liquid is used, the dough is slack (loose) and the scones tend to spread and lose their shape during baking.

Make a well in the centre of the mixture and pour in almost all the liquid to bind (plus any liquid flavouring if used). Using a palette knife, work the liquid(s) into the mixture to make a soft dough. Do this lightly and quickly as over-mixing toughens the scones. Stir in the remainder of the liquid if the consistency is too dry.

Gather the dough together with your hand to form a ball—the sides of the bowl should be left clean—and turn the dough on to a lightly floured board. Knead until the dough is smooth and free from cracks. The dough should be slightly springy to the touch (the cooking term for this is an elastic dough). The kneading must be thorough, but lightly and quickly done. Insufficient kneading can lead to scones with a rough surface when cooked. On the other hand, heavy handling toughens the dough and makes a heavy scone.

ROLLING OUT

Roll out the dough on the lightly floured surface to a round 1.2 cm [½"] thick. Turn the dough 45° to your left after each rolling to keep it in shape and evenly thick. Take care not to stretch the dough.

Alternatively you may prefer to dispense with the rolling pin altogether. Instead, shape the dough into a round and, using the palms of your hands, press it out lightly until 1.2 cm [½"] thick.

Either method is perfectly suitable, although scones cut from dough which has been shaped by hand will not have such a smooth top. If you have a large quantity of dough, it is quicker to roll it out with the rolling pin rather than pressing it out by hand.

CUTTING OUT THE SCONES

Use the size of cutter specified in the recipe. To stop the dough sticking, the cutter is lightly coated with flour before each round is stamped out. To do this, dip the cutter into a bag of flour, then shake the cutter to remove excess flour.

The correct way to use the cutter is to press it sharply and firmly down through the dough. Don't twist the cutter as this will distort the shape of the scone. Shake the cutter gently to release the scone. Stamp out as many scones as possible at a time as each successive kneading and rolling out toughens the dough.

Gather the trimmings together and knead gently. Roll out again and cut out more scones.

Place the scones on the baking tray(s) (greased if necessary), spacing them about 2.5 cm [1"] apart to allow for expansion.

GLAZING AND BAKING

Scones made with white flour may appear rather pale when cooked, so they are usually glazed before baking. Milk, melted butter, beaten egg or egg white can all be used and will also enhance scones made with brown flour. Warmed syrup or honey can also be used to give a shiny brown, sticky finish to sweet and plain scones but is unsuitable, of course, for savoury scones. Simply warm a little syrup in a heavy-based saucepan over a low heat—don't let it boil. Remove the pan from the heat and dip your pastry brush into the syrup, then glaze the uncooked scones.

Bake the scones for 12-15 minutes. If you are using two baking trays do not place them directly beneath each other. Place one tray on the shelf second from the top and towards the right-hand side of the oven. Place the second tray on the middle shelf towards the left-hand side. This allows the hot air to circulate freely.

To test whether the scones are cooked, tap the underside with your finger or knuckle—it should sound hollow.

Turn the cooked scones on to a wire rack, allow to cool for a few minutes and serve.

SWEET AND SAVOURY SCONE MIXES

All sorts of different ingredients can be incorporated into the basic mix to produce a variety of results. Powdered ingredients, such as spices, are sifted with the flour and salt to ensure even distribution. Dry in-

Here are some of the good things you can use to make flavoured scones.

Step-by-step traditional scones

225 g [½ lb] self-raising flour
2.5 ml [½ teaspoon] salt
50 g [2 oz] butter or margarine
150 ml [¼ pt] milk

1 Position shelf and heat oven. Sift flour (and raising agent if plain flour is used) with salt.

2 Cut fat into flour, then rub in until mixture resembles even-sized breadcrumbs.

3 Make a well, add most of the milk and work in to make a soft dough. Add rest of milk if needed.

4 Gather the dough together with your fingers and turn out on to a lightly floured board.

5 Knead lightly and quickly until the dough is smooth and free from cracks.

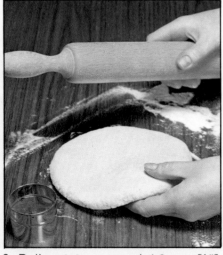

6 Roll out to a round 1.2 cm [½"] thick, turning dough 45° to your left after each rolling.

7 Using a 5 cm [2"] floured cutter, stamp out scones. Press cutter firmly and sharply—do not twist.

8 Place scones on baking tray 2.5 cm [1"] apart. Brush with glaze and bake for 12-15 minutes.

74

RAISING AGENTS IN SCONES

	Flour	Raising agent	Salt	Fat	Liquid
Basic plain scone mix	225 g [½ lb] self-raising flour	—	2.5 ml [½ tsp] salt	50 g [2 oz] butter or margarine	150 ml [¼ pt] fresh milk or cream
	225 g [½ lb] plain flour	15-20 ml [3-4 tsp] baking powder*	2.5 ml [½ tsp] salt	50 g [2 oz] butter or margarine	150 ml [¼ pt] fresh milk or cream
	225 g [½ lb] plain flour	5 ml [1 tsp] bicarbonate of soda 10 ml [2 tsp] cream of tartar	2.5 ml [½ tsp] salt	50 g [2 oz] butter or margarine	150 ml [¼ pt] fresh milk or cream
Plain scone mix with an acidic liquid	225 g [½ lb] self-raising flour	—	2.5 ml [½ tsp] salt	50 g [2 oz] butter or margarine	150 ml [¼ pt] sour milk, yoghurt, buttermilk or sour cream
	225 g [½ lb] plain flour	15-20 ml [3-4 tsp] baking powder*	2.5 ml [½ tsp] salt	50 g [2 oz] butter or margarine	150 ml [¼ pt] sour milk, yoghurt, buttermilk or sour cream
	225 g [½ lb] plain flour	5 ml [1 tsp] bicarbonate of soda 5 ml [1 tsp] cream of tartar	2.5 ml [½ tsp] salt	50 g [2 oz] butter or margarine	150 ml [¼ pt] sour milk, yoghurt, buttermilk or sour cream

*According to manufacturer's instructions

gredients (including sugar, dried fruit and nuts) are stirred into the rubbed-in mixture before the liquid is added. Liquid additions, honey for example, are added together with the liquid used to bind. Whenever a liquid flavouring is used, less other liquid is needed to bind the mixture to a soft dough.

You can have fun inventing your own recipes, or try some of the following ideas. The weights of ingredients listed below are for the basic recipe, using 225 g [½ lb] self-raising flour.

● For sweet scones add 50 g [2 oz] caster or soft brown sugar to the basic recipe. Or use 60 ml [4 tablespoons] honey, syrup or treacle instead of the sugar and reduce binding liquid accordingly.
● Flavour sweet scones with the finely grated zest of any citrus fruit.
● For banana scones, mash a large banana and stir this into the rubbed-in mixture together with 25 g [1 oz] caster sugar.
● For extra flavour and nutritional value, replace 25 g [1 oz] flour with the same amount of unprocessed bran.
● For nutty delights, use plain brown flour plus 5 ml [1 teaspoon] bicarbonate of soda and 10 ml [2 teaspoons] cream of tartar, and add

50 g [2 oz] chopped nuts. (Try pistachio, almond or cashew.)
● For spiced scones, add 2.5 ml [½ teaspoon] ground spice and 50 g [2 oz] caster sugar.
● For fruity scones, use 50 g [2 oz] of any chopped dried fruit.
● For extra-crumbly scones, replace up to half the amount of flour (white or brown) with oatmeal.
● For bacon savouries, crumble 50 g [2 oz] crisply fried bacon and stir this into the rubbed-in mixture.
● For peanut treats, substitute 50 g [2 oz] smooth peanut butter for the fat and add 50 g [2 oz] chopped salted peanuts.
● For a sweet surprise, soak sugar cubes in orange cordial until saturated. (This only takes a few seconds; don't leave them too long or they will dissolve.) Press a sugar lump into the centre of each stamped-out scone and bake as usual.

STORING AND FREEZING
Scones don't keep well but you can freshen up 1-2-day-old scones—either heat them through in a warm oven, 160°C [325°F] gas mark 3, for 5-10 minutes, or cut the scones in half and toast under the grill.

Freshly baked plain scones can be successfully frozen for 6 months, provided they are wrapped and frozen as soon as they are completely cold. Wrap in a heavy-duty polythene bag or place them in an airtight container. Thaw unopened for 1 hour at room temperature

Handy hints
● Sour milk gives scones a lovely light texture and makes an excellent (and inexpensive) alternative to sour cream. You cannot buy sour milk but it is terribly easy to make at home. To sour 275 ml [½ pt] milk, simply stir in 15 ml [1 tablespoon] lemon juice or vinegar and leave to stand for a few minutes.
● If you do not have a cutter, or if you want different-shaped scones for a change, you can cut out the scones with a sharp knife. Flour the blade as you would a cutter and cut the dough into strips about 5 cm [2"] wide. Then cut the strips diagonally to make diamond shapes.

COBBLERS

A cobbler is a sweet or savoury dish which has a dough topping. The dough is made in exactly the same way as for plain or flavoured scones and then rolled or pressed out 1.2 cm [½"] thick. The dough can be laid in one piece over the filling as a complete covering and scored into a decorative pattern with a knife. Alternatively, you can cut out individual scones and arrange them over the filling. Traditionally the scones are placed around the inside edge of the dish so that they slightly overlap one another and the filling in the centre of the dish is left uncovered.

If you are going to lay the dough in a single piece over the filling you will need 225 g [½ lb] dough for a 20 cm [8"] pie dish. Press the dough out to the shape of the dish and, using the rolling pin to lift, transfer the dough and unroll it to cover the filling. There's no need to seal the dough to the rim—just let it lie loosely on top of the filling. Glaze the dough and score the surface to make the dish more attractive.

BAKING

Cobbler toppings (whether in a single piece or overlapping pieces) need a slightly longer cooking time than ordinary scones to ensure that the underside of the dough (which is on top of the filling) is cooked. Usually 20-25 minutes is about right

and gives the topping a crisp brown surface. Because of the longer cooking time, both sweet and savoury toppings are baked at the lower temperature, that is, 220°C [425°F] gas mark 7.

FILLINGS

Any pre-cooked filling—sweet or savoury—can be used. Alternatively, you can add the topping to a dish which is being cooked in the oven towards the end of its cooking time.

The filling should be firm and moist, but not liquid or the topping will be soggy.

For extra interest, flavour the scone dough with an ingredient which complements the filling. For example, make a cinnamon dough to top a mixture of apple and blackberries, or make a cheesy scone dough to go over a fish filling.

PEACH PRUNE COBBLER

Here is an excellent emergency pudding which can be made quickly and easily using ingredients from your store cupboard. There is no need to soak the prunes—they are finely chopped and mixed into the cream cheese, making a chewy layer to go over the soft peaches.

SERVES 6
400 g [14 oz] canned peach slices
10 prunes

225 g [½ lb] cream cheese
25 g [1 oz] caster sugar
30 ml [2 tablespoons] lemon juice

For the topping:
225 g [½ lb] plain flour
5 ml [1 teaspoon] bicarbonate of soda
5 ml [1 teaspoon] cream of tartar
50 g [2 oz] butter or margarine
25 g [1 oz] caster sugar
about 150 ml [¼ pt] buttermilk or sour milk
milk for glazing

1 Grease a 20 cm [8"] pie dish.

2 Drain peaches, reserving syrup, and place in prepared dish.

3 Stone and chop the prunes.

4 Beat together the cream cheese, sugar, lemon juice and 30 ml [2 tablespoons] of the reserved syrup. Stir in the chopped prunes.

5 Spread the cream cheese mixture over the peaches and set the dish aside while you prepare the topping.

6 Position shelf above centre and heat oven to 220°C [425°F] gas mark 7.

7 Sift flour and raising agents into a mixing bowl. Cut the fat into the flour and rub in until the mixture resembles fine breadcrumbs. Then stir in the sugar.

8 Make a well in the centre of the mixture and pour in most of the buttermilk. Mix to a soft dough adding the remaining buttermilk if necessary.

9 Gather the dough into a ball with your fingers, turn out and knead until smooth.

10 Roll out to a round 1.2 cm [½" thick. Then use a 5 cm [2"] floured pastry cutter to cut out the scones.

11 Arrange the scones over the filling, around the inside of the rim of the dish, so that they partially overlap one another. Glaze and bake for 20-25 minutes.

WHOLEWHEAT HERB ROUND

Sieving wholewheat flour separates out the bran, so in this recipe the baking powder is sieved together with the salt and pepper then brown flour is added and thoroughly stirred in. Because yoghurt is an acidic liquid, less cream of tartar is needed to make the dough rise.

Split the wedges apart and serve with cheese for a delicious and nutritious snack.

MAKES 6 WEDGES
225 g [½ lb] plain wholewheat
    flour
5 ml [1 teaspoon] bicarbonate
    of soda
5 ml [1 teaspoon] cream of
    tartar
2.5 ml [½ teaspoon] salt
large pinch freshly ground
    pepper
50 g [2 oz] butter or margarine
5 ml [1 teaspoon] dried mixed
    herbs
150 ml [¼ pt] natural yoghurt
milk for glazing

1 Position shelf and heat oven to 220°C [425°F] gas mark 7.

2 Sift raising agents, salt and pepper into a mixing bowl, add flour and stir until thoroughly mixed.

3 Cut fat into flour, then rub in until the mixture resembles even-sized breadcrumbs.

4 With a metal spoon stir in the mixed herbs.

5 Make a well in the centre of the mixture and pour in almost all the yoghurt. Work to a soft dough, adding the remaining yoghurt if necessary.

6 Gather the dough together with your fingers and turn on to a lightly floured board. Knead until smooth.

7 Shape the dough into a round and press until 1.2 cm [½"] thick.

8 Place the round of dough on the baking tray.

9 Flour the blade of a sharp knife. Then score the scone round into 6 portions, as though cutting a cake,

but do not cut right through the dough.

10 Glaze surface of the dough with milk and bake the round for 20-25 minutes.

CHEESE SCONES

These delicious savoury scones are so quick and easy to make you can even prepare them for breakfast! They are also excellent crumbled into hot broths to make an easy, handy family lunch or supper. Because Cheddar cheese is strongly flavoured, margarine can be used instead of butter and less salt is added.

MAKES 12-14
225 g [½ lb] plain white flour
1.5 ml [¼ teaspoon] salt
5 ml [1 teaspoon] mustard
    powder
20 ml [4 teaspoon] baking
    powder
50 g [2 oz] margarine or butter
125 g [¼ lb] Cheddar cheese
about 150 ml [¼ pt] milk
milk for glazing

1 Position shelf and heat oven to 230°C [450°F] gas mark 8.

2 Grease baking tray(s) and set aside. Grate the cheese.

3 Sift flour, salt, mustard and baking powder into a mixing bowl.

4 Cut in the fat until the pieces are walnut-sized and well coated with flour. Rub fat into flour until the mixture resembles fine breadcrumbs.

5 Stir in the cheese. Make a well in the centre of the mixture and pour in almost all the milk.

6 Mix to a soft dough, adding the remaining milk if necessary.

7 Gather the dough into a ball with your fingers. Turn out and knead until smooth.

8 Roll out on a lightly floured surface to 1.2 cm [½"] thick. Using a 5 cm [2"] floured plain pastry cutter, cut out the scones.

9 Place the scones on the prepared tray(s) leaving 2.5 cm [1"] space between each. Brush the surface of each with milk and bake for 12-15 minutes.

TREACLE SCONES

Treacle is acidic, so less cream of tartar is needed than usual for this recipe and the binding liquid is reduced since treacle is a liquid. Remember that sweet scones need a greased baking tray to prevent sticking. They are baked at a lower temperature than plain or savoury scones to prevent the sweetener from crystallizing during baking.

For a change, the scones are not stamped out with a round cutter but cut into diamond shapes with a knife. The blade of the knife is floured to prevent the dough sticking.

MAKES 12-14
225 g [½ lb] plain white flour
5 ml [1 teaspoon] cream of
    tartar
5 ml [1 teaspoon] bicarbonate
    of soda
pinch of salt
25 g [1 oz] butter or margarine
50 g [2 oz] treacle
about 60 ml [4 tablespoons]
    milk
milk for glazing

1 Position shelf and heat oven to 220°C [425°F] gas mark 7. Grease baking tray(s) and set aside.

2 Sift flour, cream of tartar, bicarbonate of soda and salt into a mixing bowl.

Freshly baked scones and scone rounds transform tea-time into a feast.

3 Cut the fat into the flour and rub in until the mixture resembles fine breadcrumbs.

4 Make a well in the centre of the mixture. Add the treacle and most of the milk. Work in to give a soft, manageable dough, adding the rest of the milk if necessary.

5 Gather the dough into a ball with your fingers, then turn on to a lightly floured board and knead until smooth.

6 Roll out the dough until 1.2 cm [$\frac{1}{2}$"] thick. Use the floured blade of a sharp knife to cut the dough into 5 cm [2"] wide strips. Cut the strips diagonally to make diamond shapes.

7 Place the scones on the prepared tray(s) and brush with milk. Bake for 12-15 minutes.

FRUITY SCONE ROUND

Instead of cutting out individual scones, you can shape the dough into a single large round. The dough is pressed out by hand and then scored into 6 portions. A round takes longer to

cook than individual scones but the test is the same: the round is cooked if the underside sounds hollow when tapped. To serve the round, simply pull the warm edges apart with your hands.

Gently warm the honey to glaze in a heavy-based saucepan as this makes it easier to brush over the surface of the scones.

MAKES 6 WEDGES
225 g [$\frac{1}{2}$ lb] self-raising flour
2.5 ml [$\frac{1}{2}$ teaspoon] salt
50 g [2 oz] butter or margarine
25 g [1 oz] caster sugar
50 g [2 oz] dried fruit
about 150 ml [$\frac{1}{4}$ pt] milk

For the glaze:
15 ml [1 tablespoon] honey

1 Position shelf and heat oven to 220°C [425°F] gas mark 7. Grease the baking tray and set aside.

2 Chop any large dried fruit and set aside.

3 Sift flour and salt into a mixing bowl, then cut the fat into the flour

and rub in until the mixture resembles fine breadcrumbs.

4 Stir in caster sugar and dried fruit.

5 Make a well in the middle of the mixture and pour in most of the milk. Stir the liquid into the mixture to make a soft dough, adding the remaining milk if necessary.

6 Gather the dough into a ball with your fingers and turn on to a lightly floured board. Knead the dough until smooth and free from cracks.

7 Shape the dough into a round and press out until 1.2 cm [$\frac{1}{2}$"] thick.

8 Place the round on the prepared baking tray.

9 Dip the blade of a sharp knife into flour, shake to remove excess then score the round into 6 portions but do not cut right through the dough.

10 Glaze the surface of the round with honey and bake for 20-25 minutes

girdle cookery

No-bake baking

Girdle cookery is an old-fashioned way of making scones, well worth preserving. The method of preparation and the ingredients are the same as for oven-baked scones, but these cakes are cooked on a girdle or hot plate on top of the cooker instead of in the oven.

The basic recipes, the rubbing-in method and the preparation of scones and girdle cakes are all basically the same. The only real difference between them is the method of cooking—the girdle instead of the oven. There's an old saying about scone making that is equally true of girdle cookery—'very cold making, very hot baking'.

Girdle cookery is done on a heated flat iron surface, which is proved and lightly greased, then placed over the source of heat. It has remained

unchanged over the years, evolving from a patchwork of traditional country recipes, that even in these modern times produce delicious home-made flavours and textures.

The girdle is the predecessor of the modern stove top or hot plate. The girdle—a flat iron plate with a long hooped handle—was hung over an open fire in the kitchen, and lowered into position when needed for cooking. Scones and cakes were cooked on it.

With the advent of the kitchen

range, girdle recipes were baked on the flat metal plate that formed part of the top of the cooker. This, rather aptly, was named a griddle after the girdle which it resembled.

Today, solid fuel and some electric cookers include a griddle. Girdle cookery has reverted back to using the traditional girdle which can be used on top of any domestic cooker.

Scrumptious fruity girdle scones served with lashing of butter.

Girdle cookery is still a live tradition in many areas throughout the British Isles. The traditional girdle recipes which were at one time made throughout the British Isles are today mainly to be found in the north of England and Scotland, made, eaten and enjoyed just as they were over a hundred years ago.

Traditional recipes originated from festivals while others were derived from local produce or evolved from local customs. As the ingredients and cooking method were both limited, it is not difficult to see why the same recipe appears in various parts of the same country under different names. Singin' hinny is the peculiar name given to a delicious girdle cake—perhaps the most famous of all. It originated in Northumberland, where it is still a high-tea speciality, and is often called Northumberland farmhouse girdle cake. The name singin' hinny evolved because of the way the fat sizzles on the girdle as the cake cooks. This sizzling sound increases as the cake cooks.

Sweet or savoury cakes are delicious eaten straight from the girdle. Plain or sweet girdle cakes are unbeatable simply split and spread with butter or lashings of thick cream and home-made preserves. Traditional potato scones are tasty served straight from the girdle, piping hot with a rasher of crispy bacon, though these are more of a knife and fork job because they tend to be soft.

Oatcakes, most frequently called bannocks, are another traditional type. These were made and baked in wedges which were called farls. Their slightly chewy texture makes them ideal to serve with soup, fish, cheese and bacon for high-tea or supper.

EQUIPMENT
Girdle scones and cakes are made by the rubbing-in method (in the same way as oven-baked scones), so they are very simple to make. For details, see pages 72–73.

In addition to the usual equipment for rubbed-in mixtures, only a girdle, heavy-based frying-pan or solid iron plate (known as a griddle) are needed. A small palette knife is useful for turning the cakes or scones during cooking.

Girdle
A girdle is a thick, round, iron plate with a half-loop handle. The handle is there for convenience when in use, making it easier to transport to the top of the cooker. The use of the top of the cooker for scone and cake making is quite an economy on fuel, compared with heating the oven, especially for a small batch of cakes.

Solid-plate
The solid-plate griddle, which forms part of some solid fuel and electric cookers, may be used in place of a girdle. This must be cleaned and prepared as for a girdle.

Heavy-based frying-pan
If you don't own a girdle or a cooker with a griddle, improvise by using a heavy-based frying-pan. A lighter frying-pan is not suitable because it will burn when heated for the long period of time that girdle cooking requires.

PREPARING A GIRDLE
Never wash a girdle in between cooking, simply clean and prove immediately prior to using. Washing could very easily result in the girdle rusting during storage.

After using a girdle, simply dust away any particles of food adhering to the surface. The cleaning process is all part of the proving and this takes place before the girdle is used.

Place the girdle on top of the cooker with the half-hoop handle standing upright. Have an oven glove ready for transporting the hot girdle from the cooker at the end of the cooking process. Turn on the heat under the girdle, but keep this low. A high heat would result in uneven heating of the girdle and the possibility that the cakes would cook unevenly and burn.

Clean the girdle by sprinkling with 5 ml [1 teaspoon] salt. Sprinkle the salt all over the surface of the girdle and rub with a thick pad of kitchen paper. Rub lightly but evenly using circular motions until the salt seems to disappear. Using a fresh pad of kitchen paper, dust away any remaining salt from girdle. At this point, the girdle should be completely clean and free from any signs of rust or brown staining.

If the girdle is very dirty or has not been used for a long time, repeat this process until it is completely clean.

Heat the girdle, still over a low heat, for 20 minutes. This initial heating period ensures an even heat over the whole surface of the girdle. (If using a heavy-based frying-pan, prepare as for a girdle. A solid plate or griddle, if this is not already hot, will only need heating for about 10 minutes.)

Heating a girdle correctly is all-important. If it is too hot, the outside of the cake will form an over-browned crust, while the centre of the cake will remain uncooked and raw.

Before attempting to bake on the heated and proved girdle, always test that the correct heat has been achieved. One way to test is to sprinkle a little white flour on to the surface of the girdle. If the heat is correct the flour should turn a deep brown in three minutes. Brush away the browned flour immediately. Alternatively, sprinkle a few drops of cold water on to the heated girdle. If it is ready, the water will start to dance about on the surface. Wipe away the water with kitchen paper.

Once the correct temperature has been reached, the girdle needs light greasing with melted fat before cooking scones or cakes. For oatcakes, no greasing is necessary.

BASIC INGREDIENTS

Starch
Plain flour with the addition of raising agents will make the most successful scones and girdle cakes. However, self-raising flour gives satisfactory results.

A proportion of ground rice is a traditional ingredient in some girdle cakes. When rice is used it is substituted for a proportion of the flour, which must be reduced accordingly. Ground rice is usually added to replace not more than 50 g [2 oz] of the total amount of flour.

Scones may be based on freshly made, hot mashed potato. When this is used it forms the major ingredient; 450 g [1 lb] of potato is used with the addition of 100 g [¼ lb] self-raising flour.

Oatcakes are made using seven parts oatmeal to one part plain flour.

Raising agents
When self-raising flour is used additional raising agents must still be added. This is because, for girdle cookery, the proportion of raising agent to flour required for a scone dough must be higher than that already present in self-raising flour.

When using plain flour, to every 225 g [½ lb] flour add 2.5 ml [½ teaspoon] bicarbonate of soda and 2.5 ml [½ teaspoon] cream of tartar or 5 ml [1 teaspoon] baking powder. If self-raising flour is used, add 2.5 ml [½ teaspoon] bicarbonate of soda, or the same amount of baking powder or cream of tartar.

Fat
Use the same proportions as for oven-baked scones—50 g [2 oz] of fat to each 225 g [½ lb] flour (see page 72).

Salt
Use the same proportions—2.5 ml [½ teaspoon] to each 225 g [½ lb] flour—as for oven-baked scones.

Liquid
A liquid is added to bind the mixture together to make a soft dough, except when bannocks are being made. It is essential to use an acid liquid, such as milk, buttermilk, soured milk or cream to obtain the rich flavours and textures associated with girdle cookery.

If you intend to use fresh milk, you must increase the amount of raising agent by 5 ml [1 teaspoon]. This is because fresh milk lacks the raising qualities present in the more acidic liquids. A tablespoon of black treacle (which is also acidic) may be added to the liquid to aid the raising.

Sugar
Sugar is always added to sweet girdle cakes and scones. Use 50 g [2 oz] caster sugar or soft brown sugar per 225 g [½ lb] flour.

ROLLING OUT
Girdle scones are rolled 12 mm [½"] thick on a lightly floured board. They can be cut into wedge shapes (traditionally called farls), rounds or squares. Again, the same rules that apply to oven-baked scones apply to girdle scones. They should be made and then baked as quickly as possible.

COOKING
All girdle scones and cakes should take no longer than five minutes to

Step-by-step to preparing a girdle

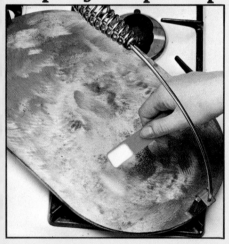

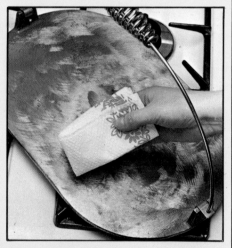

1 Place the girdle on top of the cooker over a low heat. Leave to heat for one minute then sprinkle with 5 ml [1 teaspoon] salt.

2 Rub salt lightly but thoroughly over the surface of the girdle with a thick pad of kitchen paper. Rub the surface until it is clean.

3 Dust away salt from surface of girdle until fresh pad of kitchen paper does not colour brown. Heat over a low heat for 20 minutes.

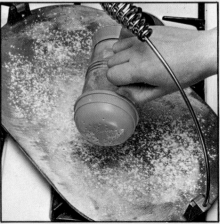

4 To test heat, sprinkle white flour on to surface. If ready, the flour will brown within 3 minutes. Brush off flour.

OR sprinkle a few drops of cold water on to surface. If ready, the water should dance about on the surface. Dry off.

5 Before cooking commences the girdle needs to be greased. Brush surface of girdle lightly with melted fat.

Step-by-step to girdle scones

225 g [½ lb] plain flour
2.5 ml [½ teaspoon] salt
5 ml [1 teaspoon] baking
    powder
50 g [2 oz] butter or
    margarine
50 g [2 oz] caster sugar
150 ml [¼ pt] buttermilk,
    soured milk or thin cream

1 Heat and prepare girdle as shown in the step-by-step instructions. Sift flour, salt and baking powder into a bowl.

2 Cut fat into flour, then rub in until mixture resembles even-sized breadcrumbs.

3 Stir sugar into rubbed-in mixture. If adding any additional flavourings, stir in with sugar.

4 Make a hollow in the middle of the mixture, pour in liquid. Work in to make a soft, but not sticky dough.

5 Gather the dough together with your fingers and turn out on to a floured board. Knead lightly and quickly.

6 Roll out dough to a round, 12 mm [½"] thick, Using a long-bladed knife, cut dough into eight wedges (farls).

7 Carefully transfer wedges (farls) to heated girdle and bake for 5 minutes, or until well risen and light brown underneath.

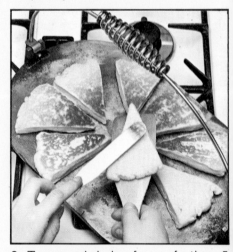

8 Turn and bake for a further 5 minutes until evenly browned and hollow sounding when tapped.

cook on each side. There is no need to space them as they will not spread during baking.

Place cakes or scones on prepared and greased girdle and bake for five minutes. Carefully lift to check that undersides are evenly browned before turning with the aid of a small palette knife. The scones or cakes should have risen slightly which indicates that they are baking evenly. Once turned, cook for a further five minutes.

To test if the cakes or scones are cooked, tap the underneath of one. It should sound hollow.

FLAVOURINGS

Any number of flavouring ingredients can be used; these are added to the basic mixture. Traditionally, dried fruits and some sweet spices are added as a variation and, while these are delicious, there is no reason why you should not make up your own flavouring ideas. If powdered flavourings, such as spices, cocoa or coffee powders, are used sift these with the dry ingredients, adding approximately 2.5 ml [$\frac{1}{2}$ teaspoon] per 225 g [$\frac{1}{2}$ lb] flour.

Dry flavouring ingredients, such as dried fruit, should be stirred into the rubbed-in mixture with the sugar.

Liquid or semi-liquid additions, such as treacle, honey, syrup or jam are considered as part of the liquid. An adjustment must therefore be made to the amount of liquid given in the basic recipe. Add these to the liquid in the measuring jug to bring it to the specified quantity. The liquid is then added to the rubbed-in mixture after any sugar has been added.

SERVING IDEAS FOR SCONES

Try the following variations on the basic scone mixture.
● For fruity girdle scones, sift 2. 5 ml [$\frac{1}{2}$ teaspoon] ground nutmeg with the dry ingredients and stir 50 g [2 oz] mixed dried fruit into the rubbed-in mixture.
● For caraway girdle scones, stir in 2.5 ml [$\frac{1}{2}$ teaspoon] caraway seeds to rubbed-in mixture.
● For crunchy hazel girdle scones, sift 2.5 ml [$\frac{1}{2}$ teaspoon] ground cinnamon with the dry ingredients and stir 50 g [2 oz] finely chopped toasted hazelnuts into the rubbed-in mixture.

POTATO SCONES

The best way to eat potato scones are straight from the girdle, piping hot and spread with lots of butter. Always use freshly made mashed potato for best results—cold mashed potato will result in heavy scones with an unpleasant texture. If time is short, use instant mashed potato as an alternative to freshly cooked potato.

MAKES 12–14
450 g [1 lb] potatoes
10 ml [2 teaspoons] salt
50 g [2 oz] butter
oil
100 g [4 oz] self-raising flour
2.5 ml [$\frac{1}{2}$ teaspoon] bicarbonate of soda

1 Peel and boil potatoes in lightly salted water for 20–25 minutes, depending on size.

2 Drain potatoes, add salt and butter. Mash thoroughly until light and fluffy.

3 Heat and prepare girdle as shown in the step-by-step instructions. Lightly grease girdle with oil.

4 Sift flour and bicarbonate of soda together, fold flour into potato to make a soft dough.

5 Gather the dough together with your fingers. Turn out on to a lightly floured board. Knead lightly and quickly.

6 Roll out or pat dough to 12 mm [$\frac{1}{2}$"] thick. Using a 5 cm [2"] floured plain pastry cutter, cut out scones.

7 Place the scones on prepared girdle and bake for 5 minutes, or until well risen and light brown underneath.

8 Turn and bake for a further 5 minutes until evenly browned and quite dry.

Variations
● Chop 4 spring onions finely and fold into mashed potato before adding flour.
● For a continental flavour, use sweet potatoes. Omit salt and replace with 2.5 ml [$\frac{1}{2}$ teaspoon] ground cinnamon and 15 ml [1 tablespoon] soft brown sugar.
● Grate 100 g [4 oz] Cheddar cheese

and stir into mashed potato with a dash of anchovy essence or Worcestershire sauce.
● Finely chop 30 ml [2 tablespoons] parsley and add to mashed potato with butter.
● Stir 30 ml [2 tablespoons] tomato purée into mashed potato with 2.5 ml [$\frac{1}{2}$ teaspoon] dried oregano and 1 small finely chopped onion.

BANNOCKS

Bannocks are oatcakes that originated in Scotland where, up until the last century, they were made to celebrate every Highland quarter day as well as for weddings and birthdays. They may be eaten spread with butter and marmalade for breakfast or served with soup, fish, bacon, or cheese. Bannocks are delicious eaten straight from the girdle, if there are any over, store in an airtight container and reheat on a girdle or toast before serving.

MAKES 12
200 g [7 oz] medium ground oatmeal
25 g [1 oz] plain flour
2.5 ml [$\frac{1}{2}$ teaspoon] salt
2.5 ml [$\frac{1}{2}$ teaspoon[baking powder
50 g [2 oz] lard or soft bacon dripping
75 ml to 90 ml [5 to 6 tablespoons] hot water

1 Heat and prepare girdle as shown in the step-by-step instructions. Do not grease.

2 Place oatmeal, flour, salt and baking powder in a bowl. Stir.

3 Cut fat into flour, then rub in until mixture resembles breadcrumbs.

4 Make a hollow in middle of the mixture and pour in water, a tablespoon at a time, to make a soft dough.

5 Scatter a board with oatmeal and turn out dough on to prepared board. Knead lightly and quickly.

6 Sprinkle with a little more oatmeal if the dough sticks. Roll out dough to 6 mm [$\frac{1}{4}$"] thick and cut into squares, rounds or wedge shapes.

7 Transfer oatcakes to heated girdle and bake for 5 minutes, turn and bake for a further 5 minutes.

SINGIN' HINNY

This delicious Northumberland speciality that 'sings' as it cooks on the girdle is ideal for tea-time. Serve piping hot, split and buttered. This traditional recipe uses 50 g [2 oz] ground rice which makes it extra light and tasty. If ground rice is unavailable, use all self-raising flour.

SERVES 8

350 g [¾ lb] self-raising flour
2.5 ml [1 teaspoon] baking powder
50 g [2 oz] ground rice
5 ml [1 teaspoon] salt
50 g [2 oz] butter
50 g [2 oz] caster sugar
75 g [3 oz] currants
250 ml [½ pt] thin cream and milk mixed

1 Heat and prepare girdle as shown in the step-by-step instructions.

2 Sift flour, baking powder, ground rice and salt into a bowl.

3 Cut fat into flour, then rub in until mixture resembles even-sized breadcrumbs.

4 Stir sugar and currants into rubbed-in mixture.

5 Make a hollow in the middle of the mixture and pour in cream mixture. Work to make a soft, but not sticky, dough.

6 Gather the dough together with your fingers and turn out on to a lightly floured board. Knead quickly and lightly.

7 Roll out dough to a 23 cm [9"] circle approximately 6 mm [¼"] thick.

8 Lightly grease prepared girdle and transfer singin' hinny to girdle with the aid of a fish slice and palette knife.

9 Bake for 4–5 minutes or until risen and brown underneath.

10 Turn and bake for a further 4–5 minutes or until evenly browned and quite dry in centre.

11 Transfer cake to a warmed serving plate cut into wedges, split in half and spread with butter.

Variations

●Sift in 5 ml [1 teaspoon] mixed spice with dry ingredients and stir in 75 g [3 oz] mixed dried fruit to the rubbed in mixture.

●Sift 5 ml [1 teaspoon] ground cinnamon with dry ingredients. Use 50 g [2 oz] chopped hazelnuts and only 25 g [1 oz] currants in place of dried fruit.

Small is beautiful

A series of delectable small cakes can be made from rich sponge mixture. These may be plain or fancy. They may be cut from a larger cake or baked separately, but all will prove irresistibly tempting.

Small cakes are easy to handle and are popular with children and adults alike. They are infinitely adaptable and there is one to suit almost every occasion: they are perfect for weddings and birthday parties, they round off a meal with a sweet treat or they will give the family a welcome extra to fill up after a rather slim supper.

Small cakes may be baked separately in paper cases or bun tins, or they may be cut from a slab of a larger cake in a variety of decorative shapes. The rich sponge mixture given on pages 12–13 is ideal for these cakes and they can be iced in many of the ornamental ways which are given on pages 35–46.

Small cakes baked separately and shapes cut from a larger cake with ornamental cutters are iced one by one. If a larger cake is to be cut with a knife to make smaller iced fancies, the larger cake is iced first and then divided afterwards.

Outlined here are the general rules for making small ornamental cakes and some lovely individual recipes.

EQUIPMENT AND ITS PREPARATION

Equipment for making, baking the basic sponge and icing it is described on pages 8–14 and 35–46. For small cakes you will also need paper cases, bun or tartlet tins. For some special cakes, dariole tins (sometimes known as castle pudding moulds) are used. If you regularly bake small cakes, individual small cake tins are a necessary investment.

Bun tins should not be confused with tartlet tins, which are used for pastry cases. Bun tins are oblong or square with a number of indentations in them to hold the cake mixture. Bun tins come in various sizes (depending on the number of indentations) which are usually called 'holes'. Tins are sold in combinations of 6-, 9- and 12-hole sizes.

Paper cases are the easiest to use when baking small round cakes as they are ready to use, pre-greased and require no initial outlay on extra baking equipment. They can, of course, be used once only, but they are generally economical to buy and add a professional and attractive touch. Cakes can be baked on a flat baking sheet. Not all paper cases are strong enough to ensure that the cake is a regular shape once baked. A little trick of the trade to ensure they keep their shape is to place the cases very close to each other, or touching. When they are baked each cake supports the adjacent one and this prevents them becoming lopsided or out of shape as the mixture expands.

You can use a paper case in conjunction with bun or tartlet tins, placing one case in each hole. The sides of the case are then kept rigid and upright by the tin.

Dariole moulds (castle pudding moulds) are individual metal tins which resemble a miniature bucket in appearance. Although they are mainly employed in the making of puddings, they are used when making traditional madeleines— those delicious sponge cakes coated in jam and sprinkled with coconut.

Preparing the tins
All small cake tins should be brushed lightly with melted fat or oil to ensure

Step-by-step to cutting small cake shapes

1 Place the cake on a wooden board or work surface and cut away the baked cake edges.

2 For round cakes, press plain or fluted pastry cutters through the cake with one firm action.

OR place a round template on top of the cake and cut around the template to make circular cakes.

AND using a long-bladed knife, cut across the fingers of sponge to make square shapes.

4 For oblongs or fingers, cut across the fingers at intervals either greater or less than the width.

5 For diamond-shaped cakes, cut across the fingers diagonally at equal intervals.

SMALL CAKES: QUANTITIES FOR DIFFERENT TINS

Butter or margarine	Caster sugar	Medium-sized eggs	Self-raising flour	Tin	Oven temperature	Baking time
50 g [2 oz]	50 g [2 oz]	1	50 g [2 oz]	a 9-hole bun tin or 9 paper cases	200°C [400°F] gas mark 6	10–15 minutes
100 g [¼ lb]	100 g [¼ lb]	2	100 g [¼ lb]	18 cm [7"] square shallow tin or 18 paper cases	200°C [400°F] gas mark 6	20 minutes
				or 12 dariole tins	190°C [375°F] gas mark 5	20 minutes
175 g [6 oz]	175 g [6 oz]	3	175 g [6 oz]	a 28 × 18 cm [11 × 7"] swiss roll tin	180°C [350°F] gas mark 4	35–40 minutes

3 For square cakes, cut the cake lengthways into equal-sized fingers, the width of one cake.

6 For triangles, cut the cake into squares. Cut these diagonally one way then the other.

that the cake mixture does not stick to the tin during the baking. If large cakes are made for subsequent cutting, prepare the tin by greasing, lining and regreasing.

When using non-stick tins for the first time, follow the manufacturer's instructions for seasoning the new tin. Otherwise, the tins can be used without any pre-greasing or lining.

CLEVER CUTTING

If you do not own bun tins and don't have paper cases at hand, there are several interesting ways in which you can cut a larger cake to make several smaller ones. It is important to bake the cake in a shallow tin. Any of the following shapes can be cut from an 18 cm [7"] square shallow tin or a 28 × 18 cm [11 × 7"] swiss roll tin.

The first thing to do is to make and bake the cake. The chart gives you a guide to the quantities you will need for the different types of tin that are suitable for small cakes. Double up for larger quantities. The chart also gives you the different baking times and temperatures you will need.

Make sure that the cake is completely cold before cutting it. It is quite a good idea to use one day-old cake as it cuts better than an absolutely fresh one. Place the cake on a wooden board or work surface and trim the edges of the cake with a long-bladed sharp knife. The reason for this is that the edges tend to be rather more browned and harder than the centre. If these were left on the cake, the harder edges could very well spoil the shape of the cakes.

Round cakes

It is very easy to cut shapes from a round cake; all that is needed is a round pastry cutter and a firm hand. Place the pastry cutter (plain or fluted) on the top of the cake and press down in one action so that the resulting cut leaves a clean side. Cut the next shape as close to the first one as possible, planning so there is the minimum of wastage. Use the trimmings for trifles and no-cook puddings.

If you do not have pastry cutters, cut out a small round template from thin card and use it as directed on page 18. Small round, or fluted cakes cut from a larger one are always iced individually, after cutting.

Square and rectangular cakes
Square and rectangular cakes can easily be sliced with a sharp knife into a number of different shapes. Since these all have straight sides it is usual to ice the cake first before slicing to save time.

Square cakes: decide on the size of the square cake you want then cut the cake into fingers the width of one side of the cake. Cut each finger of cake at intervals to form a square.

Oblongs and fingers: the first cut is made as for square cakes. Adjust the length of the cutting intervals to make different sized cakes.

Diamonds: these shapes look extremely attractive once decorated and are easier to make than they first appear. Cut the cake into fingers as for the squares. Cut across a finger of cake at intervals, diagonally, thus dividing the cake into diamond shapes.

Triangles: cut the cake into even-sized squares. Cut the squares diagonally, first one way and then the other to form even-sized triangles.

IDEAS FOR SMALL CAKES

The following ideas are for small cakes all cut from one large cake. A few are iced before cutting: the majority are decorated after cutting.

●Cover the top of a 28 × 18 cm [11 × 7"] rich sponge cake with lemon-flavoured glacé icing and sprinkle with chopped pistachio nuts. Cut the cake into 4 cm [1½"] strips, lengthways. Cut each strip into squares, triangles or diamond shapes.

●Cut a 28 × 18 cm [11 × 7"] chocolate-flavoured sponge into squares. Coat each square with chocolate-flavoured butter-cream icing and coat with chocolate vermicelli. Pipe a small star of chocolate-flavoured butter-cream icing on top of each cake.

●Coat triangles of coffee-flavoured sponge cake with melted apricot jam and coat with toasted desiccated coconut.

●Coat the sides of small round cakes with melted strawberry jam and coat with crushed praline or digestive biscuits. Spread top of each cake generously with strawberry jam and pipe small shells of vanilla-flavoured butter-cream icing around the top outer edge of each cake.

●Cut a selection of fancy shapes from a 28 × 18 cm [11 × 7"] rich sponge cake. Brush the top of each cake with melted apricot jam. Using the same cutters as you used to cut the cakes, cut out matching shapes from thinly rolled-out marzipan. Place the corresponding marzipan shapes on top of each cake. Cover each one with glacé icing (flavoured and coloured to your taste). Decorate the top of each cake with stars of flavoured and/or coloured butter-cream icing, walnut halves, glacé cherries, chopped nuts, small sugar coated sweets or glacé fruits.

●Coat the sides of small heart-shaped cakes with melted apricot jam and chocolate vermicelli, following the step-by-step instructions on page 44. Now cover the top of each cake with peppermint-flavoured glacé icing. Fill a small greaseproof paper piping bag with melted chocolate and on to the top of each cake pipe any of the following: straight lines, 'S' shapes, a trellis design or a continuous figure-of-eight design.

●Coat squares of chocolate and mint-flavoured marble cake with green-coloured peppermint glacé icing. Dip a peppermint cream sweet into melted chocolate to half cover

the sweet and place one on top of each cake.

●Using a set of decorative metal cutters, cut a variety of shapes from a 28 × 18 cm [11 × 7"] plain or flavoured sponge. Place the cakes on a wire rack about 2.5 cm [1"] apart. Place three small balls of marzipan on top of each cake and coat each cake entirely with plain or coloured glacé icing.

●Coat the sides of small round sponge cakes with chocolate-flavoured butter-cream icing and coat in chocolate vermicelli. Fill a medium-sized piping bag (fitted with a small shell or star nozzle) with vanilla-flavoured butter-cream icing or crème au beurre.
Pipe lines of icing to cover the top of each cake, then pipe a border of small shells or stars around the top outer edge of each cake. Stand small triangles of chocolate (or chocolate discs) in the icing, so that they radiate from the centre of the cake in a circle.

●Brush the sides of diamond- or triangle-shaped cakes with melted apricot jam and coat with finely chopped nuts. Fill a piping bag fitted with a star nozzle with orange-flavoured crème au beurre or butter-cream icing. Pipe icing in a zig-zag design over the top of each cake and sprinkle with chocolate caraque.

●Cut a 28 × 18 cm [11 × 7"] sponge cake into strips about 4 cm [1½"] wide. Cut the strips into 5 cm [2"] long fingers. Coat half the total amount of fingers with lemon curd and place another finger of sponge on top. Place the cakes on a wire rack and entirely coat each sandwich with melted chocolate or chocolate-flavoured glacé icing. Drain a small can of mandarin oranges and dry each segment. Place about 4 orange segments lengthways down each finger. Brush the orange segments with melted apricot jam.

MADELEINES

The cheerful appearance of these cakes make them popular with children and they are the ones that the 19th century French author Proust remembered so well.

MAKES 9 MADELEINES
100 g [¼ lb] self-raising flour
2 medium-sized eggs
100 g [¼ lb] butter or margarine
100 g [¼ lb] caster sugar

175 g [6 oz] red jam
50 g [2 oz] desiccated coconut
halved glacé cherries

1 Brush inside of 9 dariole (castle pudding moulds) tins with melted fat or oil. Stand the tins on a baking tray.

2 Heat oven to 190°C [375°F] gas mark 5. Sift flour into a bowl and reserve. Break the eggs into another bowl and lightly whisk together.

3 Place the fat in a mixing bowl and beat until light and creamy. Add the sugar and beat until light in colour and fluffy in texture.

4 Beat in the eggs, a little at a time, beating well after each addition. Fold in the flour, one-third at a time using a metal spoon.

5 Two-thirds fill the prepared tins with the mixture. Bake just above the centre of oven for 20 minutes, until golden brown.

6 Leave the cakes to cool in tins for 5 minutes, then turn out the cakes on to a wire rack to cool.

7 Using a small sharp knife, cut the 'risen tops' from each cake to form a flat base which will keep the cake upright.

8 Place the jam and 60 ml [4 tablespoons] water into a small saucepan over a low heat until jam has melted. Remove pan from the heat.

9 Sprinkle coconut on to a large sheet of greaseproof paper or foil. Insert a skewer into the cut end of a madeleine and hold the cake over the jam.

10 Brush the entire surface with the jam then roll the cake in the coconut so that it coats the sides of the cake.

11 Repeat with the remaining cakes. Place a halved glacé cherry, cut side down, on top of each cake.

CAULIFLOWER CAKES

These unusual little cakes resemble miniature cauliflowers—hence the name! Traditionally they are made with green-coloured marzipan. There is no reason why you should not abandon the cauliflower idea and colour the marzipan with whatever colouring you have available, especially if you are serving them by themselves and want an attractive selection.

MAKES 15 CAKES
175 g [6 oz] quantity of rich sponge mixture (see chart)

For the decoration:
**225 g [½ lb] marzipan
few drops of green food colouring
175 g [6 oz] apricot jam
275 ml [½ pt] thick cream**

1 Make sponge mixture as directed on pages 12–13, using quantities based on 175 g [6 oz] flour used in the chart on page 87. Bake the mixture in a 28 × 18 cm [11 × 7"] swiss roll tin at 180°C [350°F] gas mark 4 for 35–40 minutes.

2 Knead the marzipan until soft and pliable. Add a few drops of green food colouring. Knead this into the marzipan until it is evenly coloured a pale green.

3 Roll out the marzipan thinly. Using a 5 cm [2"] plain round cutter, cut out 90 circles from the marzipan. Reserve.

4 Heay apricot jam in a small saucepan with 45 ml [3 table-spoons] water. Sieve melted jam.

5 Whisk the cream until thick and place in a large piping bag fitted with a medium-sized star nozzle.

6 Cut the cooled cake into 15 circles using a 5 cm [2"] plain round cutter.

7 Brush one side of marzipan circles with apricot jam.

8 Using six circles of marzipan per cake, overlap the marzipan circles around the side of each cake to completely cover.

9 Use the piping bag to pipe stars of whipped cream to cover the top of each cake.

CARIBBEAN PINEAPPLE CAKES

These unusually decorated individual cakes are suitable for any special occasion and are good enough to create a special occasion just to try them. If you don't own 8.5 cm [3½"] tartlet tins, bake the same quantity of mixture in a 28 × 18 cm [11 × 7"] oblong tin and cut out the rounds using a plain 7.5 cm [3"] round metal cutter.

MAKES 6 CAKES
175 g [6 oz] quantity of rich sponge mixture (see chart)

For the decoration:
**6 canned pineapple rings
45 ml [3 tablespoons] apricot jam
250 g [½ lb] plain chocolate
75 ml [3 fl oz] thick cream
6 maraschino or glacé cherries**

Madeleines are tiny sponge cakes baked in dariole moulds. They are coated with jam, then covered with desiccated coconut and topped with a cherry.

1 Make sponge mixture as directed on pages 12–13, using the quantities given in the chart on page 87, with 175 g [6 oz] flour. Bake the mixture in 3 tartlet tins or in an oblong tin, following the temperatures given in the chart.

2 When the sponge is cold, either cut the individual cakes into two horizontally or, if using an oblong tin, cut out eight circles.

3 Melt the chocolate in a small bowl over hot water. Spread the sides of each cake.

4 Place the cakes on a wire rack. Drain and reserve the syrup from the canned pineapple. Dry the pineapple rings on kitchen paper.

5 Place 30 ml [2 tablespoons] pineapple syrup in a small saucepan and add the sieved jam. Heat over a low heat until melted.

6 Spoon a little of the remaining pineapple syrup over each cake and top with a pineapple ring.

7 Whisk the cream until stiff. Place it in a small nylon piping bag fitted with a star nozzle.

8 Brush the top of each pineapple ring with apricot jam.

9 Pipe a large swirl of cream into the centre of each pineapple ring and place a whole cherry on top of each swirl of cream.

CHOCOLATE BOX CAKES

These very sophisticated little cakes are just the thing to impress guests. Do not be put off by their complicated look as they are far simpler to make than they look. The chocolate squares can even be made in advance, ready for you to stick on the cakes when made. Crème au beurre is used for decoration.

MAKES 16 CAKES
450 g [1 lb] plain chocolate
90 g [3½ oz] self-raising flour
15 g [½ oz] cocoa powder
2 medium-sized eggs
100 g [¼ lb] butter or margarine
100 g [¼ lb] caster sugar
milk
225 g [½ lb] vanilla-flavoured crème au beurre

1 Break up the chocolate and place in a bowl. Put the bowl over a saucepan of hot, but not boiling, water. Stir from time to time until the chocolate has melted.

2 Pour the chocolate on to waxed or silicone paper. Spread it with a palette knife until it is about 6 mm [¼"] thick and even, then leave it to set.

3 Heat oven to 190°C [375°F] gas mark 5. Prepare an 18 cm [7"] square shallow tin by greasing, lining and regreasing.

4 Make and bake cake as directed on pages 12–13, and in the chart on page 87.

5 When the cake is completely cold, cut it into four strips, 4.5 cm [1¾"] wide. Cut each strip of cake into 4 equal-sized squares to make 16 squares.

6 Spread the sides of each cake with two-thirds of the crème au beurre.

7 Place the last of the crème au beurre in a medium-sized piping bag fitted with a star tube and reserve.

8 Using a sharp, long-bladed knife, cut the chocolate into 80 squares each 4.5 × 3 cm [1¾ 1¼"]. Reserve these.

9 Press a chocolate square against the side of each cake, leaving the top of each cake open.

10 Pipe stars of crème au beurre to cover the top of each cake. Then place a chocolate square at an angle on top of each cake, so that the piped crème au beurre shows through.

Variations
●Cut only 64 squares of chocolate as 'lids' will not be needed. Make the cakes as directed but fill and coat the sides with thick whipped cream. Place a whole strawberry on top of each cake.
●Make as directed but use a peppermint and chocolate marble cake as the base. Flavour the crème au beurre with a few drops of peppermint extract and colour it with a few drops of green food colouring, then make the cake as directed.

Melting moments

Cake making by the melting method really is a piece of cake because it requires the minimum of effort. This method is specially designed to cope with extra sweeteners needed to make soft and sticky traditional cakes such as gingerbread and parkin.

Melting-method cakes have a characteristic tacky, sticky texture throughout the cake, and it is this that has made cakes like gingerbread so very popular and has given them such a high place in traditional baking. This stickiness is achieved by increasing the proportion of sweetening agents to other ingredients in the cake.

To handle the extra volume of sweetener, a special method is used—one entirely different to the method covered on previous pages on cakes. With this method the fat is melted with the sweetener before the flour is added. Before cooking the cake mixture has a tacky texture and a consistency similar to a thick batter, rather than the soft dropping consistency of cake mixtures made by the all-in-one or creaming methods.

INGREDIENTS
Proportions
Like all cakes, the amount and the choice of ingredients depend on the method you are using, the flavour and the texture you wish to achieve and/or the recipe you have chosen. The average proportions, however, for cakes made by the melting method are one-third fat to the total amount of flour; one-third sugar to the total amount of flour; and one to two-thirds of sweetener to the total amount of flour.

One extremely important factor when making cakes by this method is the exact weighing of the ingredients for the individual recipes. As long as there is a correct balance of ingredients to start with, perfect results will follow.

Flour
There are no hard and fast rules about the type of flour to use. As a basic guide, plain flour is best used, because then you can control the amount of raising agent which is important to the mixture. Self-raising flour may be used for certain recipes, but as you have no control over the raising agent you can never be sure whether it is too much or too little for the purpose of making cakes by this method. Certain brown flours can be used depending on your taste. Never use a strong plain flour (the type recommended for bread making), because this will produce a tough and heavy-textured cake. You should never substitute one flour for another in a given recipe, because this could upset the overall balance.

Raising agents

Bicarbonate of soda is the raising agent most often used in this method of cake making as it combines successfully with plain flour. When this chemical raising agent is heated, it gives off a carbon dioxide which produces the rise. Baking powder, another chemical raising agent, is used where self-raising flour is included. The quantities are usually small because of the amounts already in a self-raising flour. Baking powder is added, nevertheless to boost the rising. If you are using a brown flour, you must use baking powder in larger quantities than with self-raising flour. Brown flour is so much heavier than white flour and needs the extra rise that a larger quantity of baking powder will give.

Fat

When making melting-method cakes you can use margarine just as successfully as butter without fear that the flavour will be less satisfying. With this method, the fat is used purely as a binding medium and nine times out of ten the flavour from the fat is disguised by the flavourings and sweeteners in the recipe. Of course, butter can be used, should you prefer it, but any hard margarine, lard or a clarified dripping can be used with equal success.

Because the fat is always melted there is no need to bring it to room temperature before use, as is necessary with the other cake methods. If you are using a hard fat, just cut it into small pieces. This will make it easier to handle and will, of course, mean that it will melt faster.

Sweeteners

There are two kinds of sweeteners that can be used in the melting-method cake: liquid sweeteners, such as treacle, syrup or honey, or sugar.

Liquid sweeteners are the first choice of sweetening agent with this type of cake. This is not only because of their characteristic flavours, but also because the whole melting method has been designed to incorporate and blend them in their liquid form most conveniently. Black treacle alone gives a very handsome colour. Golden syrup will give more of a golden colour and, of course, a very sweet flavour. Other liquid sweeteners, including honey and malt extract may be used.

Sugar: soft brown or a Demerara sugar is generally used if sugar is being included, because of its rich flavour and colour. Caster and granulated sugar are more often used for other types of plainer cakes, but both are suitable for this method.

Combinations: you may also come across a recipe that uses a combination of liquid sweeteners or one that combines liquid and sugar sweeteners.

Eggs

Eggs do not play an important part in cakes made by this method; they are generally only used in small quantities. The enriching qualities of the cake are amply provided for by the sweetener when liquid sweeteners are used. The egg is not, therefore, included to enrich the cake, as with the creaming-method cakes. In a melted-method cake using sugar rather than all liquid sweetener, an egg does provide richness because it works with the flour in the recipe to form the structure of the cake (usually when there is fruit in the cake).

Liquids

Liquids are added to some, but not all cakes made by the melting method. Before cooking, melting-method cakes must have the consistency of a thick batter (one that is easy to pour, but thick enough to spread slowly). To achieve this consistency, extra liquid is sometimes added to melted ingredients, plus any eggs used. Milk and/or water are most usual additions; milk will give a slightly softer texture than water. However other liquids may be used for additional flavour (see flavourings).

Flavourings

A variety of flavouring ingredients may be used, some for taste and some to give an interesting contrast of textures.

Dry flavourings: spices play a vital role in many melting-method cakes particularly gingerbreads. As well as imparting their own enticing flavour, they play a secondary but important role of disguising the sometimes bitter flavour left when bicarbonate of soda is used.

Ground ginger is, of course, the traditional spice for gingerbreads: but it is best combined with another spice because of its pungency. Combined with ground cinnamon or mixed spice the flavour is detectable but much more subtle. Never be afraid to adjust the quantity of spices (ground ginger in particular) to suit your family's taste—it will not affect the balance of ingredients. Always sift any spice used with flour to ensure even distribution in the cake.

Citrus zest must always be finely grated. It is an excellent flavouring, as it helps to offset the sweetness often associated with cakes made by the melting method.

Nuts chopped or ground, depending on the recipe, add extra texture and moisture. Any type of nut can be used, as long as it is prepared according to the recipe.

Glacé or crystallized fruits and even preserved fruit, make a delicious addition especially to gingerbreads. Finely chop the fruit, unless otherwise directed. When using a preserved fruit, drain the syrup from it and pat it dry before chopping.

Dried fruit may be used successfully. If the fruit is large, chop it to a uniform size.

Liquid flavourings: when these are used, a corresponding reduction must be made of the milk or water used in the recipe. If this is not done, the recipe will be unbalanced and the batter will be too thin. When flavouring extracts are used, however, the amounts are usually so small that they will not disturb the proportions.

● Plain or flavoured yoghurt will give a lighter slightly tangy result.

● Beer, brown ale or stout are ideal and give a rich flavour.

● A little syrup from a jar of preserved fruit is a delicious and economical addition. If using the syrup from preserved ginger, take care not to use too much, as this is particularly strong.

EQUIPMENT

Accurate measuring equipment heads the list in priorities for making cakes by the melting method. In addition you will need a heavy-based saucepan to actually melt the fat and sweetener and a wooden spoon to amalgamate the melting ingredients.

A sieve and a large mixing bowl are essential for the dry ingredients and a small basin for whisking the eggs. A tablespoon is neccessary for blending the melted and dry ingredients together. Be sure to use a metal spoon as the sharp edge of the metal is best for cutting through the ingredients quickly and efficiently.

Avoid using a wooden spoon, because there is always the temptation that you will beat the mixture together. Beating is to be avoided at all costs because it produces a tough cake.

A rubber spatula is handy when it comes to turning the mixture into the cake tin as you can be sure that every last drop will be used.

Preparing the tin
The cake mixture should be baked as soon as it is made, so always choose and prepare your bakeware before you start. Square or rectangular tins are traditionally used for gingerbreads because they are usually served cut into squares. Tea-breads, like bread, are baked in loaf tins so that they can be cut into slices for serving. Provided it is of the right capacity, there is no reason why a round tin cannot be used.

Whatever tin you choose be particularly careful about preparing it correctly. Because you are dealing with a batter there is more chance than usual that the cake will stick during baking. The tin must be completely greased, lined and greased again (see on pages 29–30 for lining tins). If using a loaf tin, grease it and only line the base before regreasing.

THE BASIC METHOD
The melting method is extremely straightforward and practically foolproof. Follow the basic rules and there will be no problems. Measure carefully and accurately, taking particular care over the raising agent. Being over generous with the raising agent will cause the cake to rise too quickly during baking; it could then collapse in the centre.

Melting
When melting the fat and sugar or liquid sweetener, take care that it does not become overheated. Always melt over a slow heat and never a high one. If the melted ingredients are allowed to boil, the results will be more like toffee and totally unmanageable. If you are interrupted, it is wiser to turn off the heat and remove the pan from the heat to ensure that no mishaps occur.

As soon as the fat and sugar are completely melted remove the saucepan from the heat and allow the mixture to cool slightly.

Dry ingredients and egg
While the melted ingredients are cooling, measure the dry ingredients and whisk the egg. Make a well in the centre of the flour.

Adding the melted ingredients
It is very important that the melted mixture is allowed to cool sufficiently before it is added to the dry ingredients. A good test of whether the melted mixture is ready is if you can comfortably place your hand against the side of the saucepan. Do not use the melted mixture before this point, or the dry ingredients will cook slightly before you have had a chance to combine them. Pour the melted mixture plus 1 egg and liquid (if used) into the centre of the dry ingredients all in one go. Using a metal spoon and a light cutting action, combine the ingredients together until the mixture is smooth and batter-like in consistency.

When the mixture has reached this stage, stir in any flavourings used.

OVEN TEMPERATURE AND TIMING
Once you have the tin prepared, the cake is relatively quick to make. For this reason, it is of prime importance that the oven shelves are positioned and the correct temperature reached before the cake is prepared.

Because of their high sugar content, melting-method cakes require a warm oven only—even a slow oven in some cases—otherwise they will most certainly burn. As a general guide, 160°C [325°F] gas mark 3 is suitable, but the richer the cake the lower the temperature.

Always stick to the recommended oven temperature. Should you be tempted to turn up the temperature to speed the cake along, all you will achieve is a cake that is peaked in the centre, which in turn will crack and look unsightly. Apart from the deformed shape of the cake, there is a pretty good chance that the cake will burn before it has had a chance to cook through.

Step-by-step to melting-method cake

1 Position oven shelf and heat oven. Grease, line and re-grease a baking tin.

2 Place fat and sweetener in a heavy based saucepan over a low heat. Stir gently, until melted.

5 Pour melted mixture into bowl together with eggs and any liquid. Stir lightly with a metal spoon.

6 Stir in any additional flavouring ingredients and pour the batter into prepared tin.

Oven times

The cooking time will depend on the size and depth of the cake, as well as the ingredients, so there are no hard and fast rules. As a general guide, a cake made with 225 g [½ lb] flour will require 1¼–1½ hours at a warm temperature. Always follow the time given in the recipe you are using.

Handy hints

● Always leave the cake undisturbed in the oven during baking. Opening the oven door to have a peep will produce a cake that has sunk in the centre.
● Carefully peel away the lining paper from the cake while still hot—the surface of these cakes is particularly sticky. If the paper is left on until the cake is cold, you will find that the paper will have become stuck to the surface of the cake.

GINGERBREAD

No Scottish clan would call themselves complete without their own particular recipe for making gingerbread. This gives you just some idea how many recipes there are for it. A true Scottish gingerbread should be sticky, rich and above all eaten at least one day after it is made. Eating it when it has time to mature means that all those delicious flavours have had time to mingle and complement each other.

Gingerbread will quite happily store for two days before it is eaten and, if it lasts that long, up to two weeks after it has been baked.

MAKES 16 SQUARES
oil or fat for greasing
50 g [2 oz] black treacle
50 g [2 oz] golden syrup
100 g [¼ lb] margarine or butter
100 g [¼ lb] soft brown sugar
225 g [½ lb] plain flour
a pinch of salt
10 ml [2 teaspoons] ground
    ginger

5 ml [1 teaspoon] bicarbonate
    of soda
1 medium-sized egg
45 ml [3 tablespoons] milk

1 Position shelf to the centre of the oven. Heat oven to 160°C [325°F] gas mark 3.

2 Brush a 17.5 cm [7"] deep square tin with melted fat or oil, fully line and re-grease.

3 Place the treacle, syrup, margarine or butter and the sugar in a heavy-based saucepan.

4 Place the saucepan over a low heat and stir until the fat has melted and the sugar has dissolved. Remove the pan from the heat and put aside to cool.

5 Sieve the flour, salt, ginger and bicarbonate of soda into a large bowl. Make a well in the centre of the dry ingredients.

6 Whisk the egg and milk together lightly.

7 When the melted mixture has cooled sufficiently (test with your hand on the side of the saucepan), pour into the dry ingredients with the egg and milk.

8 Using a metal spoon, stir the ingredients together until smoothly blended and butter-like in consistency.

9 Pour batter into prepared tin and bake for 1¼ hours.

10 Test by pressing cake, it should feel firm and slightly springy.

11 Leave cake to cool for 10 minutes in the tin. Turn out and place on a wire rack. Remove lining paper.

Variations

● For a really dark gingerbread, omit the golden syrup and use all black treacle.
● For the reverse, a light gingerbread, omit the black treacle and use all golden syrup.
● For a celebration gingerbread, brush the surface of the cake with warmed golden syrup while the cake is still warm, and decorate with pieces of any crystallized fruit.
● Make a gingered gingerbread by

3 Remove mixture from heat, when melted. On no account let it boil. Put aside to cool.

4 Sift flour and raising agent into a bowl. Make a well in dry ingredients. Whisk egg lightly.

Bake cake for recommended time. To test, it should feel firm when lightly pressed.

8 Allow cake to cool in the tin for 10 minutes, turn out and remove lining paper, leave to cool.

adding 50 g [2 oz] chopped crystal-lized ginger or drained, chopped stem ginger at the end of step 8.

●With celebrations still in mind, make an almond gingerbread by stirring in 50 g [2 oz] of blanched, chopped almonds at the end of stage 8. When the cake is cooked, but still warm, brush the top of the cake with warmed black treacle and decorate with whole blanched almonds.

●For the beer lovers in the family, omit the milk and use the same amount of brown ale and stir in 100 g [¼ lb] sultanas at the end of stage 8.

●For an upside-down gingerbread that is more of a pudding than a cake, try a surprise gingerbread. Grease but do not line the tin. Cream to-gether 50 g [2 oz] butter with 50 g [2 oz] caster sugar and spread over the base of the tin. Peel, core and neatly slice 2 medium-sized pears. Arrange the pear slices over the creamed mixture. Pour the gingerbread mix-ture over the fruit and bake as direc-ted. When cooked allow the ginger-bread to cool in the tin for five minutes then invert on to a warmed serving plate and serve with custard.

●Gingerbread people can be made by baking the mixture in a 28 × 17.5 cm [11 × 7″] swiss roll tin for 30 minutes. Leave the cake to cool for 5 minutes then turn out and leave until completely cold. Using a special gingerbread people cutter, cut as many figures as you can get from the cake. Make up 100 g [¼ lb] glacé icing using half the amount of liquid—15 ml [1 tablespoon]. Place the icing in a greaseproof paper icing bag fitted with a small plain tube. Pipe the gingerbread people.

PARKIN

The north of England is famous for this special type of ginger-bread called parkin. It is very similar to gingerbread except that oatmeal is used in place of a proportion of the flour. Make parkin at least two days before eating to allow the flavours to develop and the cake to moisten up. In the north it is traditionally served on Guy Fawkes night around the bonfire.

MAKES 8–12 PIECES
oil or fat for greasing
100 g [¼ lb] black treacle
100 g [¼ lb] soft brown sugar
100 g [¼ lb] margarine or butter
100 g [¼ lb] plain flour
a pinch of salt
5 ml [1 teaspoon] ground ginger
5 ml [1 teaspoon] mixed spice
2.5 ml [½ teaspoon] bicarbonate of soda
100 g [¼ lb] oatmeal
1 medium-sized egg
75 ml [5 tablespoons] milk

1 Position the shelf in the centre of the oven. Heat oven to 160°C [325°F] gas mark 3.

2 Brush a deep 15 cm [6″] square tin with melted fat or oil, fully line and re-grease.

3 Place the treacle, sugar and fat in a heavy-based saucepan.

4 Place the saucepan over a low heat and heat gently, stirring from time to time until the fat has melted and the sugar dissolved. Remove the pan from the heat and allow to cool.

5 Sift the flour into a bowl with the salt, spices and bicarbonate of soda. Stir in the oatmeal.

6 Make a well in the centre of the dry ingredients. Whisk the egg and milk together lightly.

7 When sufficiently cooled, pour the melted mixture into the dry ingredients.

8 Using a metal spoon, stir the ingredients together until smooth-ly blended.

9 Pour the batter into the prepared tin and bake for 1–1¼ hours until the cake is firm to the touch.

10 Leave cake to cool in tin for 10 minutes. Turn cake out on to a wire rack and remove lining paper. Leave to cool.

Variations

●For an orange- or lemon-flavoured parkin, omit the spices and use 10 ml [2 teaspoons] finely grated lemon or orange zest.

●For a lighter cake, use honey or golden syrup instead of treacle.

WHOLEMEAL PEANUT LOAF

This is a chewy, protein-packed loaf with an attractive rough surface. Like most of the melted-method cakes, this one is also best eaten a good twenty-four hours after it is made. Serve cut into slices and thickly buttered or made into sweet sandwiches for an unusual lunchbox filler.

The mix is much stiffer than usual, but do not worry; this is because it has to support the weight of the peanut which is a heavy addition.

MAKES A 900 G [2 LB] LOAF
oil or fat for greasing
350 g [¾ lb] self-raising wholemeal flour
a pinch of salt
50 g [2 oz] golden syrup
75 g [3 oz] soft brown sugar
75 g [3 oz] butter or margarine
3 medium-sized eggs
60 ml [4 tablespoons] milk
175 g [6 oz] crunchy peanut butter
25 g [1 oz] chopped salted peanuts

1 Position the shelf in the centre of the oven. Heat oven to 160°C [325°F] gas mark 3.

2 Brush a 900 g [2 lb] loaf tin with melted fat or oil and line the base, re-grease.

3 Sift the flour and salt into a bowl. Tip any bran left in the sieve back into the bowl and stir in lightly.

4 Place the syrup, sugar and fat in a heavy-based saucepan.

5 Place the saucepan over a low heat and heat gently, stirring from time to time until the fat has melted and the sugar dissolved.

6 Remove the pan from the heat and allow to cool.

7 Make a well in the centre of the dry ingredients. Whisk the eggs and milk together lightly.

8 Pour the melted mixture and the egg mixture into the dry ingredients.

9 Using a metal spoon, stir the ingredients together until evenly blended.

10 Stir in the peanut butter until completely amalgamated.

11 Pour the mixture into the prepared tin and sprinkle the surface of the mixture with the peanuts.

12 Bake for 1½ hours until the cake is risen and golden brown.

13 Leave cake to cool in tin for 10 minutes, turn out on to a wire rack and remove lining paper.

14 Leave cake until completely cold.

Variations
● If wholemeal flour is not available use white self-raising flour. Reduce the milk to 30 ml [2 tablespoons].
● To make a wholemeal date and walnut loaf, omit the crunchy peanut butter and peanuts. Flavour with a pinch of cinnamon instead of the salt. Stir in 75 g [3 oz] chopped, stoned dates and 75 g [3 oz] chopped walnuts at the end of stage 9.
● For a wholemeal sultana loaf, omit the peanut butter and peanuts. Sift 5 ml [1 teaspoon] mixed spice with the flour. Stir in 175 g [6 oz] sultanas at the end of stage 9.

Biscuits for beginners

For tea or coffee breaks, a packed lunch, picnic or afternoon tea at home, nothing goes down quite so well with the family as crisp, fresh home-baked biscuits. If you have never made biscuits before, start here and discover how simple and mouthwateringly delicious home-baked biscuits can be.

Baking biscuits at home is much cheaper than buying them. If you work out the cost of ingredients and cooking and compare it to the cost of a packet of biscuits, you will find that quite a saving can be made. Savings are even greater if you own a freezer as you can make up a large quantity of the basic biscuit mixture then divide and flavour it in various ways. The mixture can then be frozen and used as needed; it will keep for two months in the freezer.

Quick and very easy to make, rubbed-in biscuits are made using a similar method to rubbed-in cakes (pages 72–73). Biscuits made by the rubbed-in method include well-known favourites, such as short-bread and digestives, plus lesser-known but just as good Linzer biscuits, Danish butter biscuits and many others which you will find in this course. There are non-sweet biscuits too—such as delicious home-made water biscuits to serve with soup, pâté or cheese.

One important thing to keep in mind when making your own biscuits is that you are not trying to compete with their commercial equivalent. Home-made biscuits may not look the same or be as uniform in size and

colour as the bought variety, but they will certainly taste every bit as good if not better.

BASIC INGREDIENTS
The basic ingredients for rubbed-in biscuits are flour, salt, fat, sugar, eggs and liquid.

Flour
The flour for biscuits is usually plain as biscuits, unlike rubbed-in cakes, are not required to rise. You may, however, find some recipes where a self-raising flour or a combination of plain flour and a raising agent is used. This gives the biscuits a softer, more cake-like texture.

To achieve this, the cooking time will probably be longer than for the basic biscuit to ensure even baking and a crisp biscuit. The flour should be sieved before use. Part of the flour is sometimes replaced with rice flour or cornflour to give biscuits a crumbly texture, and combinations of white and brown flour are often used, particularly for digestive biscuits. Brown flour is never used alone, only with other flours, as using all brown flour would produce a very heavy textured cake or biscuit.

Salt
Salt is essential even in sweet biscuits to bring out flavour. A pinch up to 225 g [$\frac{1}{2}$ lb] flour is usually enough. The salt is sieved with the flour to ensure even distribution.

Fat
The fat for rubbed-in biscuits can be either butter or margarine. Butter of course gives the best flavour but a margarine with a high butter content is an economical alternative. Lard is sometimes used but never on its own, usually combined with butter or margarine.

The fat should be firm enough for it to rub evenly into the flour until the mixture resembles fine breadcrumbs. As a rule rubbed-in biscuits use the same proportions as rubbed-in cakes: the fat should be about half the total weight of the flour.

Sugar
Caster sugar is best for biscuits because it blends in easily and melts at the low temperature employed in biscuit baking. Granulated sugar can be used but it does not dissolve so easily as caster sugar. A golden rule

to remember is that for sweet biscuits made by the rubbed-in method, you always use the same amount of sugar as fat, unless dried fruit is used or the recipe dictates otherwise. Because dried fruit contains a high proportion of sugar the amount of sugar in fruit biscuits is reduced slightly. In savoury biscuits a little sugar is sometimes included to bring out the flavour of the other ingredients.

Eggs
Not all rubbed-in biscuits use eggs to bind and/or enrich the mixture. However, where biscuits are enriched by the addition of eggs, they are usually crumblier. Rubbed-in biscuits made without the addition of eggs tend to be much crisper.

Where eggs are used they should be at room temperature. The size will depend on the recipe. They should be lightly whisked before being added to the dry ingredients.

Liquid
Where an egg is not used, the biscuit mixture is bound with a liquid. This is usually either milk or water and just enough is added to make a stiff paste. Sometimes fruit juice or squash may be used instead to give the biscuits flavour.

FLAVOURINGS
Other ingredients may be used to flavour and add texture to the biscuits. You can try any of these with the basic mixture given in the step-by-steps to rubbed-in biscuits.

Dried fruit
Dried fruit can be stirred into the rubbed-in mixture before the addition of any liquid. This will make what are often referred to by small boys as 'squashed fly biscuits'. Small or very finely chopped fruit is best. Large pieces will make the biscuit mixture difficult to cut once rolled out. Usually about 50 g [2 oz] of dried fruit is used to 225 g [$\frac{1}{2}$ lb] flour.

Nuts
Ground or finely chopped hazelnuts or almonds are very good. When using ground nuts, replace 50 g [2 oz] of the stated amount of flour with the nuts, use as described for dried fruit. Chopped hazelnuts or walnuts give very crunchy biscuits, particularly when toasted. For savoury biscuits, finely chopped salted peanuts are a

good addition. When these are used, salt should be omitted.

Fruit zest
Grated orange or lemon zest gives the basic rubbed-in mixture a delicious tangy flavour. About 10 ml [2 teaspoons] finely grated zest will be sufficient to every 225 g [$\frac{1}{2}$ lb] flour.

Cheese
Grated cheese is often used in savoury biscuits in place of the sugar. Use a hard grated cheese such as Cheddar or Parmesan.

Oats
To give biscuits a crunchy texture, part of the flour is sometimes replaced with coarse oatmeal or rolled oats. The amount of oats never exceeds 50 g [2 oz] per 225 g [$\frac{1}{2}$ lb] flour.

Drinking chocolate or cocoa powder
To make chocolate biscuits, 30 ml [2 tablespoons] of the flour may be replaced with cocoa powder, drinking chocolate or a malted powder. If drinking chocolate is used, reduce the sugar by about 30 ml [2 tablespoons] as the drinking chocolate is ready sweetened.

Spices
A pinch of mixed spice, nutmeg, cinnamon or ginger gives biscuits individual flavour. About 5 ml [1 teaspoon] spice will be sufficient to flavour biscuits made with 225 [$\frac{1}{2}$ lb] flour.

EQUIPMENT
As well as the usual mixing bowl, scales, rolling pin, wire rack etc, there are several other important pieces of equipment needed for biscuits.
Cutters: metal scone or biscuit cutters are best because they give a cleaner cut than plastic ones. Use a size that suits you or one that the recipe suggests. Always remember to dry cutters carefully after use, especially the smaller ones, or they may rust at the seams. Leaving cutters on top of a warm cooker after washing and drying will ensure that they are perfectly dry before storage. For sandwiched biscuits which have a hole in the upper half so that filling can show through (as in Linzer biscuits), small petit four cutters are ideal. If you do not have one of these,

a thimble or an apple corer will make a neat round hole. A wine glass is always a handy standby if cutters are not available. You can also use a sharp, long-bladed knife to cut squares, oblongs and diamond shapes from a rolled-out mixture.

Baking trays: biscuits are baked on flat trays or baking sheets. These should be heavy and preferably aluminium as this is a good conductor of heat. Large trays are best as you can get a good quantity of biscuits on them. Baking biscuits on small trays usually mean that the quantity of biscuits will not all fit on to one and will have to be baked on different shelves in the oven which makes accurate timing difficult.

Fish slice or palette knife: to transfer the biscuits off the trays after baking to a cooling rack you will need a palette knife or a fish slice.

MAKING THE BISCUITS
Sifting the dry ingredients
The flour and salt (plus spice or powdered flavouring if used) must first be sieved into a medium-sized bowl. Sieving the salt and spices with the flour ensures even distribution throughout the mixture. If you use a wholewheat flour remember to tip the bran which remains in the sieve after sifting into the rest of the flour and lightly mix.

Rubbing-in
The butter or margarine which, as for rubbed-in cakes, should be quite firm is then cut into the flour, using a palette or round-bladed knife. Rub the fat into the flour until the mixture resembles fine breadcrumbs. The only exception to this is when you are making richer biscuits, such as shortbread, where the proportion of butter is high. In these mixtures, the crumbs will be larger.

If you are adding fruit, nuts or citrus zest, stir into the mixture at this point with the sugar.

Adding egg or liquid
If an egg is being used to bind the mixture, whisk lightly with a fork before adding to the other ingredients. To add the liquid or egg, make a well in the centre of the mixture and pour in. Using a knife, draw the dry ingredients into the liquid with a stirring motion, until the mixture sticks together in the bowl to form a stiffish dough.

Kneading
When the mixture sticks together in a ball, knead it gently into a ball which is smooth and free from cracks. This light kneading is essential otherwise the biscuit mixture will not roll evenly and smoothly. Should the dough be rather too soft and difficult to roll, wrap in foil or greaseproof paper and firm up in the refrigerator.

Rolling and cutting
The next stage is the rolling of the dough. This is best done on either a wooden board or smooth work surface. Dust the surface lightly with flour to prevent the dough sticking. It is a good idea to lightly flour the rolling pin too. Rolling in one direction, roll out the dough until it is about 6 mm [¼"] thick or as in the recipe.

Using the cutter of your choice, cut out the biscuits using one firm press so that you can get a clean cut. Lightly flour the cutter to prevent it sticking to the dough. Cut out as many biscuits from the dough as you can, then transfer them with a fish slice or palette knife and place on a prepared, greased baking tray. Re-knead dough scraps and roll out. Repeat until you can cut no more biscuits from the dough.

Glazing and topping
If wished, biscuits may be brushed with lightly beaten egg and sprinkled with chopped nuts, poppy or caraway seeds before baking.

Baking
When all the biscuits have been cut out, you can prick the surface of plain, flat ones with a fork. This gives a decorative finish and also helps the biscuits to cook evenly. Bake just above the centre of the oven for 10 to 15 minutes or for the time given in the recipe.

The temperature for cooking biscuits varies from low, for the richer ones containing more butter, to moderate for hard, dry biscuits.

Depending on the amount of fat in the mixture, the biscuits may still be soft when they come out of the oven; do not worry about this. They firm very quickly. Always leave biscuits for 5 minutes on the baking tray before transferring them to give them time to set. Cool biscuits on a wire rack and always make sure they are absolutely cold before storing in airtight containers.

This basic biscuit dough can be used to make all kinds of biscuits. Add fruit, nuts, spices or fruit zest, as wished, following the guidelines in the ingredients section.

3 Rub the fat into the flour until mixture resembles even-sized breadcrumbs. Stir in the sugar. Make a well in centre of mixture.

7 Dip a 7.5 cm [3"] cutter into flour and cut out biscuits. Transfer each biscuit on to the prepared tin.

Step-by-step basic rubbed-in biscuits

MAKING ABOUT 24 7.5 CM [3"]
BISCUITS
225 g [½ lb] plain flour
pinch of salt
100 g [¼ lb] butter or margarine
100 g [¼ lb] caster sugar
1 large egg

1 Heat oven to 160°C [325°F] gas mark 3. Grease a large baking tray and set aside.

2 Sift flour and salt (plus spices or powdered flavouring if used) into a large bowl. Cut fat into flour until all pieces are pea sized.

4 Lightly beat the egg. Pour into the well and draw in the dry ingredients with a fork, until mixture sticks together.

5 Knead gently until the mixture forms a smooth ball, then turn on to a lightly floured board.

6 Using a lightly floured rolling pin roll out to a round 3 mm [⅛"] thick.

8 Re-knead dough scraps into a ball, roll out again and use to cut more biscuits. Transfer to prepared tray.

9 Prick the surface of the biscuits lightly with a fork or glaze. Place on a shelf just above the centre of the oven.

10 Cook for 13–15 minutes until lightly browned. Leave biscuits for 5 minutes to set on tray. Transfer to a wire rack to cool.

Step-by-step to fancy biscuits

1 For jam sandwich biscuits, cut two rounds. Using a petit four cutter or thimble, cut a hole in the centre of one of the rounds.

AND cook the biscuits. When cold, spread jam or butter cream on the whole round. Sift icing sugar over 'tops' then place these on top.

2 For choc-top biscuits place 5 ml [1 teaspoon] of melted chocolate on each cooked biscuit. Spread lightly with a hot knife.

AND top with a walnut half or almonds or sprinkle with chopped nuts or desiccated coconut for decoration.

3 For forked biscuits, roll mixture into walnut-sized balls. Place on tray then press each ball lightly with a fork.

4 After baking, biscuits can be decoratively iced with thin glacé or butter-cream icing and topped with sweets or nuts.

DANISH BUTTER COOKIES

To give these crisp little biscuits a real Danish flavour, Danish butter should be used. Failing this, you can use ordinary butter but not margarine, as this will not give the correct flavour and texture. In Denmark, these biscuits are made for Christmas.

MAKES 18 5 CM [2"]COOKIES
**100 g [¼ lb] self-raising flour
pinch of salt
75 g [3 oz] butter
75 g [3 oz] caster sugar
1 large egg
a few drops of vanilla extract
25 g [1 oz] flaked almonds**

1 Heat the oven to 190°C [375°F] gas mark 5. Grease two small or one large baking tray.

2 Sift the flour and salt into a bowl.

Cut butter into the flour until all the pieces are pea sized and coated with flour.

3 Rub into the flour until the mixture resembles breadcrumbs.

4 Stir in sugar and lightly whisk egg. Make a well in the centre of mixture and add 30 ml [2 tablespoons] of whisked egg and the vanilla extract.

5 Draw the dry ingredients into the liquid with a fork until mixture sticks together.

6 Knead the dough gently until it forms a smooth ball free from cracks. Turn on to a lightly floured surface. Roll out to 6 mm [¼"] thick.

7 Using a floured 5 cm [2"] biscuit cutter, cut out the biscuits, re-rolling as necessary.

8 Brush the biscuits with the remaining egg and sprinkle each one with flaked almonds.

9 Bake in the centre of the oven for about 9 minutes or until golden brown. Leave on tray to set for 5 minutes then transfer to a wire rack to cool.

Variation

●For butter biscuits with chocolate fudge topping, make the mixture as above. Press the mixture into a slab cake tin measuring 28 × 17.5 cm [11 × 7"] and about 5 cm [2"] deep, which has been well greased. Cook as above. Heat 50 g [2 oz] butter and 50 g [2 oz] soft brown sugar in a saucepan. Heat gently for about 4 minutes until the sugar dissolves. Stir in the contents of a 425 ml [14 fl oz] can of sweetened condensed milk. Bring to the boil and stir continuously until the mixture forms a soft ball when a teaspoonful is poured into a saucer of cold water. Stir in 50 g [2 oz] plain chocolate until melted. Remove pan from heat and beat until mixture cools and thickens. Pour over the cooked, cooled biscuit base still in the tin and spread evenly. Leave to cool. While the fudge is cooling, melt 100 g [¼ lb] plain or cooking chocolate. Pour melted chocolate over the fudge and tap the tin on a hard surface to level the chocolate. Leave in the refrigerator for about 1 hour to set and then cut into fingers.

WATER BISCUITS

Water biscuits have been a firm favourite to eat with cheese for many years. Because the biscuits are very dry, only a little butter is used.

MAKES 24
100 g [¼ lb] plain flour
pinch of salt
25 g [1 oz] butter or
 margarine

1 Heat the oven to 200°C [400°F] gas mark 6 and grease a large baking tray.

2 Sift the flour and salt into a bowl. Use a round-bladed knife or palette knife to cut fat into flour until all pieces are pea sized and coated with flour.

3 Rub the fat into the flour until mixture resembles even-sized breadcrumbs.

4 Make a well in the centre of the mixture. Pour in 30 ml [2 tablespoons] water. Using a fork, draw the dry ingredients into the water until the mixture sticks together.

5 Knead gently until the mixture forms a smooth, crack-free ball.

6 Roll out to 6 mm [¼"] thick. Use a 5 cm [2"] cutter to cut out the biscuits, re-rolling as necessary.

7 Using a rolling pin, gently roll each biscuit out to thinner circles about 10 cm [4"] diameter.

8 Bake just above centre of oven for about 8 minutes until golden and puffy. Leave biscuits to set on tray for 5 minutes, transfer to a wire rack to cool.

LINZER BISCUITS

These pretty little continental biscuits are rich and buttery. Unless serving immediately, store unfilled and sandwich with jam of your choice just before serving. A plain buttercream icing can also be used for a filling. If you do not have a clover-leaf petit four cutter, use an apple corer or a thimble to cut holes in the centre of the biscuits. The biscuits are very small so it is wise to make quite a large amount at one time. Because these biscuits are sandwiched, the dough is rolled thinner than normal.

MAKES 20
150 g [5 oz] self-raising
 flour
pinch of ground cinnamon
pinch of ground cloves
100 g [¼ lb] butter or
 margarine
75 g [3 oz] caster sugar
1 small egg
raspberry jam to fill
icing sugar to sift over

1 Heat the oven to 160°C [325°F], gas mark 3. Grease two baking trays or one large tray.

2 Sift flour and spices into a bowl. Cut the butter into the flour until pieces are pea sized and evenly coated with flour. Rub in until the mixture resembles breadcrumbs.

3 Stir in the sugar. Break the egg into a bowl and whisk lightly with a fork. Make a well in the centre of the dry ingredients.

4 Pour in whisked egg. Using a fork, draw the dry ingredients into the egg, until the mixture sticks together.

5 Knead the dough gently until the mixture forms a ball free from cracks. Lightly flour a board and a rolling pin.

6 Roll the dough out to 3 mm [⅛"] thick. Using a 6 cm [2½"] cutter, cut out 40 rounds, re-rolling as necessary.

7 Using a clover-leaf petit four cutter or an apple corer, cut out the centre of half of the rounds. Transfer to prepared trays.

8 Bake in the centre of the oven for 10–12 minutes until pale golden in colour. Leave biscuits to set for 5 minutes before transferring to a wire rack to cool.

9 When cold, spread each whole biscuit with about 2.5 ml [½ teaspoon] jam. Sift the tops lightly with icing sugar. Place a cut-out biscuit on top so that the jam shows through.

Bake a batch of delicious Linzer biscuits, sandwiched together with raspberry jam.

DIGESTIVE BISCUITS

Delicious with cheese or honey, buttered or just by themselves, digestives have always been a family favourite. These home-made biscuits are just as tasty as the bought variety and much cheaper.

MAKES 30
100 g [¼ lb] plain flour
225 g [½ lb] wholemeal flour
2.5 ml [½ teaspoon] salt
75 g [3 oz] butter or margarine
75 g [3 oz] lard
50 g [2 oz] caster sugar
1 medium-sized egg

1 Heat the oven to 200°C [400°F] gas mark 6. Grease one large or two small baking trays.

2 Sift the flours and salt into a bowl. Tip the bran from the sieve into the flour. Cut the butter and lard into the dry ingredients until pieces are

Handy hints

Storing biscuits
To prevent biscuits losing their crispness and going soft, store them in an airtight tin or plastic snap-top container in a cool place. Biscuits freeze well. Pack them in plastic bags, expel air and seal them. They will keep for 6 months in the freezer, making batch-baking a practical, money saving proposition.

pea sized and evenly coated with flour.

3 Rub the fat into the flour until the mixture resembles breadcrumbs.

4 Stir in the sugar. Whisk the egg and 60 ml [4 tablespoons] water together. Make a well in the centre and pour in the egg mixture.

5 Use a fork to draw in the dry ingredients until the mixture sticks together. Knead to form a ball which is free from cracks.

6 Turn on to a lightly floured surface. Using a lightly floured rolling pin, roll out to 6 mm [¼"] thick. Dip a 5 cm [2"] cutter into flour and use to cut out the biscuits. Re-roll as necessary.

7 Bake just above centre of the oven for 15 minutes until golden brown. Leave biscuits to set for 5 minutes on the tray(s), then transfer to wire rack to cool.

Variation
● For chocolate digestives, spread the cooled biscuits with melted chocolate. You will need about 75 g [3 oz] chocolate.

Beautiful biscuits

Rich, tempting, crumbly biscuits made by the creaming method are a treat to eat, and they are easy to make, too. The method is the same one used for creaming cakes. The basic biscuit mixture can be turned into a large and colourful variety of tempting flavours, shapes and colours; piped fingers, whirls, bars, some glazed and some sandwiched together. Flavours vary from sophisticated coffee whirls, to crunchy peanut biscuits which are always a firm favourite with the family.

The word biscuit comes from the French, meaning 'twice-cooked'. Biscuits were originally twice cooked to ensure that they would be crisp, dry and last for a long time. Nowadays, the biscuits are only cooked once, as they keep well in modern airtight containers—if there are any left after greedy hands have been on them!

The big advantage of biscuits is the sheer convenience. Biscuits are right for a wide range of occasions, when you feel you need something extra—from a tea-party, to just inviting friends or neighbours round for a cup of tea or coffee. They are quick to make—valuable when time is short.

It is easy to be a good biscuit baker. Information on page 98 covers the rubbed-in method and basic techniques. Here we cover making biscuits with a more professional finish. The creaming method, which is explained on page 8, is used.

When using the creaming method to make biscuits, it is important to pay attention to detail in order to obtain good results. Given below are the main points to observe.

The way in which the ingredients are creamed is slightly different if biscuits are made instead of cakes. When a mixture is creamed for a cake, the maximum amount of air must be incorporated into the mixture, this means beating the butter and sugar very vigorously. Biscuits are not required to rise as much as cakes so beating in air is not quite so

important. This means that less effort is needed to make biscuits. For biscuits, the fat and sugar need only be softened—no more of that arm-aching beating that cooks unfortunate enough not to own an electric mixer go through when making creamed mixtures.

It is important to cook biscuits thoroughly if they are to store well. For this reason, biscuits should be cooked slowly.

BASIC INGREDIENTS

The basic ingredients for creamed biscuits are much the same as for rubbed-in biscuits (see page 99).

Flour and salt

Plain flour is used for traditional biscuits, since they are not required to rise. However, for some biscuits a raising agent is included with the plain flour, or self-raising flour is used. Use 5 ml [1 teaspoon] baking powder to every 225 g [½ lb] plain flour if not using self-raising flour.

Approximately double the amount of flour to fat and to sugar is used both for biscuits that are 'blobbed' straight out of the spoon on to the tray and for rolled-out biscuits.

As with rubbed-in biscuits, part of the flour is sometimes replaced with rice flour, cornflour or oats, and brown flour is sometimes used in combination with white. The flour is often sifted with a pinch of salt which brings out the flavour.

Fat

Butter or margarine can be used. The fat should be at room temperature to allow it to be creamed easily. If possible, take the fat out of the refrigerator at least 1 hour before use to allow it to soften. There are no hard and fast rules about the quantity of fat to flour used in this type of biscuit. Quantities depend largely on the richness required in each individual recipe. However, biscuits that are to be piped always contain a fairly high proportion of fat. This is because a softish mixture is necessary for smooth piping. If the mixture is dry, it will break up when forced out through the piping nozzle.

Flavourings

The basic creamed biscuit mixture can be flavoured in the same way as rubbed-in biscuits (see on page 99). Small or finely chopped fruit, ground or finely chopped nuts, grated orange or lemon zest all make good additions.

Coarse oatmeal, rolled oats or muesli mixture give the biscuits a crunchy texture and spices add individual flavour.

EQUIPMENT

You will need much the same equipment for creamed biscuits as for rubbed-in biscuits—a mixing bowl, scales, rolling pin, wire rack, cutters (metal or plastic), flat baking tray and a fish slice or palette knife.

You will also need a medium or large vegetable star nozzle for piping some biscuit mixtures, and a sandwich tin for baking some biscuits.

THE BASIC METHOD

The basic method for creaming biscuits can be divided into a few simple stages.

Sifting the dry ingredients

Sift the flour (and salt if using) together with spice or powdered flavouring into a bowl and set aside. Any bran left in the sieve after sifting wholewheat flour should be tipped into the sifted mixture and lightly incorporated.

Creaming fat

The softened butter is now creamed in a separate mixing bowl to make it light and to release its flavour. Cream the butter until it is soft but not light and fluffy.

Adding the sugar

As soon as the butter is soft add the sugar, all at once. Beat the sugar with the butter until it is light and fluffy and no longer feels gritty. Scrape the mixture down from the sides of the bowl from time to time so that all the sugar is smoothly blended into the butter.

Adding liquid flavourings

If you are using flavouring essences they are added at this stage. Simply beat them into the butter and sugar mixture so that the flavour is evenly distributed. Citrus zest, if used, is also added at this stage. Once again, beat well.

Adding eggs

If the recipe includes egg it is added at this stage. If using a whole egg, lightly beat it first. If using egg yolk put it directly into the mixture and beat it until it is thoroughly incorporated. Unlike creaming cakes, there is no danger of the mixture curdling because the proportion of egg to fat and sugar is so much lower.

Adding the flour

The sifted flour, and other dry ingredients, such as cocoa powder and raising agent if used, are now added to the creamed mixture. As with the initial creaming process, less care is needed in this operation than in creaming cakes. Add the flour all at once to the creamed mixture and stir in briskly until thoroughly incorporated. There is no need to fold it in, because the mixture does not need to be so light and airy.

Further additions

Once the flour has been added, further flavouring ingredients such as chopped nuts or dried fruit may be stirred in. The bulky type of flavourings should never be used for biscuits that are to be piped because their lumpy texture will stick in the piping nozzle and the mixture will refuse to come out.

Creaming with a mixer

To cut down time and effort the mixture can be creamed in a mixer. Place the butter and sugar together in a bowl and cream together using a hand-held electric whisk or table-top electric mixer. From time to time, turn off the mixer and scrape the mixture down the sides of the bowl to make sure it is all thoroughly mixed.

SHAPING THE BISCUITS

If the dough is too soft to handle chill it for 1 hour. The biscuit dough can be shaped by dropping or piping the mixture directly on to the tray, rolling the mixture out and cutting into shapes or pressing into a sandwich tin.

It is important that the biscuit mixture is well spaced on the tray before baking, because the biscuits flatten and expand during cooking and may well join together if they are placed too close to each other.

Piping

Fit a large nylon piping bag with a large nozzle (usually a vegetable star nozzle) then fill the bag with the mixture, no more than three-quarters full. Have ready a greased baking tray and pipe the mixture with a firm and steady hand into the required shapes.

Dropping

This method is used when the biscuit mixture is too soft for rolling and when you do not wish to pipe. The simplest way of making dropped biscuits is simply to let the mixture fall from a spoon on to a tray. There should be 5 cm [2"] between the little heaps of mixture to allow for spreading. For neater shapes, the mixture can be rolled into little balls. Flour your hands before doing this. Biscuit mixture formed into balls can also be forked. To do this, press lightly on the ball of mixture with the prongs of a fork. Space as above.

1 Position oven shelf above centre and heat the oven to given temperature. Grease a baking tray.

4 If using whole egg, whisk lightly then beat into the mixture. Beat yolks directly into the mixture.

OR pile the mixture into a piping bag fixed with a star nozzle and pipe on to a greased baking tray.

Rolling and cutting

If the biscuit mixture is stiff it may be rolled and cut into shapes in the same way as for rubbed-in biscuits. Roll out the dough on a lightly floured surface with a floured rolling pin, to a thickness of about 6 mm [$\frac{1}{4}$"] or as specified in the recipe.

Lightly flour your chosen cutter before firmly pressing into the dough to make biscuit shapes. Continue until you have finished all the dough, lightly kneading scraps and rolling out to make a few more at the end. Transfer the mixture to a prepared, greased baking tray with a fish slice or palette knife.

Making bars

Press the biscuit mixture into a lightly greased sandwich tin, and flatten the top with a small palette knife or the back of a spoon. This is cut into bars after it has been baked.

Toppings

If the recipe calls for it, whole or chopped nuts may be pressed on the top of the biscuits before baking.

BAKING

The oven must be preheated to the correct temperature before the biscuits are placed in it. The best shelf position is just above the centre of the oven. Temperature varies from moderate to fairly hot depending on the type of biscuit you are cooking.

After 10-20 minutes the biscuits will be done. Take them from the oven and allow them to 'rest' for 5 minutes on the baking tray to allow them to firm up. Then transfer them to a wire rack to cool. Lift them carefully with a palette knife or fish slice. Biscuit mixtures cooked in sandwich tins are allowed to cool in the tin before being cut into bars.

Step-by-step to creamed biscuits

Sift flour (plus spices or powdered flavourings if used): reserve. Beat softened butter until light.

3 Add sugar to the fat and cream it with a wooden spoon until light in colour and fluffy in texture.

OR place the fat and sugar together in a bowl and cream together with a hand-held electric whisk.

With a rubber spatula scrape the mixture down the side of the bowl and off the spoon. Beat again.

6 Stir in the sifted flour using vigorous actions until it is thoroughly incorporated.

7 Drop mixture on to tray in spoonfuls 5 cm [2"] apart. Flatten with prongs of warm, wet fork if wished.

OR roll out the mixture to about 6 mm [¼"] thick. Cut out and place on prepared tray 2.5 cm [1"] apart.

OR press mixture into a prepared, greased sandwich tin and smooth top.

8 Cook 10-20 minutes. Leave for 5 minutes to set on tray. Cut into bars if necessary. Cool on a wire rack.

GINGER NUTS

These are the traditional hard, ginger-flavoured biscuits with the 'cracked' tops. They have very good keeping qualities.

MAKES 30 BISCUITS
175 g [6 oz] plain flour
10 ml [2 teaspoons] bicarbonate of soda
10 ml [2 teaspoons] ground ginger
1.5 ml [¼ teaspoon] ground cloves
90 g [3½ oz] softened butter
75 g [3 oz] caster sugar, plus a little extra for topping
1 medium-sized egg
90 ml [6 tablespoons] molasses or black treacle

1 Sift the flour together with the rest of the dry ingredients into a bowl and set aside.

2 Cream the softened butter. Add the sugar and cream again until light and smooth.

3 Lightly beat the egg and add with the molasses to the mixture. Beat until light and fluffy.

4 Beat in the sifted dry ingredients. Cover the bowl and chill for 1 hour.

5 Position shelf just above centre and heat the oven to 180°C [350°F] gas mark 4. Grease two small or one large baking tray.

6 Use your hands to shape the mixture into balls the size of a small walnut. Roll in a little caster sugar until evenly coated.

7 Place on prepared trays at least 5 cm [2"] apart, flatten into rounds with the flat side of a knife.

8 Bake for 12-15 minutes, Leave on tray for 5 minutes then transfer to a cooling rack.

HAZELNUT BARS

If you cannot buy ground hazelnuts, grind whole nuts in an electric grinder or chop them as finely as possible. Other nuts, such as walnuts may be used instead.

MAKES 8-10 BARS
100 g [¼ lb] self-raising flour
50 g [2 oz] softened butter
100 g [¼ lb] caster sugar
1 small egg
50 g [2 oz] ground hazelnuts

1 Position the shelf just above centre and heat the oven to 180°C [350°F] gas mark 4. Grease a sandwich tin 17·5 cm [7"] square.

2 Sift the flour into a bowl and set aside.

3 Cream the softened butter. Add the sugar and cream again until light and smooth.

4 Lightly beat the egg, then add to the mixture. Stir in the flour together with the hazelnuts.

5 Press the mixture into the prepared tin. Level the top with a small palette knife.

6 Bake in the centre of the oven for 25 minutes. Allow to cool for 5 minutes then cut into bars and transfer to cooling rack.

OATY CRISPS

Porridge oats add texture and flavour to these biscuits. The oats are incorporated in an unusual way— by forming the biscuit mixture into balls and then rolling in oats to coat.

MAKES 24 BISCUITS
75 g [3 oz] plain flour
2.5 ml [½ teaspoon] salt
1.5 ml [¼ teaspoon] bicarbonate of soda
100 g [¼ lb] softened butter
50 g [2 oz] caster sugar
50 g [2 oz] porridge oats

1 Sift the first three ingredients into a bowl and set aside.

2 Cream the butter. Add the sugar and cream again. Beat the flour into the butter mixture.

3 Position a shelf just above the centre and heat the oven to 190°C [375°F] gas mark 5. Grease one large or two small baking trays.

4 Form the biscuit mixture into walnut-sized balls using floured hands. Sprinkle oats on a plate. Roll balls in oats to coat. Place on prepared trays spacing them 5 cm [2"] apart.

5 Bake for 10-15 minutes or until a light golden colour.

Variation
●For nutty oat biscuits, work in 50 g [2 oz] chopped almonds to the biscuit mixture before forming into balls.

CHOCOLATE PEANUT BISCUITS

A butterscotch flavour is given to these biscuits by the use of soft brown sugar. The mixture is studded with unsalted peanuts and baked in little rounds until crisp and golden.

MAKES ABOUT 15 BISCUITS
75 g [3 oz] self-raising flour
7.5 ml [1½ teaspoons] cocoa powder
50 g [2 oz] softened butter
65 g [2½ oz] soft brown sugar
1 small egg
100 g [¼ lb] unsalted peanuts

1 Position the shelf just above the centre and heat the oven to 180°C [350°F] gas mark 4. Grease one large or two small baking trays.

2 Sift the flour and cocoa.

3 Cream the butter. Add the sugar and cream again.

4 Lightly beat the egg then add to the mixture. Stir in the sifted flour and cocoa, then the nuts.

5 Drop teaspoonfuls on to the prepared tray(s) 5 cm [2"] apart.

6 Bake for about 15 minutes. Leave on tray for 5 minutes then transfer to a wire rack to cool.

Store your home-made biscuits in airtight tins to keep them crisp and fresh.

CHOCOLATE ORANGE FINGERS

These delicious little biscuits are rich in butter to give a smooth, soft texture for piping. Icing sugar is best for the same reason. The cooked biscuits are brushed with apricot jam and glazed with orange icing and then popped back in the oven to allow the icing to 'set'. The chocolate ends complement the orange flavour of the fingers.

MAKES 18 BISCUITS
100 g [¼ lb] plain flour
100 g [¼ lb] softened butter
25 g [1 oz] icing sugar
1 medium-sized orange

For the topping:
30 ml [2 tablespoons]
**   apricot jam**
25 g [1 oz] icing sugar
100 g [¼ lb] plain
**   chocolate**

1 Sift the flour and the 25 g [1 oz] icing sugar into a bowl and set aside.

2 Cream the softened butter in a bowl with a wooden spoon.

3 Grate the zest from the orange, squeeze and reserve the juice. Add icing sugar and orange zest to the butter and cream until light and smooth.

4 Beat in the sifted flour and icing sugar.

5 Fit a piping bag with a large star nozzle and spoon in the mixture.

6 On to the prepared baking tray(s) pipe fingers about 9 cm [3½"] long. Space them about 5 cm [2"] apart. Chill for 1 hour.

7 Position the oven shelf just above centre. Heat the oven to 160°C [325°F] gas mark 3. Grease two small or one large baking tray.

8 Bake for 15-20 minutes or until golden brown.

9 Meanwhile, place the jam in a saucepan over low heat. Sift the icing sugar into a bowl. Heat 15 ml [1 tablespoon] of orange juice to boiling point, then gradually add it to the icing sugar, stirring all the time.

10 When the biscuits are golden brown, remove them from the oven. Brush the tops with apricot jam, then immediately with orange icing. Return to the oven for 5 minutes to 'set' the icing.

11 Remove from the oven, leave on the tray for 5 minutes then transfer to a wire rack and leave until cold.

12 Melt the chocolate in a bowl over a pan of hot water on a low heat.

13 Remove the bowl of melted chocolate from the heat and dip the ends of each biscuit into it.

14 Allow to set on a wire rack.

CHOCOLATE AND WALNUT DROPS

These crunchy drop biscuits have a deliciously rich glaze of buttery chocolate, which is topped by walnut.

MAKES 24 BISCUITS
175 g [6 oz] plain flour
15 ml [1 tablespoon] cocoa
200 g [7 oz] softened butter
75 g [3 oz] caster sugar
1.5 ml [¼ teaspoon] vanilla
**   extract**
100 g [¼ lb] cornflakes

For the topping:
100 g [¼ lb] plain chocolate
7 g [¼ oz] butter
about 24 walnut halves

1 Sift the flour and cocoa powder into a bowl and set aside.

2 Cream the butter. Add the sugar and vanilla extract and cream again until light and smooth.

3 Beat in the flour and cocoa, then add the cornflakes and beat again until everything is thoroughly mixed.

4 Position the shelf just above centre and heat the oven to 180°C [350°F] gas mark 4. Grease two small or one large baking tray.

5 Drop the mixture in small spoonfuls on to the prepared tray, leaving 5 cm [2"] space between them.

6 Bake for 15-20 minutes. Leave on tray for 5 minutes and then transfer to a wire rack. Leave until cold.

7 Melt the chocolate in a bowl over a pan of hot water on a low heat. Away from the heat, stir in the butter.

8 Put a small spoonful of chocolate over the top of each biscuit and immediately top with a walnut half, pressing it in lightly to secure.

CURRANT BISCUITS

This is a fairly firm biscuit mixture enriched with eggs, studded with raisins and rolled out and cut into shapes. Each biscuit is brushed with whisked egg white and dusted with sugar before baking to give a crunchy glazed top and to prevent the biscuit softening.

MAKES 30 BISCUITS
225 g [½ lb] plain flour
salt
150 g [5 oz] softened butter
  or margarine
1 lemon
100 g [¼ lb] caster sugar
2 medium-sized eggs
50 g [2 oz] currants
15 g [½ oz] caster sugar

1 Sift the flour and salt and reserve. Put the butter in a mixing bowl and cream with a wooden spoon.

2 Grate the zest from the lemon. Add it and 100 g [¼ lb] sugar to the butter and cream lightly.

3 Separate the eggs, keeping one egg white aside for use later. Beat the yolks a little at a time into the creamed mixture.

4 Beat the flour all at once into the mixture. Stir in the currants. The mixture should be of a stiff consistency. If soft, refrigerate for one hour.

5 Position shelf just above centre and heat the oven to 190°C [375°F] gas mark 5. Grease two small or one large baking tray.

6 Turn the mixture out on to a lightly floured board and roll out to 6 mm [¼"] thick.

7 Using a floured 5 cm [2"] biscuit cutter, cut out the biscuits, re-rolling as necessary. Transfer to baking tray.

8 Whisk the reserved egg white until it stands in soft peaks.

9 Using a pastry brush, brush each biscuit with the egg white, then sprinkle with remaining sugar.

10 Bake for about 15 minutes or until golden brown. Leave on tray to set for about 5 minutes then transfer to a wire rack to cool.

COFFEE WHIRLS

A rich buttery mixture is piped into attractive rosette shapes and sandwiched together with a coffee-flavoured filling to make these coffee whirls. The sophisticated flavour is much appreciated by adults.

MAKES 24 WHIRLS
225 g [8 oz] butter or margarine
50 g [2 oz] icing sugar
15 ml [1 tablespoon] coffee
  essence
175 g [6 oz] plain flour
50 g [2 oz] cornflour

For the filling:
75 g [3 oz] butter
175 g [6 oz] icing sugar
15 ml [1 tablespoon] milk
5 ml [1 teaspoon] coffee essence

1 Cream the butter until softened. Add the icing sugar and cream until well blended.

2 Beat in the coffee essence. Sift the cornflour and flour together.

3 Heat the oven to 190°C [375°F] gas mark 5. Lightly grease two baking trays.

4 Gradually fold the cornflour and flour mixture into the butter and sugar mixture.

5 Put the mixture into a piping bag fitted with a 12 mm [½"] star nozzle.

6 Pipe the mixture into rounds on to the greased baking tray. Bake for 10–15 minutes.

7 Leave for 5 minutes then cool on a wire tray. Cream butter, icing sugar, milk and coffee essence together.

8 Sandwich the biscuits with the coffee filling.

Melt-in-the-mouth biscuits

Crispy brandy snaps, luscious chocolate-coated Florentines, chewy flapjacks—in fact all the delights of the cake shop window—can appear on your tea table when you know how to make biscuits by the melting method.

Made in a similar way to melting-method cakes (see the details on page 92), melting-method biscuits offer some of the best of traditional baking. Sophisticated Florentines and brandy snaps, economical gingersnaps and flapjacks are all made by this method so there is lots of scope for the keen baker.

One of the joys of biscuits made by this method is that they are quick and reasonably foolproof. There is no creaming or rubbing in to worry about and some of the biscuits can even be left uncooked—as you will see from the short section on no-cook biscuits given at the end of this course. What kind of biscuits can you make? Using the melting-method, you can make a mixture which can be rolled into balls, pressed into a tin and cut into fingers after cooking, simply dropped on to a baking tray in rough heaps or, in the case of brandy snaps, rolled after cooking to make a shell, which can be filled with cream and served either alone, or with fruit, or used as a cake decoration (see page 46).

INGREDIENTS

There are so many different types and textures of biscuit made by the melting method, that it is impossible to give hard and fast rules on the balance of ingredients. You will find here a guide on what kind of ingredients to use. For amounts, always follow recipes carefully as proportions do vary.

Dry ingredients
Flour

The flour for melting-method biscuits is usually self-raising as this gives the biscuits a light, crisp texture. You may find some recipes however where plain flour and baking powder or bicarbonate of soda are used instead.

Cereals

Rolled oats are sometimes used to replace all or part of the flour in cooked melting-method biscuits. Be sure you get rolled oats and not oatmeal, the results will not be at all the same. Breakfast cereals are sometimes included for texture.

Fat

The fat in melting-method biscuits is always melted. As you might expect, butter gives the best flavour but margarine makes an acceptable substitute. Don't use soft margarine—it will not melt.

Sweetener

The usual sweeteners for biscuits made by this method are honey, golden syrup or treacle. All of these combine easily with the melted fat and dry ingredients. Sugar if used can be caster, granulated, brown or Demerara.

Eggs

Eggs are very rarely used in melting-method biscuits and there is unlikely to be more than one egg in a recipe. An example of how eggs can be used for this method is shown in the recipe for Jinny's gingersnaps.

Flavourings

Spices are a popular flavouring for melting-method biscuits. Ground ginger, nutmeg and cinnamon are the most commonly used.
Chocolate is sometimes used for cooked melting-method biscuits but is a more common feature in the uncooked kind (see page 123). The best kind of chocolate to use is the plain dessert variety, rather than cooking chocolate, as it gives a better flavour.
Fruit and nuts: chopped glacé fruit and chopped nuts (such as almonds, hazelnuts, walnuts or unsalted peanuts) are sometimes mixed into biscuits to give a crunchy texture. The recipe for Florentines shows how this is done. Whole nuts or cherries are sometimes used to top biscuits. Desiccated coconut either plain or toasted is a more unusual addition. Chopped preserved dates are a traditional choice for a richly flavoured biscuit.

EQUIPMENT

To make melting-method biscuits, you will need exactly the same equip-

ment as described for melting-method cakes (see the details on page 92).

Baking tins

You will need baking sheets or trays for your biscuits. Pay particular attention to preparing them correctly as melting-method biscuits do tend to stick if they are baked on unprepared tins.

Preparing the tins: for the plainer mixtures, the tins need only be lightly brushed with melted fat or oil. Take care not to over-brush the tin with fat or oil or the biscuits will 'fry' rather than bake.

Biscuits with a high proportion of fat and sugary ingredients are best baked on tins with a non-stick coating. Failing this, line the tins with greased greaseproof paper as you would if you were lining a swiss roll tin.

MAKING THE BISCUITS

Making the biscuits can be divided into four easy-to-follow stages.

Sifting dry ingredients

Sift the dry, fine ingredients, such as flour, spices, cocoa powder, on to a sheet of greaseproof paper. This will make the task of adding the dry ingredients to the pan of melted ingredients easier. Chop nuts or glacé fruit, measure oats or other cereal additions and set aside.

Melting fat and sweetener

So that the fat will melt quickly, cut it into small pieces. If you are using chocolate break it into squares or chop into rough pieces. Place fat, chocolate if used, and the sweetener in a heavy-based pan big enough to hold the dry ingredients and stir continuously over low heat until the ingredients have just melted and blended. Don't let the mixture boil or you will end up with toffee! Remove from heat as soon as the mixture has melted.

If an egg is being used, beat it and combine quickly with the melted fat and sweetener. Do not add the egg to the pan whole or the white will start to set before the egg has been fully incorporated.

Adding dry ingredients

The next step is to incorporate the dry ingredients with the melted fat and sweetener. Add all the dry ingredients to the pan at once then

Step-by-step to

1 For bar biscuits, press the mixture into a baking tray. Cut into bars after cooking while the mixture is still soft.

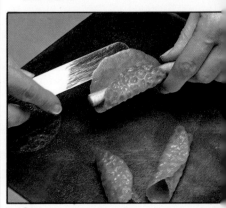

5 Slip spoon handle under edge. Roll up quickly and withdraw spoon. If snaps become too hard before you have rolled them all, reheat for 2–3 minutes.

gently stir into the melted mixture until smoothly blended.

Shaping

There are three ways to shape the mixture.

Pressing into a tin

For biscuits to be cut into bars after cooking, the mixture is pressed or poured into a baking tray. The only point to make sure of here is that the mixture is an even thickness in the tin. The mixture must be cut into bars soon after cooking or it will set too hard for cutting.

Making into balls

Some melting-method biscuit mixtures can be formed into walnut-sized balls. During cooking, these spread out to make a flattish biscuit about 5 cm [2"] diameter. Before you start forming the balls, flour your hands. This will prevent sticking. If the mixture is very soft, chill it in the

shaping melting-method biscuits

2 For round biscuits, form mixture into walnut-sized balls using floured hands. Space 2.5–3.75 cm [1–1½"] apart on baking sheet.

3 For dropped biscuits, drop the mixture on to baking sheets 5 ml [1 teaspoon] at a time. Space 7.5–10 cm [3–4"] apart.

4 To roll brandy snaps, brush the handle of a wooden spoon with oil. Ease up edge of cooked, but still soft, snap using a palette knife.

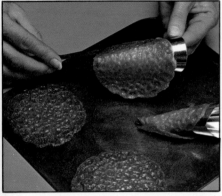

OR wrap the snaps around an oiled cream horn mould to make a cornet to fill with fruit and cream or ice-cream.

OR make baskets to hold ice-cream, fresh fruit or other cold desserts, by shaping around a well-oiled ramekin dish or an oiled wineglass.

OR for a large basket, make an extra large snap and mould around an oiled sandwich cake tin. Fill the brandy snap with fruit and ice-cream for a delicious dessert.

refrigerator for 1 hour to make it workable. Try to make all the balls roughly the same size or the smaller biscuits will be baked before the larger ones. Space the balls 3.75 cm [1½"] apart to allow for spreading.

Dropped biscuits
A very soft mixture is always dropped on to the baking sheets, 5 ml [1 teaspoon] of mixture is sufficient for each biscuit. Use another teaspoon to push the mixture off the measuring spoon on to the tray. Dropped mixture spreads quite a lot so space your biscuits 7.5–10 cm [3–4"] apart to allow for this.

BAKING
Biscuits are usually baked in a moderate oven but sometimes a lower temperature is used. The oven should have reached the correct temperature before you put the bis-

cuits in. Bake the biscuits on the centre shelf. If you have two sheets, place one on the shelf below and change positions half way through cooking so that both sets of biscuits are ready at the same time. Cooking times vary but are usually between 10 and 35 minutes.

SHAPING AFTER BAKING
Brandy snap mixture is always shaped after baking, either into the traditional cylinder shape or into one of the more enterprising variations shown in step-by-step to shaping. After cooking, the mixture is very thin and pliable. It hardens quickly though, so unless you want to keep putting the snaps back into the oven to soften you will have to be fairly speedy at shaping. Traditionally, the snaps are rolled around an oiled wooden spoon handle to make a

cigar shape which can be filled with cream or chopped fruit. You can, however, wrap the cooked brandy snap around oiled cream horn moulds to make cornets, or around ramekins or wineglasses to make baskets for cold desserts.

COOLING
Biscuits made by the melting method will still be slightly soft when they come out of the oven. They will harden however, in the cooler air of your kitchen. Leave on the baking sheet for 2 minutes then when beginning to firm, transfer to cooling racks with a palette knife or fish slice.

STORAGE
Store your biscuits in an airtight tin. Biscuits made by the melting method will keep for about 10 days.

JINNY'S GINGERSNAPS

These ginger biscuits are paler in colour and not quite as rock hard as gingernuts. Although the mixture is quite stiff, it is dropped on to the tins.

MAKES 24 BISCUITS
225 g [½ lb] self-raising flour
5 ml [1 teaspoon] ground ginger
75 g [3 oz] butter or margarine
100 g [¼ lb] caster sugar
100 g [¼ lb] golden syrup
1 large egg

1 Sift flour and ginger on to a piece of greaseproof paper. Heat the oven to 180°C [350°F] gas mark 4. Lightly oil two baking sheets.

2 Cut butter or margarine into small pieces and place in a heavy-based pan with the sugar and syrup. Stir over low heat until all ingredients have melted and combined. Remove from heat. Beat the egg.

3 Mix the dry ingredients and egg alternately into the melted fat and sweetener. Mix until well blended.

4 Drop in heaps on to baking sheets, 5 ml [1 teaspoon] at a time. Space at least 7.5 cm [3"] apart.

5 Bake in the centre of the oven for 15 minutes until golden. Leave for 2 minutes to firm. Remove from trays using a palette knife or fish slice and cool on wire trays.

BURNT BUTTER BISCUITS

Butter is always used for these biscuits. Needless to say, it is not literally burnt but simply heated until pale golden in colour. This gives the biscuits a delicious and distinctive flavour. The butter is not melted with the sugar as this would cause burning.

MAKES 30 BISCUITS
100 g [¼ lb] butter
100 g [¼ lb] caster sugar
1 large egg
175 g [6 oz] self-raising flour
50 g [2 oz] split almonds

1. Heat the oven to 180°C [350°F] gas mark 4. Sift the flour on to a sheet of greaseproof paper. Lightly oil or grease 2 baking sheets.

2. Cut the butter into small pieces. Place in a heavy-based saucepan over low heat.

3. Allow the butter to melt until pale golden in colour, not dark brown and burnt.

4. Remove from heat, stir in the sugar. Allow to cool slightly.

5. Beat the egg. Beat into the butter and sugar mixture. Gradually beat in sifted flour.

6. Drop in teaspoonfuls on to baking trays. Space about 7.5 cm [3"] apart on baking trays. Top each drop with an almond.

7. Bake in the centre of the oven for 12-15 minutes until golden. Allow to firm for 2 minutes then transfer to cooling racks.

ANZAC BISCUITS

These biscuits are a well-established family favourite in New Zealand. They are baked at a fairly low oven temperature.

MAKES 24 BISCUITS
50 g [2 oz] plain flour
50 g [2 oz] rolled oats
50 g [2 oz] desiccated coconut
100 g [¼ lb] caster sugar
75 g [3 oz] butter
15 ml [1 tablespoon] golden syrup
2.5 ml [½ teaspoon] bicarbonate of soda

1. Heat the oven to 150°C [300°F] gas mark 2. Lightly oil or grease 2 baking trays. Sift flour, combine with other dry ingredients except bicarbonate of soda and set aside.

2. Cut the butter into small pieces. Place with syrup in a heavy-based saucepan. Melt together, stirring. Remove from heat.

3. Combine bicarbonate of soda with 15 ml [1 tablespoon] boiling water. Blend with syrup and butter.

Shown from left to right are: Jinny's gingersnaps, muesli biscuits, Anzac biscuits and burnt butter biscuits.

4. Gradually mix in dry ingredients. Drop mixture on to baking trays 5 ml [1 teaspoon] at a time, spacing 7.5 cm [3"] apart.

5. Bake in the centre of the oven for 20 minutes. Cool slightly then transfer to wire trays.

MUESLI BISCUITS

Any commercial muesli can be used to make these biscuits or if you make your own, you can use that. The biscuits are thin and crisp—ideal for a mid-morning snack. For these biscuits, sugar is mixed with the other dry ingredients instead of being melted.

MAKES 24 BISCUITS
100 g [¼ lb] caster sugar
50 g [2 oz] plain flour
75 g [3 oz] muesli
50 g [2 oz] butter or margarine
7.5 ml [½ tablespoon] golden syrup
2.5 ml [½ teaspoon] bicarbonate of soda

1. Heat the oven to 150°C [300°F] gas mark 2. Sift sugar and flour on to a sheet of greaseproof paper. Oil two baking sheets.

2. Cut butter or margarine into small pieces. Place in a heavy-based pan with the syrup over low heat and melt, stirring. Remove from heat.

3. Mix the bicarbonate of soda with 22.5 ml [1½ tablespoons] boiling water. Stir into syrup and butter mixture.

4. Stir dry ingredients into this mixture. Drop mixture on to prepared trays 5 ml [1 teaspoon] at a time, spacing at least 3.75 cm [1½"] apart.

5. Bake for 20 minutes. Leave for 2 minutes then transfer to cooling trays using a palette knife or fish slice.

FLAPJACKS

These chewy, golden biscuits are traditionally baked in one piece, making them exceptionally easy to prepare. Remember to cut them into the required shapes once the mixture is baked but still warm.

Whole oats, one of the two cereals used in this recipe, may sometimes be bought under the name of 'Jumbo' oats.

MAKES 10–12 BISCUITS
75 g [3 oz] butter or margarine
50 g [2 oz] golden syrup
100 g [4 oz] Demerara sugar
75 g [3 oz] whole oats
75 g [3 oz] porridge oats

1 Heat oven to 180°C [350°F] gas mark 4. Lightly brush a 20 cm [8"] square tin with melted fat or oil.

2 Cut the fat into small pieces and place in a heavy-based saucepan. Add the golden syrup and sugar and place saucepan over a low heat.

3 Mix the ingredients together, then stir, continuously, with a wooden spoon until the fat has melted and the sugar has just dissolved.

4 Remove the pan from the heat and stir in the whole and porridge oats.

Flapjacks and fruity lemon fingers are both cut up after cooking.

Mix together until the mixture is evenly combined.

5 Turn the mixture into the prepared tin and smooth the surface flat with the back of a metal spoon.

6 Bake in the centre of the oven for 20 minutes, until the surface is golden brown.

7 Place the tin on a wooden board and, using a sharp knife, cut the biscuit into 10–12 wedge shapes. Leave the biscuits in the tin until completely cold before removing.

Variations
● For traditional flapjacks, omit whole oats and use all porridge oats.
● For extra crunchy flapjack biscuits omit porridge oats and use all whole oats.
● For honey-flavoured flapjacks, omit the golden syrup and use the same quantity of clear honey.
● For extra special munchie-type flapjacks, use only 150g [5 oz] whole or porridge oats and 25 g [1 oz] of your favourite chopped nuts. Almonds, brazil nuts and hazelnuts will all do.

FRUITY LEMON FINGERS

These bar biscuits are unusual and attractive because they are iced. It is best to leave icing until about 30 minutes before the biscuits are to be served. This gives the icing time to set but won't make the biscuits soggy as icing too far in advance would. This mixture does not set hard so there is no need to cut into fingers before cooling.

MAKES ABOUT 18 FINGERS
225 g [½ lb] self-raising flour
1 large egg
pinch of salt
100 g [¼ lb] butter or margarine
100 g [¼ lb] caster sugar
150 g [5 oz] mixed fruit

For the icing:
15 g [½ oz] butter
15 ml [1 tablespoon] lemon juice
175 g [6 oz] icing sugar
5 ml [1 teaspoon] grated lemon zest
75 g [3 oz] flaked almonds

1 Heat the oven to 180°C [350°F] gas mark 4. Lightly oil or grease a slab cake tin measuring 22.5 × 27.5 cm [9 × 11"].

2 Sift the flour and salt on to a sheet of greaseproof paper and set aside.

3 Beat the egg. Cut the butter into small pieces. Place in a heavy-based pan over low heat. Melt

gently. Stir in the sugar and remove from the heat.

4 Stir in beaten egg, flour and mixed
fruit alternately. Stir until well
blended.

5 Spread mixture into the prepared
tin. Bake in the centre of the oven
for 20 minutes. Allow to cool
slightly then turn out on to a
cooling rack.

6 To make the icing, place the butter
with 15 ml [1 tablespoon] boiling
water in a heavy based pan over
low heat. Remove from heat when
butter has melted.

7 Add lemon juice and zest. Sift the
icing sugar and add gradually,
mixing to a smooth icing.

8 Pour over the cooked biscuit mixture. Smooth with a palette knife.
Sprinkle with almonds.

9 Cut into fingers before serving.

BRANDY SNAPS

*These biscuits are traditionally rol-
led up for serving. They can be filled
with whipped cream or, for a real
summer treat, fill with fresh strawberries or raspberries then pipe a blob of
cream at each end.*

MAKES 12
50 g [2 oz] plain flour
2.5 ml [½ teaspoon] ground
ginger
grated zest of ½ lemon
50 g [2 oz] golden syrup
50 g [2 oz] caster sugar
50 g [2 oz] butter or
margarine
5 ml [1 teaspoon] brandy

For the filling:
275 ml [½ pt] thick cream

1 Heat the oven to 180°C [350°F] gas
mark 4. Sift the flour and spice on
to a sheet of greaseproof paper.
Add lemon zest. Line two baking
sheets with greased greaseproof
paper.

2 Place syrup, caster sugar, butter
and brandy in a heavy-based
saucepan over low heat.

3 Stir until melted and blended.
Remove from heat and stir in dry
ingredients.

4 Drop mixture on to prepared trays
5 ml [1 teaspoon] at a time. Space
at least 10 cm [4"] apart. Bake for 8
minutes.

5 Shape the mixture by rolling
around the oiled handle of a wood-

en spoon or in any of the other ways shown in step-by-step to shaping melting-method biscuits.

6 Whip the cream and fill the biscuits using a star nozzle or fill as desired.

Variations

●For fruity snaps, omit ground ginger and add 25 g [1 oz] chopped glacé fruit.

●For nutty snaps, omit ground ginger and add 25 g [1 oz] nibbed almonds.

FLORENTINES

These special occasion biscuits are well worth the extra effort needed in their preparation. They look and taste so special, they are ideal to wrap in a decorative box and give as a present, or to serve with coffee.

MAKES 18-20 BISCUITS
75 g [3 oz] golden syrup
75 g [3 oz] butter
30 ml [2 tablespoons] plain flour
25 g [1 oz] sultanas
50 g [2 oz] glacé cherries, chopped
75 g [3 oz] flaked almonds
5 ml [1 teaspoon] lemon juice
100 g [4 oz] plain dark chocolate

1 Heat oven to 180°C [350°F] gas mark 4. Brush two baking sheets with melted fat or oil and line with greased greaseproof paper.

2 Cut the butter into small pieces and place in a heavy-based saucepan with the syrup. Place over a low heat and stir with a wooden spoon until the butter has melted.

3 Remove the pan from the heat and allow to cool slightly. Sift the flour and add to the saucepan. Stir the flour into the melted mixture with a metal spoon.

4 Add the sultanas, cherries, flaked almonds and lemon juice and stir with a metal spoon until just combined.

5 Using a teaspoon, drop heaps of the mixture on to the prepared baking sheets leaving approximately 10 cm [4"] between each heap of mixture.

6 Bake in the centre of the oven for 15 minutes. Allow the cooked biscuits to cool completely on the baking sheets.

7 When completely cold, carefully peel the biscuits from the sheets and place on a wire rack.

8 Melt the chocolate in a bowl over hot water.

9 Allow the chocolate to cool slightly so that it thickens.

10 Using a palette knife, spread the flat underside of each biscuit with the melted chocolate to completely cover.

11 Place the biscuits, chocolate side up on a wire rack. When all the biscuits are coated with the chocolate and just on the point of setting, mark the chocolate into wavy lines with the prongs of a fork. Allow to set.

NO-COOK BISCUITS

Using a method similar to the melting method, you can make biscuits which need no baking. Refrigerator biscuits, as they are sometimes called, are made when dry ingredients, such as crushed biscuits, nuts, fruit or cereals, are stirred into a melted ingredient such as chocolate or golden syrup which will set on cooling. A chocolate refrigerator cake is a good example, made with crushed biscuits.

The easiest and best known way of using this method is to mix breakfast cereal with melted chocolate then drop heaps of the mixture into paper cake cases. There are however several different types of biscuit which you can make by this method, as you will see from the recipes given here. Always make sure the biscuits are firmly set before serving and that there is sufficient melted ingredient to bind the dry ingredients together well.

Chocolate bubbles.

CHOCOLATE BUBBLES

To give these biscuits a good flavour, the coconut is lightly toasted. To do this, spread the coconut out on a piece of greaseproof paper and brown under the grill for about 2 minutes.

MAKES 12 FINGERS
225 g [½ lb] plain dark chocolate
50 g [2 oz] butter or margarine
15 ml [1 tablespoon] clear honey
25 g [1 oz] desiccated coconut, browned
50 g [2 oz] puffed rice

1 Break the chocolate into pieces and place in heavy-based saucepan. Add the butter or margarine and the honey. Melt over gentle heat, stirring.

2 Off the heat fold in the coconut and puffed rice and stir until evenly coated.

3 Press the mixture into a shallow 17.5 cm [7"] square tin and level the top. Leave to set.

4 Cut the set mixture into 12 fingers using a sharp knife.

CHOCOLATE MUNCHIES

Simple to make, these biscuits are an established favourite with children. If wished, cornflakes may be used in place of puffed rice.

MAKES 10 BISCUITS
50 g [2 oz] butter or margarine
30 ml [2 tablespoons] clear honey
50 g [2 oz] caster sugar
30 ml [2 tablespoons] cocoa powder
25 g [1 oz] puffed rice

1 Cut the fat into small pieces and place in a heavy-based saucepan with the honey and sugar.

2 Place the saucepan over a low heat and stir continuously with a wooden spoon until the fat has melted and the sugar has just dissolved.

3 Remove the saucepan from the heat and place on a wooden board. Sprinkle in the cocoa powder and stir until well blended.

4 Using a metal spoon, carefully stir in the puffed rice until evenly coated with the mixture.

5 Divide the mixture between 10 small paper cases. Chill until firmly set.

Variations
● For apricot munchies, add 15 ml [1 tablespoon] dried, chopped apricots with the cereal.
● Syrup can be used in place of the honey but the biscuits will not be as firm.
● Raisin munchies are always a favourite with the children and can be easily made by adding 15 ml [1 tablespoon] of raisins (chopped if large) with the cereal.
● For a more sophisticated taste, simply add 15 ml [1 tablespoon] chopped walnuts with the cereal.

short-time yeast breads
Bread winners

Few things can compare with the inviting aroma of freshly baked bread filling the house. Crusty topped loaves and rolls, all with that unique home-baked flavour, are easy to achieve. The method given here is quicker than the traditional one and will put a loaf on the table in under 2 hours.

Bread making is undoubtedly an art but, contrary to some opinions, it is an art that can easily be mastered, when you understand the role of each of the ingredients. The basic bread making rules will soon become a matter of simple commonsense. Once you have learnt a few bread making knacks you will be well on your way.

Making and baking your own weekly supply of bread is one of the most enjoyable and relaxing types of baking. It is fast gaining popularity because of the superior qualities of home-made loaves.

Bread making has an old and fascinating history dating back as far as 2000 BC, when bread was so highly prized it was used as a form of money. The Romans introduced wheat for bread making and the grinding processes which milled raw wheat into an early form of flour. They also discovered that ground flour could be sifted to produce variations such as wholemeal, bran and white flour. The Romans also experimented by adding grapes and honey to bread, producing tea-bread and fruit loaves of a type which are still very popular today.

Bread-making techniques have

progressively become more sophisticated. The advent of the sliced loaf, sold by the large bakeries, meant a decline in the popularity of baking bread at home. Now, however, interest in home bread making is ever increasing.

SHORT-TIME BREAD MAKING

The common objection when bread making is discussed is the long time needed to make it. However, the short-time method described here does much to overcome this problem. The technique is a reminder of the new bread-making methods that are constantly under development.

When the short-time method is used for baking bread, a batch of bread can be ready to eat in under $1\frac{3}{4}$ hours. The magic ingredient which makes this possible is called ascorbic acid, also known as vitamin C.

Small quantities of ascorbic acid, added in tablet form, speed up the fermenting and rising processes by acting as a catalyst. These rising processes are essential to a good yeast bread, but they can easily prove tediously lengthy for busy cooks when the traditional methods are employed.

FLOURS

The flour you choose for bread will be the one that gives you the type of loaf you most enjoy. However, there are certain flours that make bread making easier; these give better results too.

Broadly speaking, flours are defined by something called the rate of extraction. This means the percentage of the whole grain left in the flour after it has been milled. The name of the flour is a guide to the amount of whole grain it contains.

Wholemeal flours, as the name suggests, contain the whole of the cleaned wheat grain, nothing added or taken away.

Wheatmeal flours contain between 80–90 per cent of the original cleaned wheat grain. Merely by looking at the colour, you can see that brown wheatmeal flours contain some of the

Add variety to baking day and use a new flour for a change. The flours shown here are, in descending order, strong white, wholemeal, wheatmeal, stone-ground wheatmeal and rye.

bran and germ.

Wholemeal and brown flours are available in a variety of textures: coarse, medium and fine ground. The texture is determined by the amount of bran or germ they contain. The more bran there is in a flour, the darker in colour it will be. A wholemeal flour that is sold as 'coarse' will contain all the bran and germ in the wheat grain.

White flours usually contain around 70–72 per cent of the cleaned wheat grain. The milling process removes much of the bran and germ and this gives the flour its white colour.

The extraction rate of white flour is flexible. There are fine white flours which contain between 40–50 per cent of the whole grain.

Flours to choose

White: for best results in bread making, choose a strong plain flour—sometimes called 'bread flour' by bakers. This strong flour will absorb more liquid than a soft flour. A dough made with a strong flour will develop quickly into a firm elastic dough when it is kneaded and therefore gives a larger volume and lighter texture to the baked bread.

Wholemeal: bread made with a wholemeal flour will have a good nutty flavour and a close texture. If you are not fond of a close-textured bread, but like the flavour and colour that a wholemeal flour gives, then wholemeal and strong plain flour can be mixed together. When strong plain flour is included in wholemeal bread, usually as half the weight of flour, you will have the flavour of the wholemeal and the lighter texture of plain flour dough.

Soft flour is a very unsatisfactory choice when bread making—all self-raising flours come into this category. They are soft because the quantity of raising agent in them is not sufficient to raise a dough. Soft flours absorb less liquid, giving a smaller volume and a shorter texture to the baked bread—these are all qualities not wanted in bread making.

Speciality flours

Brown flours may be either wholemeal or wheatmeal flours. You can buy them coarsely or finely ground. Different types vary in flavour and strength.

Stone-ground flours are usually more expensive to buy. They are available mainly from health food and vegetarian shops. They tend to be more expensive because the process of grinding the grain is a slow one and is done by hand nowadays, between two stones whereas ordinary flours are ground between metal rollers.

Bakers' flours: small quantities of flours are also available for making speciality bread. These mixtures are usually only available from the baker, but nowadays some health food and vegetarian shops are selling flour mixes that contain varying amounts of bran, wheat germ, soya flour and malt flour. In addition to these flours, some mixes contain cereals such as rye and barley.

Rye and barley: before yeast was introduced as the raising agent, rye and barley were integral ingredients of bread. Now rye and barley are seldom used, because they inhibit the rise induced by yeast. Used in large amounts, rye or barley produces an overpowering flavour and a heavy texture. Therefore, they must be used in small quantities together with another flour.

Gluten and how it works

When you are bread making, the most important element of flour is the gluten. This is formed when the protein reacts with water, and it gives the dough its elasticity.

Gluten forms the structure of the bread, stretching to contain the air bubbles as these expand and forming the walls of the bubbles. The elastic properties of the gluten are therefore most important for a good rise in bread making. The gluten holds the shape of the bread until the temperature in the oven sets it.

There is a larger quantity of gluten in a strong flour than in a soft one. The strong flour will therefore absorb more water and this, in turn, means that strong flour will make more dough than the same weight of soft flour.

Additions affecting the gluten

Other elements added to the flour have the effect of either softening or strengthening the gluten.

Cereals such as bran and wheatgerm, which you may want to include for flavour, will inhibit the stretching qualities of the gluten. They tend to soften it and limit its rising abilities. This is why bread made from these cereals tends to be unleavened. When making leavened (risen) bread which include bran or wheatgerm,

the quantity of cereal added must be small.

The addition of sugar to the dough will have a softening effect on the gluten. The sugar must, however, be included to feed the yeast.

Gluten is strengthened by the addition of salt. If you forget to add the salt, you will get a very sticky dough that is extremely difficult to handle. If short-time bread is being made, and ascorbic acid is being included, the latter also strengthens the gluten.

Strengthening the gluten

More than anything else, handling gluten will strengthen it. This handling is called kneading. Bread is kneaded to make it more elastic and thus ensuring a good rise. With kneading, the gluten structure in the dough becomes stronger. This kneading process offsets the softening effect of any ingredient.

YEAST

Yeast is the raising agent that makes the bread rise. It comes in two forms, fresh and dried—each with its loyal advocates. Baker's yeast must not be confused with brewer's or tonic yeast, neither of which can be used for bread.

Because yeast is a living plant, it needs food and comfort in which to live and carry out its 'rising' duties. As the yeast grows, it gives off carbon dioxide and it is this gas within the dough that raises it. As the gas expands, the elastic cell walls of the gluten in the flour stretch to form the risen structure. The food that the yeast needs to do this job must be supplied as another ingredient in the bread recipe. The comfort is supplied in the form of a warm temperature.

Fresh yeast

Fresh yeast is by far the easiest to use but not always the easiest to purchase. Because it is perishable, and there is not a colossal demand for it, it is only available from bakers and some health food stores or supermarkets.

Choosing fresh yeast: fresh yeast is perishable, so it is essential that it is 100 per cent fresh when you buy it. Purchase it, therefore, from somewhere that has a fast turnover to ensure fresh stock. Usually sold by the 25 g [1 oz] weight, fresh yeast can be recognized by the following characteristics. It must be creamy or

putty coloured, without signs of browning around the edges where it may have dried out. It should also be cool to the touch. When crumbled between the fingers, it should be easily breakable, while it should have a slightly pungent smell. Avoid yeast that is streaked with brown or dark yellow, or any that is sticky to the touch or smells unpleasant.

To store fresh yeast, wrap it in 25 g [1 oz] portions in foil or keep it in a screw-top jar in the refrigerator for up to 4 days. It will store, wrapped in foil, in the ice compartment of a refrigerator for up to 4 months and in a deep freezer for up to one year.

Dried yeast

Dried yeast is more readily available because it stores well. It looks like millet seed and is usually sold in small packets, drums or tins. It has the same raising properties as a fresh yeast, but it is inert because it has been dehydrated. Dried yeast is available from most large supermarkets, chemists and health food stores. Like fresh yeast, it should not be confused with a tonic or brewer's yeast which has no raising power.

Using dried yeast: dried yeast must be reactivated for use, and this is achieved by mixing it with a liquid. Add the yeast slowly to at least four times its own weight of water. Use a proportion of the liquid given in the recipe. If you wish to use dried yeast for short-time bread use the entire quantity of liquid specified in the recipe. The liquid must be at about blood heat. Leave the yeast in a warm, draught-free place to react for about 10–15 minutes. It will become frothy when ready. Stir lightly and use.

In traditional bread making, (long-rise bread), a very small amount of sugar is added to the water before putting in the dried yeast. If dried yeast is to be used for short-time bread, however, the sugar is not included with the liquid, but is added with the dry ingredients, as described on the next page.

Dried yeast is twice as strong as fresh yeast. Remember, therefore, that if fresh yeast is given in a recipe, and you propose to use dried yeast, you only need half the given amount.

Storing: stored properly on a cool, dry shelf, dried yeast will keep in good condition for at least six months. If you do not bake your own bread regularly and it is uneconomical to buy larger quantities, buy the packets which are sold in 25 g [1 oz] and 50 g [2 oz] sizes. If using dried yeast from a drum or tin, make sure that, after you have removed some, there is no air space between the lid and the yeast. As you use the yeast, transfer it to a smaller tin or screw-top jar. If you do not do this, the dried yeast will gradually lose some of its potency and its valuable rising qualities will be lost.

For short-time bread: it is inadvisable to use dried yeast for short-time bread. This is not because dried yeast does not work with the ascorbic acid—you will get a successful loaf using dried yeast, if you want to experiment with this method. It is simply a question of time. The great advantage of the short-time method is that it cuts down baking time; if you then have to wait for the yeast to reactivate, this will increase your baking time again.

Quantities to use

For short-time dough, use 50 g [2 oz] fresh yeast (or 25 g [1 oz] dried yeast) with 1.4 kg [3 lb] white flour. Wholemeal flour is heavier and needs double the amount of yeast to raise the same amount of flour. As small amounts of yeast are difficult to measure, the quantity is not proportionately reduced below half the amounts. You may find it easier to measure small amounts of dried yeast in spoonfuls. For 15 g [½ oz] use 15 ml [1 tablespoon].

ASCORBIC ACID

The short-time method of bread making is a good example of the new methods of bread making being developed. The main disadvantage of making bread at home has been the time it can take. When ascorbic acid is used, this time is considerably reduced.

Ascorbic acid tablets are obtainable from chemists in 25 mg and 50 mg sizes. When used for bread making, they are crushed and dissolved in the yeast liquid. Acting on yeast, this magic ingredient acts as a catalyst: it automatically speeds up the fermenting and rising processes. Both these stages are essential to a well-risen bread, but can prove tediously slow when traditional methods of bread making are employed. Ascorbic acid also strengthens the gluten in the flour.

LIQUIDS

The liquids used may be milk, water or a mixture of the two. When all milk or a proportion of milk is used, the dough is strengthened. Milk improves the food value and texture of the bread and will, to a certain extent, delay staling.

The amount of liquid needed varies according to the type of flour being used. A brown flour will absorb more liquid than a strong plain (white) flour. A guide is to use a scant 250 ml [½ pt] liquid per 450 g [1 lb] of flour. The liquid is always added all at once to the dry ingredients when bread making.

Liquids must be used lukewarm. This starts the yeast working immediately by providing the all impor-

tant moist, comfortable atmosphere that it needs to carry out properly its job of rising. If water is being used, heat it until it is just warm. It must not be too hot or this will kill the yeast. The old-fashioned practice of scalding milk before use to kill bacteria is now no longer necessary.

SALT

Salt brings out the flavour of the bread and, to a certain extent, controls the action of the yeast. It is essential that the amount be carefully measured, because of its second function. If too much salt is used, this will inhibit the rise, while too little will give a sticky dough that is unmanageable. With brown flours, extra salt is added to bring out the flavour and to help form a good crust.

FAT

Small amounts of fat are used in all short-time bread. When enriched short-time bread is being made, increased amounts of fat are often used.

Fats used are margarine, butter or lard. These fats will improve the texture and increase the volume of the bread and also delay staling.

Adding a fat has the effect of softening the gluten in the flour. This in turn improves the elasticity of the gluten and results in an increased rise.

SUGAR

A small amount of sugar is added as food for the yeast. In short-time bread, a small amount of sugar is mixed in with the dry ingredients before the fat is rubbed in.

It is not advisable to add the sugar directly to the yeast (a method known as creaming). If the yeast and sugar are creamed together, some of the yeast cells are destroyed. These dead cells could give the bread an unpleasant yeasty flavour.

BREAD TINS

Metal loaf tins are sold in various sizes. The best ones are the strong, old-fashioned oblong tins with high, slanting sides. They are available in 500 g, 1 kg, 1 lb and 2 lb sizes. If you bake a lot of bread, invest in a couple of each size.

The tins must be greased before

use and during storage to prevent them from rusting. Non-stick bread tins are now available. Dark tins always absorb heat better during baking. Lightly grease non-stick tins the first couple of times they are used.

If you are making bread for the first time, or do not have bread tins, then cake tins can be used. It does not really matter what shape and size the bread tins are, provided you put the right quantity of dough into them. The dough should half fill the tin.

If the tin is more than half filled with dough the dough will rise then overflow the tin, sinking again on top. The top of the bread will crack and there is the possibility that the loaf will not cook through. If you are baking rolls or bread that do not need to be shaped by a tin, baking sheets and even swiss roll tins are useful. They should be greased before use.

OTHER EQUIPMENT

Accurate measuring equipment in the form of scales, a set of measuring spoons and a jug are essential. You will also need a pair of teaspoons, a fork and a round-bladed, as well as a sharp, knife. The mixing bowl must be big enough to hold 1.4 kg [3 lb] flour plus the fat for rubbing in without the mixture spilling out. A polythene bag is used to provide the moist atmosphere in which the dough rises. This should be big

enough to enclose the bread tin or baking sheet on which you propose to bake rolls, with plenty of room to spare. To glaze the loaf you need a pastry brush and to cool the baked bread, a cooling rack.

MAKING THE DOUGH

First assemble all the ingredients and the equipment needed. Yeast doughs should always be mixed quickly, so there should be no delays once you start mixing.

Preparing the yeast

Short-time dough uses the dissolved yeast or straight dough method. For this, the yeast is dissolved in the entire quantity of liquid being used.

Measure the liquid exactly. If water or milk is being used, this should then be heated until lukewarm. If your kitchen is cool, use the liquid at 32–38°C [90–100°F]. If your kitchen is warm, use the liquid at a temperature of 27–32°C [80–90°F]. If you have no

thermometer, you can test the heat of the liquid with a clean finger. As the temperatures given are near blood heat, your finger should feel comfortable when you insert it in the liquid.

Crumble the fresh yeast between the thumb and forefinger into the warm liquid. Crush the ascorbic acid tablet to a fine powder. The easiest way to do this is to put it in a teaspoon and press another teaspoon down on top of it. A pestle and mortar will do the same job. Sprinkle the powder into the liquid. If you are using an electric mixer to make bread, this liquid should first be placed in the largest mixer bowl.

Whisk the yeast and ascorbic acid powder with a fork, until they have completely dissolved in the liquid. The liquid will now be a cloudy brown colour.

Mixing the dough

Weigh the flour and put it with the salt and sugar in a large bowl. Weigh the fat and add it to the dry ingredients in the bowl. With a round-bladed knife, cut it into the flour until the lumps are pea sized and are all coated with flour. Rub the fat into the flour, until it is all incorporated and the mixture resembles fine breadcrumbs. This process does not take very long because only a small amount of fat is used.

Adding the yeast liquid

Yeast doughs must always be mixed quickly; the liquid should be added all at once. Make a well in the centre of the rubbed-in mixture and pour all of the yeast liquid into the well. Mix by drawing the dry ingredients into the liquid with a fork. Mix together until the dough begins to bind together and leaves the side of the bowl to form one mass. When this happens, use your hands to press the dough together.

Kneading

The dough is next kneaded to ensure a good rise and texture to the bread. When the yeast is added to the flour it has the effect of softening the gluten. Kneading will offset the softening effect. It makes the dough strong enough to hold in the gas bubbles that the yeast produces and to hold firm the structure of the dough. Kneading stretches and thereby strengthens the gluten. It interlocks the gluten strands, helping to form a firm structure to hold up the bread until it is set by baking.

Kneading is a simple process of stretching and pushing the dough. Do this either by hand or with the

MAKES 1.4 KG [3 LB] DOUGH
50 g [2 oz] fresh yeast
50 mg tablet ascorbic acid
1.4 kg [3 lb] strong, plain flour
30 ml [2 tablespoons] salt
10 ml [2 teaspoons] caster sugar
25 g [1 oz] margarine or butter

1 Warm a scant 850 ml [1½ pt] wate to blood heat. Test temperature by inserting a finger. Crumble the yeast into the liquid.

5 Make a well in the centre and add the yeast liquid. Mix together until the dough binds and leaves the sides of the bowl.

6 Turn dough on to a floure surface. Knead by stretching th dough, pushing it away from yo with the lower part of your hand.

9 Remove the dough from the bag and knock it back. To do this, flatten it by pressing down all over with your knuckles.

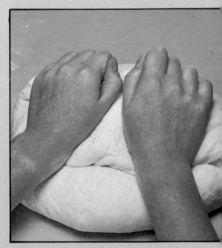

10 Knead the dough stretching it, a before, for 1 minute, pushing th dough to stretch it, folding an turning. Divide up for 2–3 loaves

130

short-time white bread

2 Crush the ascorbic tablet between two spoons. Stir powder into the yeast liquid and whisk with a fork until completely dissolved.

3 Put the flour, salt and sugar in a mixing bowl large enough for rubbing in and stir together with a round-bladed knife.

4 Cut the fat into the flour until the pieces are pea sized and coated with flour. Rub in the fat until mixture resembles breadcrumbs.

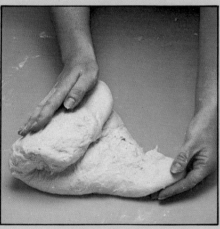

7 Give the dough a quarter turn, folding it back and kneading it. Repeat kneading and turning for 10 minutes with a rocking action.

OR use the dough hook of an electric mixer to knead the dough. Mix at speed 1 for 1 minute and then at speed 3 for 3 minutes.

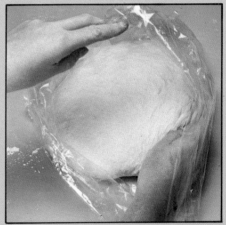

8 Put the dough in a lightly greased polythene bag and tie loosely. Put bag on a baking sheet in a warm place to rise for 5–10 minutes.

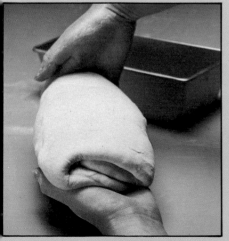

11 Shape bread dough, folding it in three lengthways. Put in greased tin, free end underneath. Shape any rolls. Put on baking sheet.

12 Replace dough, with the tin or sheet, in the polythene bag. Tie loosely and leave in a warm place 40–45 minutes until doubled.

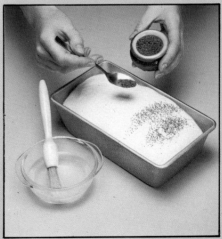

13 Remove bread from polythene bag. Paint with glaze and sprinkle with any required topping. Bake for the time given in the recipe.

dough hook of an electric mixer, until the dough feels firm and elastic. When sufficiently kneaded it should no longer feel soft or stick to your fingers.

Kneading by hand

Place the dough on a lightly floured surface and very lightly flour your hands. Keeping your fingers together, fold the dough towards you. Then push down and away with the heels of both hands stretching out the dough. Now fold it back towards you again, so that it is compact. Give the dough a quarter turn so that it will be stretched in a different direction. Repeat the process. You should develop a rocking action as you knead and turn. Continue to knead for 10 minutes. Wholemeal dough only needs kneading for 2 minutes.

Kneading with a dough hook

If you are using a mixer with a special dough hook attachment, kneading time can be reduced considerably.

Prepare the yeast liquid in the mixer bowl. Add the rubbed-in mixture directly to the liquid in the mixer bowl. Mix the dough together on the slowest speed (mark 1) for 1 minute before increasing the speed to moderate (mark 3) for a further 3 minutes.

RISING

All yeasts doughs have a period when they are left to rise. The swiftness of the rise when making short-time bread is the beneficial result of adding ascorbic acid with the yeast. The rising time allows the yeast to function and push up the dough. To do this it must have a suitable atmosphere.

Use a polythene bag that is at least twice as large as the amount of dough that is to be put inside it. This must be lightly greased or oiled inside. The easiest way to do this is to put the fat or oil inside, tie the bag loosely, then rub the bag between your hands.

Put the dough into the bag and tie it very loosely at the end, so that there is sufficient room for the dough to rise and expand. Put this on a baking sheet. If you do not have a large enough bag, use a saucepan with a lid: you will need the largest you have.

Because this rising period is a very brief one, it is essential that it takes place in a warm atmosphere, but

Earthenware flowerpots make unusual containers for bread and give a loaf of an attractive shape. These wholemeal loaves are covered with cracked wheat for texture.

specific temperatures are not required because the rising time is so short. If the oven has been used, the bread can be placed in the warming drawer or even on top of the oven.

The rising time is 5 minutes for a plain dough. The dough should increase in size by approximately a third during this short time.

KNOCKING BACK AND FINAL PROVING

After the first, brief period of rising the dough will be soft and puffy to the touch. This is because the yeast has softened the gluten.

Knocking back

To restore the dough to its previous strong state, it is flattened and re-kneaded for a period of no more than 1 minute. This disperses any large air bubbles and ensures a better rise the second time. It also gives a more even texture to the loaf without large air bubbles. This process is called 'knocking back'.

Remove the risen dough from the polythene bag or saucepan and place on a very lightly floured surface. Clench your fists together and, using the knuckles, press down, all over the surface of the dough to completely flatten it. Do this until there are no visible signs of bubbles in the dough.

Shaping the dough

The dough is now ready to be shaped into loaves or rolls. Put it into the oiled tin, remembering that the dough must come no more than half way up the tin. To ensure an even upward rise, it should fit the bottom of the tin exactly. To do this, flatten the dough to an oblong the same width as the length of the tin. Fold both ends over to make three layers and place the dough, free end underneath, in the tin. If you are making rolls, shape these and put them on a lightly oiled baking sheet. Use approximately 50 g [2 oz] dough for a medium-sized roll.

Proving the dough

This final rise, once the dough has been shaped, is called the final proof or proving.

When the dough has been shaped, it must be returned to a warm, moist atmosphere in order to rise again. This second rise is the important one and the bread must double in size before it is ready to be baked.

A lightly oiled polythene bag is employed again. Place the tin or baking sheet full of rolls inside a large polythene bag and tie it loosely, as before, so that there is enough room for the dough to double its size.

The second rising should take approximately 40–50 minutes at room temperature 21°C [70°F]. If the bread is rising in a warming drawer or on top of a warm oven, it will take approximately 30 minutes. If the temperature during rising is much less than that given, the rising time will be increased and the overall time considerably lengthened.

ATTRACTIVE FINISHES

To improve its appearance, the bread is finished off to give a loaf which is crusty, shiny or with a floury, matt surface.

If you have ever wondered how bakers manage to produce bread that is deliciously crusty, you will be interested to know that it is all done by steam. To make a similar crusty top introduce your own steam.

Place a container of water in the bottom of the oven. The steam it gives off as it evaporates helps to lift the bread and provides a steamy atmosphere which makes the crusty top.

A second method of achieving a good crust is to paint the bread surface with water or salt water. For a rich golden-brown crust, paint the bread with the top of the milk or a thin cream or brush it with lightly beaten egg. Brushing with melted margarine or butter will give a crisp, crunchy crust.

Bread made from brown flour can be given an attractive finish by painting it with a water and salt solution (approximately 1 part salt to 3 parts water) and then sprinkling with poppy seeds or cracked wheat. Cracked wheat is available from health food shops and large supermarkets. White bread looks attractive when sprinkled with poppy or sesame seeds.

BAKING

Bread always requires a very hot baking temperature—230°C [450°F] gas mark 8 and is baked in the centre of the oven.

Loaves baked in tins or on baking sheets will take between 20 to 35 minutes, depending on the size of the

loaf. Rolls will take from 10 to 20 minutes.

The hot oven kills the yeast and thus prevents the dough from rising further. The gluten is set by the heat and becomes the framework of the bread.

The bread is cooked when the crust is golden brown and the bread sounds hollow when it is tapped underneath with the knuckles. The same test is used for rolls on a tray. Bread cooked in a tin is ready when it has shrunk slightly from the sides of the tin.

Remove the bread from the tin immediately it is cooked and transfer to a wire rack to cool. Slide rolls on to a cooling rack straight away.

FLOWERPOT BREAD

Baking bread in earthenware containers, in interesting shapes like flowerpots, is traditional. Always use earthenware flowerpots and, if they are new or you are using them to bake in for the first time, test them before using. To do this, grease the insides of the flowerpots and bake in the centre of a very hot oven for 1 hour. This will season them and you will discover whether heat will crack them before putting in the dough. After the test allow them to cool at room temperature before filling with the dough and baking.

MAKES TWO 450 G [1 LB] LOAVES
25 g [1 oz] fresh yeast
25 mg tablet ascorbic acid
175 g [6 oz] strong plain flour
225 g [½ lb] wholemeal flour
10 ml [2 teaspoons] salt
10 ml [2 teaspoons] sugar
15 g [½ oz] lard
90 ml [6 tablespoons] oil
wheat or oat flakes

1 Warm a scant 250 ml [½ pt] water to blood heat and test with a finger. Crumble the yeast into the water. Crush the ascorbic acid tablet between two small spoons and sprinkle it into the water.

2 Whisk the liquid with a fork until the yeast has completely dissolved.

3 Place both the flours and the salt and sugar in a large mixing bowl. Stir all the ingredients together to combine.

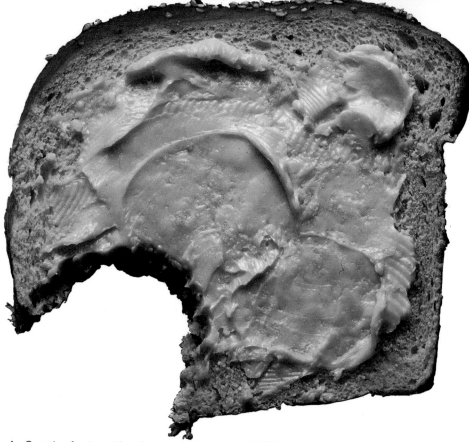

**1.4 kg [3 lb] short-time white
    bread dough
5 ml [1 teaspoon] salt
15 ml [1 tablespoon] water**

1 Thoroughly grease the sides and base of one large loaf tin and one smaller loaf tin.

2 After knocking back the dough, cut the dough into a 900 g [2 lb] piece and a 450 g [1 lb] piece with a sharp knife. Working on one piece at a time, flatten the dough to an oblong so that the width of the dough is the same as the tin length.

3 Fold the oblong of dough into three and turn it over so that the seam is underneath.

4 Smooth over the top and tuck in the ends of the dough before placing in the prepared tin. It should fit neatly in the bottom to ensure an even rise. Repeat with remaining piece of dough in the second tin.

5 Lightly brush the tops of each piece of dough with oil and place each tin in a lightly greased polythene bag.

6 Tie each bag loosely at the top to allow for expansion. Place tins on a baking sheet in a warm place until dough has doubled in size. This will take about 45 minutes.

7 Position shelf to centre and heat oven to 230°C [450°F] gas mark 8.

8 Fill a small ovenproof container with water and place this on the floor of the oven.

9 Mix the salt with 15 ml [1 tablespoon] water. Remove tins from polythene bags and carefully brush the surfaces of the bread with the salt water.

10 Bake the bread for 30–35 minutes, until it is golden and well risen.

11 Remove each loaf from its tin and tap the base with your knuckles. If the bread is fully baked, the loaf will sound hollow.

12 Cool the bread on a wire rack.

4 Cut the fat into the dry ingredients with a round-bladed knife until all the pieces are pea sized and coated with flour.

5 Rub the fat into the flour until the mixture resembles breadcrumbs.

6 Make a well in the centre of the dry ingredients and add the yeast liquid, all in one go.

7 Mix the liquid into the dry ingredients with a round-bladed knife and mix until the dough binds together.

8 Turn the dough on to a lightly floured surface. Knead the dough for 3 minutes until the surface is smooth.

9 Place the dough in a lightly greased polythene bag and tie loosely to secure. Put it on a baking tray in a warm place to rise for 5 minutes.

10 Choose two flowerpots with 12.5 cm [5"] diameter tops and lightly grease the insides. Sprinkle the insides of each flowerpot with wheat or oat flakes.

11 Remove the dough from the polythene bag and flatten with your knuckles. Knead dough for 1 minute.

12 Divide dough into 2 equal-sized pieces with a sharp knife and shape each piece to fit a flowerpot.

13 Place the dough in flowerpots and brush the top of each piece of dough with oil.

14 Place the flowerpots in two greased polythene bags big enough to allow the bread to rise. Tie the tops loosely.

15 Leave in a warm place for about 45 minutes until the dough has risen to the top of the flowerpots. Remove the pots from the bags.

16 Position a shelf in the centre of the oven and heat it to 230°C [450°F] gas mark 8.

17 Stand the flowerpots on a baking sheet and bake for 35 minutes.

18 Leave flowerpots to cool for 5 minutes after removing from the oven. Invert bread on to a cooling rack and leave to cool.

TIN LOAF

This oblong loaf is the most common bread shape of all and is ideal for slicing. Make the dough following the step-by-step instructions up to step 9. The dough must be shaped before the final rising.

Sweet and savoury parcels pastry

It's often said that perfect pastry is the mark of a good cook and pastry making is indeed a skill to be proud of. If this is your first attempt remember that there are no shortcuts to perfect shortcrust but, with practice and patience and by paying attention to a few golden rules, you'll soon master the technique and then a whole range of different dishes will be yours for the making. To start off, learn how you can make penny-saving pastry parcels which look as good as they taste.

Shortcrust is one of the most popular and versatile of pastries. It is made by the rubbing-in method (described on page 72) and then just enough water is added to the crumble mixture to bind the ingredients together to a stiff dough.

PASTRY PARCELS

One of the easiest, and most delicious, ways of using shortcrust is as a wrapping or 'case' for different tasty fillings. In fact, pastry originated as a simple flour and water dough which was used by the ancient Greeks and Romans to wrap round meats to seal in the flavoursome juices produced during cooking. The baked paste was not eaten, but with the passing of time fat was mixed into the dough to make it more appetizing. From the Middle Ages until the

nineteenth century, pastry was held in great esteem and all kinds of fillings, often containing assorted meats and fruits, were concocted to be encased in thick pastry.

Today, pastry parcels are as popular as ever. Different-shaped parcels have different names—pasty, turnover, roll, dumpling and tricorn—but the principle behind each of them is the same. The pastry is shaped, rolled out, wrapped around a sweet or savoury filling and the parcel is baked in the oven.

'MUSTS' FOR PERFECT PASTRY

As its name suggests, shortcrust pastry should be 'short', that is, crisp but not hard or tough, melt-in-the-mouth but not over-rich. To achieve the right, light texture there are certain rules which you must follow every time.

Measure your ingredients. This takes the guesswork out of balancing proportions. For shortcrust, the rule is half as much fat as flour and a little cold water to bind the ingredients together.

Too much fat gives an over-rich and crumbly pastry. Too much flour makes the pastry dry and hard. If too much water is added, the pastry will be tough and liable to shrink. On the other hand, not enough water will give a crumbly, unmanageable dough.

Coolness is another key to successful shortcrust—it helps to prevent the fat(s) from becoming oily.

Have your equipment, ingredients and hands as cool as possible. (If your hands are warm or sticky, try rinsing them under cold water and dry them before you start rubbing-in.)

Always use your fingertips to rub in because they are the coolest part of your hands.

The water to bind should be chilled, so put a small jug of water in the refrigerator 15 minutes before you start—failing that, pop some ice cubes into the jug of water.

Light handling makes light pastry. Take care not to overwork the mixture when rubbing-in or kneading the dough or it will become sticky.

Add water with caution. Blending in the water and binding the ingredients together is the most crucial stage. Adding too much water is one of the commonest causes of tough, heavy pastry. As a general rule you will need approximately 5 ml [1 teaspoon] cold water for every 25 g [1 oz] flour; but different flours absorb different amounts of water—so don't worry if you have to add a little more.

Sprinkle water, small quantities at a time, over the surface of the crumble mixture and use a round-bladed knife to blend it in after each addition.

Relaxing the dough in the refrigerator. This takes 30 minutes—but you can leave it overnight if you like. Although less important for shortcrust than for the richer pastries, this cools the dough, making it easier to handle. For easier working, and to prevent the dough cracking when rolled out, the dough must be taken out of the refrigerator and allowed to soften. The time this takes will vary but you should allow about 15 minutes if you have chilled the dough for 30 minutes and longer if you have left it overnight.

Correct rolling out. Sprinkle the working surface and the rolling pin with the minimum of flour. Too much flour worked in at this stage alters the balance of the ingredients and can spoil the pastry.

To get the shape you want and an even thickness, roll in one direction only (away from you) and turn the pastry around frequently. Random rolling produces an uneven shape and is extremely wasteful. The pastry will have to be trimmed to shape, leaving bits to be re-rolled and used up. Twice-rolled shortcrust is not as good as once rolled!

When making parcels, divide the dough into the number of parcels you are making and roll each to the shape you want. If you roll and cut out the shapes you will have to gather the trimming together to make the last parcel, which is less satisfactory.

Rely on the rolling pin to get the shape you want. Don't be tempted to stretch the pastry to shape, it might tear and anyway will only shrink back during baking.

Bake in a pre-heated oven. The contrast between the heat of the oven and the coolness of the pastry causes rapid expansion of air trapped in the dough and this gives pastry its desirable light texture.

Bake at the recommended temperature. If the oven is too hot, the pastry will burn before the filling is properly cooked; if the oven is too cool, the pastry will be tough and chewy.

INGREDIENTS

Flour: plain flour gives the best results. Self-raising flour may be used but tends to give a more spongy texture. Wholewheat flour makes a 'nutty' flavoured pastry but it is more difficult to roll out so try using half white and half wholewheat to start with for brown pastry.

Remember that whenever a recipe calls for a weight of pastry this refers to the weight of flour used to make the pastry and not to the total weight of all the ingredients.

Salt: a pinch of salt is always added.

Fat: butter, margarine, lard or cooking fat may all be used. A mixture of half butter and half lard makes excellent pastry; the butter gives a good flavour and the lard shortens the texture. Margarine may be substituted for the butter and cooking fat for the lard. If you use all butter or all margarine the flavour is good but the pastry has a firmer texture; all lard or cooking fat gives a cloying pastry.

Whichever fat (or combination of fats) you use, make sure they are firm but not hard. If the fat is very hard, take it out of the refrigerator 20 minutes before you want to use it. Hard fat is not only difficult to rub in and does not blend easily with the flour but can also result in a blistered-looking pastry. If the fats are too soft they quickly become sticky, which makes rubbing-in messy and produces an oily pastry.

Water: different flours vary in the amount of water they absorb. There is only a slight difference between white flours and 5 ml [1 teaspoon] to each 25 g [1 oz] flour is normally enough to bind a well rubbed-in mixture. Brown flour usually needs 10 ml [2 teaspoons] for each 25 g [1 oz] flour.

EQUIPMENT

To make the pastry you will need scales, a sieve, a large mixing bowl and a round-bladed knife to blend the water into the rubbed-in ingredients. If you don't have a round-bladed knife

Here are some of the kitchen tools used for pastry making. The wire pastry blender (an optional extra) prevents warm hands from coming into contact with ingredients. The pastry board scraper shown in the foreground makes the job of cleaning up much easier, but if you don't have one you can use a palette knife instead.

Step-by-step shortcrust pastry

MAKES 225 G [½ LB] PASTRY
225 g [½ lb] plain flour
2.5 ml [½ teaspoon] salt
50 g [2 oz] butter or margarine
50 g [2 oz] lard or cooking fat
approximately 40 ml
   [8 teaspoons] cold water

1 Sift flour and salt, add fat. Use a round-bladed knife to cut fat into flour until all the pieces are pea-sized and coated with flour.

2 Rub fat into flour until mixture resembles even-sized bread-crumbs. Use fingertips, lift high and let mixture fall back into bowl.

3 Shake bowl to bring lumps to the surface and rub these in until the fat is evenly distributed and all the flour is absorbed.

4 Sprinkle 10 ml [2 teaspoons] cold water over the surface of the mixture and stir this in with the round-bladed knife.

5 Sprinkle another 10 ml [2 teaspoons] cold water over the surface and stir until mixture clings together in small lumps.

6 Add another 10 ml [2 teaspoons] water but this time use the flat side of the blade to press the mixture into fairly large lumps.

7 Add remaining water. Use your fingers to test if the dough is moist enough to stick together, and to draw the dough into a ball.

8 Place the dough on an unfloured surface and knead lightly until smooth. Wrap dough and chill in the refrigerator for 30 minutes.

you can use an ordinary kitchen knife instead. A wire pastry blender can be a great help during hot weather. It works the fat and flour to the crumble stage and prevents hot sticky hands coming into contact with the ingredients.

You will also need to cover the dough while it is relaxing in the refrigerator, to prevent the surface drying out and cracking. Cling film is best, or you can use a plastic bag. But do make sure you squeeze out all the air once you have put the dough in the bag. If you don't, the warm air from the kitchen trapped in the bag condenses and gives the dough a moist surface.

You can use any clean, dry surface to roll out the dough. Remember that knives will mark a laminated surface so, if it is a unit work top, protect it with a sheet of plastic or use a large, smooth wooden board instead. If you are lucky enough to have one, the traditional marble slab makes the best surface because it keeps the pastry cool and scrapes down easily.

Use a flour dredger to sprinkle the rolling-out surface with flour. If you don't have a dredger, sieve a little flour on to the board—this makes it lighter and finer. If you do have too much flour on the board, simply brush it aside with a pastry brush.

A pastry board scraper is used by professional cooks for scraping down the work surface and certainly makes the job of cleaning up easier. Although less easy to handle, a palette knife can be used instead.

MAKING THE PASTRY

Now that you know the principles behind pastry making and have organized your equipment you can begin to make the pastry for your parcels.

If you use white flour, always sift it with the salt. This aerates the ingredients and removes the lumps. Don't sift brown flour as this separates out the bran—just measure it into the bowl and stir in the salt.

Add the firm fat (or mixture of fats) to the flour and cut into pea-sized pieces. The fat will become coated with flour as you cut it up and this is known as cutting the fat into the flour. Make sure the pieces of fat are well coated with flour before you start rubbing-in because this coating provides a barrier between the fat and the warmth of your fingers.

Remember to lift your hands well above the bowl when rubbing-in and to let the rubbed-in mixture trickle back between your fingers into the bowl. This helps to keep the mixture cool and light.

Make sure that the mixture is evenly rubbed-in—shake the bowl to bring lumps to the surface. If the flour particles are not evenly coated with fat they will absorb too much liquid and give a tough, elastic dough.

Stop rubbing-in when the mixture looks like even-sized breadcrumbs. If you overwork the mixture it will become oily and sticky.

Add the cold water little by little, using just enough to bind the mixture together—all too often tough, badly shrunken pastry is the result of using too much liquid.

The best way to add the water is to use a 5 ml [1 teaspoon] measuring spoon and to sprinkle the water evenly over the surface of the mixture. Don't add the water all in one go and in one spot or you will end up with a blistered-looking surface. Use the knife (cooler than your hands) to blend each addition of water into the crumble mixture.

When the dough is sticking together in fairly large lumps draw the pieces together with your fingers. The consistency of the mixture will tell you whether any more water is needed. It should stick together easily and feel moist but not sticky. If you do need to add more water then do so cautiously until the right consistency is reached.

Gather the dough together (it should leave the sides of the bowl clean) and place it on a cool, dry, unfloured surface. Draw the outer edges of the dough into the centre with your fingertips (this is called kneading). Knead the dough lightly for a few minutes until it is smooth and free from cracks.

Wrap the dough and place it in the refrigerator to cool for 30 minutes.

Meanwhile position your oven shelf and heat the oven to the recommended temperature.

MAKING PASTRY PARCELS

To make your parcels you will need:
● equipment for rolling out already described.
● a knife to cut the dough, a round-bladed knife is best as it will not tear the pastry.

● a ruler for measuring.
● a spoon for heaping the filling on to the pastry.
● a pastry brush for damping the pastry edges and for glazing.
● a fine skewer or a fork for making steam vents.
● a fish slice for transferring parcels.
● baking tray.

Details of how to make each different parcel are given in the step-by-step pictures. Whichever kind you make, there are certain essential points which help to ensure successful parcels, so don't be tempted to skimp them.

Remove the dough from the refrigerator 15 minutes before you want to use it so that it softens slightly for easier handling.

Use a knife to cut the dough, pat the pieces gently into shape and roll out on a lightly floured board. Use swift light strokes and turn the pastry frequently to keep it in shape and give an even thickness. (To make a circle, turn the dough slightly round in the same direction after every stroke.)

Make sure that your parcel is securely sealed—however tasty the filling, it's best inside the parcel. If it leaks out during cooking it will burn and your parcel will be spoilt. So don't use too much filling and only spread it to within 1.25 cm [½"] of the pastry edges.

Always take the trouble to brush the edges of the pastry with cold water as they are then much easier to stick together. Make sure that you press the seams firmly together to seal them. Fluting or marking the seams with a fork decorates and

Handy hints

● If you forget to remove your fats from the fridge and they are rock-hard, try coarsely grating them into the flour before rubbing in.
● Pastry should not be baked in the oven at the same time as foods which produce steam (such as roasts). The steam takes away the crispness of the pastry.
● If your pastry seems a little hard even after following the directions exactly—try 'weakening' the plain flour you use by replacing 25 g [1 oz] in every 225 g [½ lb] with cornflour.

Pasties are small savoury pies which, traditionally, have a crimped sealed edge.

strengthens the join.

Except for tricorns, which have ready-made steam vents, you must prick or cut your pastry parcels to make holes for the steam given off by the filling. If the steam is unable to get out of the parcel, some of it will be absorbed by the pastry which will become soggy and 'heavy'. Also the risk of the filling bursting the pastry seams is greater. So remember—let the steam out to keep the filling in.

If you are making dumplings, you will need to grease the baking tray. This is because their filling has a tendency to leak and greasing helps prevent sticking.

FINISHING TOUCHES
Just before baking, brush the parcels with a glaze to give the cooked pastry an attractive shine. Lightly beaten egg gives a glossy golden pastry and is usually used for savoury parcels. Egg white gives a very shiny finish to sweet parcels. Milk colours the pastry golden brown and is suitable for both sweet and savoury parcels. If you want your pastry extra-crisp, then sprinkle the sweet parcels with a little sugar after glazing.

STORING SHORTCRUST PASTRY
Store rubbed-in mixture, ready to make into pastry, in a polythene bag or plastic box for up to two weeks in a refrigerator.

Wrap prepared pastry in polythene or kitchen foil, taking care to squeeze out as much air as possible, and store in a refrigerator for one week.

To freeze pastry, cut the dough into workable pieces and wrap in heavy-duty foil or self-adhesive film. Pack all the parcels in a polythene bag and freeze. Store for up to 3 months. Remember that 225 g [$\frac{1}{2}$ lb] of pastry will take about 2 hours to thaw at room temperature.

PARCEL FILLINGS
Prepare the filling for the parcels while the dough is relaxing in the refrigerator. The choice of filling will depend on which type of parcel you are going to make.

PASTIES
These are small savoury pies which can be served hot or cold. The dough is divided, rolled out to a round, gathered round the filling and crimped (fluted) decoratively.

You must plan your filling so that it needs the same time to cook as the pastry. Slice or chop your cleaned ingredients into fine slivers. Small is beautiful: if you make the pieces too big they will not be cooked through when the pastry is done.

A small pasty will need 15-30 ml [1-2 tablespoons] filling. Use your judgement here and adapt the amount of filling to your chosen pastry size. Don't attempt to cram in too much filling or you will have to stretch the pastry and it might tear; on the other hand, all pastry and very little filling makes a disappointing pasty.

●Meat pasties are traditionally filled with a mixture of diced raw beef, onions and potatoes, but you can use pork, kidney or lamb combined with a suitable vegetable.

●Fish pasties are every bit as delicious. Simply substitute any canned fish which has been drained and flaked or any uncooked filleted

1 Heat oven to 200°C [400°F] gas mark 6. For 4 pasties, cut 225 g [$\frac{1}{2}$ lb] pastry into 4 equal pieces. Pat each into a round.

5 Starting at one end of the sealed edge, use your hands to crimp the sealed edge of pastry.

fish (skinned if preferred) for the meat.

●Vegetable pasties will delight even the most avid meat-eater. The choice of ingredients is up to you. For extra flavour and food value try adding a little cheese, grated or cut into small dice. Cheddar and Lancashire are especially good.

FISHERMAN'S PASTY

▽*Serve these cooked pasties hot or* ▲*cold, with a lemon-dressed mixed salad.*

SERVES 4
225 g [½ lb] shortcrust pastry
200 g [7 oz] canned tuna
25 g [1 oz] onion
225 g [½ lb] canned tomatoes
salt and pepper

■ Heat the oven to 200°C [400°F] gas mark 6.

2 Divide the pastry into 4 equal-sized pieces and shape each to a round.

3 On a lightly floured board, roll out a piece of pastry turning it slightly in the same direction after every stroke until you have an evenly thick round about 15 cm [6"] in diameter. Repeat with the other pieces.

4 Drain the canned tuna and turn into bowl. Peel and finely chop the onion and drain the tomatoes.

5 Add the onion and drained tomatoes to the tuna. Stir the mixture together and season to taste.

6 Place one quarter of the filling in centre of the pastry round.

7 Brush round the edges of the pastry with cold water then lift up the edges of a round to meet over

the centre of the filling. Seal edges by pressing firmly together.

8 Pinch the pastry together to flute the seam. Make other pasties.

9 Use a skewer to make a concealed hole in the fluting to allow the steam to escape.

10 Lift the pasties on to an ungreased baking tin and brush with a little beaten egg or milk to give a glaze when cooked.

11 Bake the pasties on the shelf above the centre of the oven for about 20 minutes until the pastry is crisp and golden.

Variation
●Replace the canned tuna with 2 medium-sized raw kippers (remove skins if preferred) and add 15 ml (1 tablespoon) chopped gherkin.

Step-by-step pasties

Roll out until 15 cm [6"] in diameter, turning pastry slightly in the same direction after each forward stroke to retain shape.

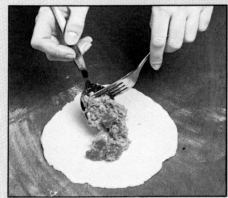

3 Spoon one quarter of the prepared filling into the centre of each circle. Brush edges of pastry with cold water.

4 Bring two opposite edges up to meet in the centre, over the filling. Press the edges firmly together with your fingers to seal.

Work along the seam until the whole seam has been decorated and firmly sealed.

7 Use a skewer to make a small hole in each pasty for the steam to escape. Lift on to an ungreased baking tray with a fish slice.

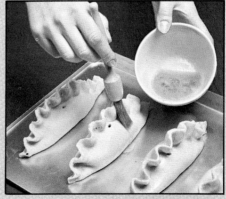

8 Brush the pasties with a little beaten egg or milk to give the pastry a shiny glaze when cooked. Bake for about 20 minutes.

TURNOVERS

A turnover is a pastry 'envelope' which lies flat on its side and has a sweet filling. Turnovers are usually semi-circular in shape but can also be triangular, rectangular or oval. The filling is placed on one half of the pastry and the other half is folded over to cover it. The seam is sealed and decorated. Baked turnovers can be served hot or cold.

You need to allow 15-30 ml (1-2 tablespoons) filling for each turnover, depending on the ingredients.
●Fresh fruit makes an ideal filling. Rhubarb and bananas as well as cooking apples, plums, pears and gooseberries are all excellent. Prepare fruit in the normal way for cooking, then slice or chop it very finely to ensure that it will be cooked at the same time as the pastry. Sprinkle with sugar to taste and dust with your favourite spice. Don't add any extra liquid as the fruit will give off its own juice during cooking. But you can spread bananas with a little syrup or jam because they contain less moisture.
●Use soft fruit in combination with any hard fruit, but not alone as it reduces to a pulp during cooking and will give a very thin filling.

Always sprinkle a very juicy fruit, such as blackberries, with a little sugar, and let it stand for 2-3 hours. Drain well before using.
●Jam is popular and needs no preparation. Choose a thick, fruity preserve, such as chunky marmalade.
●For a thicker filling, simply mix 15 ml [1 tablespoon] cottage or curd cheese with 15 ml [1 tablespoon] jam.
●A sprinkling of chopped nuts can be added to any filling and is particularly good with a wholemeal pastry made with a mixture of plain and white flour.

BANANA AND RUM TURNOVERS

◻*Quick and easy to make, these banana turnovers are particularly good served hot and accompanied with cream or ice-cream. The dough is rolled out into oval shapes to accommodate the shape of the bananas.*

SERVES 4
225 g [½ lb] shortcrust pastry
half a lemon
25 g [1 oz] butter
15 ml [1 tablespoon] Demerara sugar

Milk and Demerara sugar are used to give these tempting turnovers a sweet glaze when cooked. Dust with icing sugar to serve.

drop of rum essence
4 small bananas

For the glaze:
milk
Demerara sugar

1 Heat the oven to 200° [400°F] gas mark 6.

2 Grate the zest of the lemon into a mixing bowl. Add the butter, rum essence and sugar and mash together with a fork until creamy and evenly mixed.

3 Divide the pastry into four equal pieces and roll them to fat oval shapes about 19 × 14 cm [7½ × 5½"] long and wide enough to be able to fold over the bananas.

4 Arrange a peeled banana on one side of each piece of pastry; if the bananas are very curved, gently bend them straighter. It does not matter if they crack.

5 Spread each banana with some of the rum butter mixture.

6 Damp the edges of the pastry with cold water then fold one side over to enclose the banana; firmly press the seam together and mark it decoratively with a fork.

7 Prick the top of each turnover to make holes for steam to escape.

8 Brush the banana turnovers with milk and sprinkle with Demerara sugar, then lift them with a fish slice on to a baking sheet.

9 Cook the turnovers on the shelf above the centre of the oven for about 25 minutes until the pastry is cooked through and golden. Dust with icing sugar before serving.

Variations

Try other delicious sauces with the bananas:
●Use orange instead of lemon zest then grate a little chocolate into the rum butter mixture.
●Make the rum butter without the lemon zest and add fine slivers of stem ginger to taste.

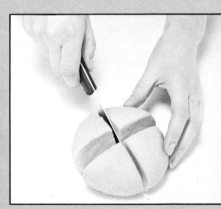

1 Heat oven to 200°C [400°F] gas mark 6. For 4 turnovers, cut 225 g [½ lb] pastry into 4 equal pieces.

5 Press the prongs of a fork along the seam to decorate and to ensure that it is well sealed.

Step-by-step turnovers

2 Pat each into a round. Roll out on a lightly floured board to circles 15 cm [6"] in diameter.

3 Spread prepared filling on half of each circle. Jam must not be within 1.2 cm [½"] of the edge.

4 Damp edges with water. Fold one half of the pastry over filling and press seam firmly to seal.

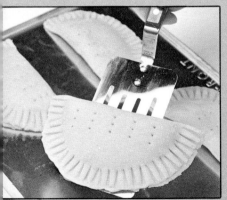

6 Prick the turnovers to make holes for steam to escape. Lift on to an ungreased baking sheet.

7 Brush with a little milk or beaten egg white and sprinkle with sugar to give a sweet glaze.

8 Bake on shelf above centre of a pre-heated oven for 20 minutes. Dust with icing sugar to serve.

ROLLS

Rolls are long sausage-shaped pastry parcels. Fillings can be meat, meat and vegetables and /or fruit, or just vegetable. The filling must be firm enough to be shaped into a long roll along the length of one half of the pastry, but not so dry that it makes the baked roll unappetizing.

The fattier cuts of meat are excellent because they have the right consistency to be shaped and will keep moist during cooking. To make sure the meat is cooked through at the same time as the pastry, always mince it finely (this also makes it easier to shape). Alternatively, use ready-minced beef, pork or veal or sausage meat.

● To offset the fattiness of the meat try adding a little sharp fresh fruit, grated or finely chopped.
● Mince vegetables where possible or chop into fine dice. Vegetables with a high water content, such as courgettes, mushrooms and tomatoes should be used sparingly. They tend to disintegrate during cooking, and too many will make the filling watery.

CHEESE, APPLE AND ONION ROLLS

⧗ *Because the ingredients for the filling are rather dry, some beaten egg is used to bind it together at the mixing stage. Use the leftover egg to glaze the rolls. Leave the baked rolls* until completely cold then slice off the pastry ends. Cut each roll in half and serve with salad as a light lunch for 4 people or into 6 small 2.5 cm [1"] rolls for cocktail savouries.

SERVES 4
125 g [$\frac{1}{4}$ lb] shortcrust pastry
100 g [$\frac{1}{4}$ lb] onion
100 g [$\frac{1}{4}$ lb] cheese
100 g [$\frac{1}{4}$ lb] cooking apple
1.5 ml [$\frac{1}{4}$ teaspoon] salt
pinch of pepper
1 medium-sized egg

For successful savoury rolls, always mince, chop or flake the ingredients for your filling very finely so they will be cooked at the same time as the pastry. Remember to make vents for the steam from the filling to escape or it will soak into the pastry and make it heavy and soggy. Leave the baked rolls until completely cold, slice off pastry ends and serve.

1 Heat oven to 200°C [400°F] gas mark 6. Peel and chop the onion and set aside. Grate the cheese.

2 Peel, core and coarsely grate the apple and set aside. Then lightly beat the egg with a fork until the yolk and white have mixed.

3 Bring a small pan of water to the boil, add the chopped onion and boil it for 2 minutes. Drain well and turn into a mixing bowl.

4 Combine all but 15 g [½ oz] of the grated cheese with the drained onion, grated apple, salt and pepper and use a little of the beaten egg to mix it together.

5 Roll out the pastry to a long thin rectangle about 15 × 36 cm [6 × 14"]. Cut it in half to make two rectangles 15 × 18 cm [6 × 7"].

6 Divide the cheese mixture between the two pieces of pastry and spread along the length of each piece, to within 1.2 cm [½"] of the sides.

7 Brush along the edges of the pastry with a little cold water then fold the pastry over and seal all the cut edges firmly to prevent the mixture oozing out.

8 Slip the two cheese rolls on to an ungreased baking sheet, brush them with the remaining beaten egg then sprinkle with the remaining cheese.

9 Make small holes at intervals along the rolls to allow the steam to escape. Bake on the shelf above the centre for about 25 minutes.

10 Leave the rolls until cold before cutting off the sealed pastry ends then slice into portions.

Variations
For ham rolls, use 125 g [¼ lb] chopped ham instead of the cheese. For corned beef rolls, omit cheese, apple and onion. Use 175 g [6 oz] flaked corned beef mixed with 75 g [3 oz] sweet corn kernels. For sardine rolls, omit cheese, apple and onion. Use 200 g [7 oz] canned sardines in tomato juice. Mash them with their juice and stir in 15 ml [1 tablespoon] tomato purée and some chopped green pepper.

Making a pastry roll

1 Roll out 125 g [¼ lb] pastry to a rectangle 15×36 cm [6×14"]. Cut in half.

2 Spoon prepared filling along one side of each rectangle. Brush pastry edges with cold water.

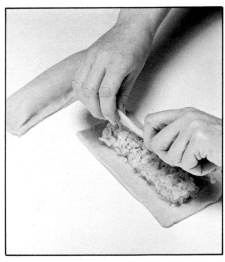

3 Lift one edge of pastry and fold over filling. Seal all the cut edges firmly and decorate if wished.

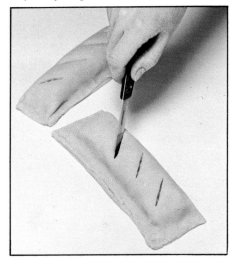

4 Use the point of a sharp knife to make small cuts along each roll to allow steam to escape.

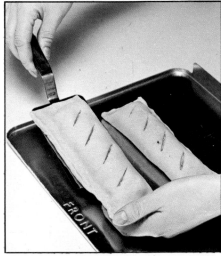

5 Carefully transfer the rolls on to an ungreased baking tray and brush with glaze before baking.

6 Leave baked rolls until completely cold before slicing off pastry ends for serving. Cut into slices.

DUMPLINGS

Dumplings are so called because the pastry is moulded round the fruit enclosed. Cooking apples are the traditional and the most suitable fruit to use. They are easy to core, and will sit firmly on their own while you shape the pastry. Choose apples of roughly the same size, so they will all be ready at the same time. Medium-sized fruit are best as they make manageable portions.

The method used to make dumplings with shortcrust pastry differs slightly from that used for dumplings with suet pastry.

Suet pastry is more pliable and has no seams after moulding, so the apples can be baked upright. With a shortcrust dumpling there is a tendency for seams to open and filling to leak out, so the parcel is placed upside down on a greased baking tray to help prevent this happening. The tray is greased in case the filling leaks out.

Peel and core each apple before putting it on a pastry square and then fill the cavity. As a rough guide, a medium-sized apple will take about 15 ml [3 teaspoons] filling, but this will vary with the size of the core cavity.

The best fillings are thick and tightly packed; have fun experimenting with your own recipes or try some of the following:
- Chopped dates, grated lemon zest and black treacle.
- Marmalade and chopped almonds.
- Honey, whole hazelnuts and a little ground cinnamon, allspice or cloves.
- Dried mixed fruit, walnut pieces and golden syrup or soft brown sugar.
- Fresh or frozen raspberries, blackberries or blackcurrants plus a little caster sugar to sweeten and a sprinkling of ground spice.

BRAMBLE AND APPLE DUMPLINGS

Fresh or frozen blackberries can be used for this recipe. Grease the baking tray to prevent sticking because the filling does tend to leak.

The dumplings are put into a hot oven to crisp the pastry and then the heat is lowered so that the pastry does not burn while the apples are cooking.

SERVES 4
225 g [½ lb] shortcrust pastry
4 small cooking apples

Cooking apples are traditionally used for dumplings because they are easy to core and will sit firmly, leaving you both hands free to shape the pastry.

20 ml [4 teaspoons] caster sugar
125 g [¼ lb] blackberries
beaten egg to glaze
4 cloves

1 Heat oven to 220°C [425°F] gas mark 7.

2 Divide the pastry into four equal pieces and on a lightly floured board roll into squares approximately 20 × 20 cm [8 × 8"].

3 Peel and core the apples.

4 Stand each apple on a square of pastry and fill each core cavity with 5 ml [1 teaspoon] caster sugar and then as many blackberries as you can push in.

5 Cut two corners off each pastry square and set these aside.

6 Damp the edges of one pastry square with cold water then gather up the edges neatly to the top of the apple, moulding the pastry round the fruit. Press edges firmly together to seal. Repeat for the other 3 dumplings.

7 Turn the dumplings, sealed edge down, on to a lightly greased baking sheet. Prick a hole in the top of each one to allow steam to escape.

8 Mark a leaf pattern on the triangle trimmings and use a little beaten egg to seal them on top of the dumplings. Pierce a clove in the centre to look like the stalk.

9 Transfer the dumplings on to a lightly greased baking tray and brush them with beaten egg.

10 Place in the oven on the shelf above the centre and bake at 220°C [425°F] gas mark 7 for 15 minutes. Then reduce the heat to 180°C [350°F] gas mark 4 and continue to bake for a further 30 minutes or until cooked.

11 Serve hot or cold with sugar to sprinkle.

1 For 4 dumplings cut 225 g [½ lb] pastry into 4 equal pieces. Roll out to squares 20 × 20 cm [8 × 8"].

5 Place dumplings on a lightly greased baking tray, sealed side down, to keep seams closed.

Making apple dumplings step-by-steps

2 Cut 2 corners off each square and set aside. Place a prepared apple in centre of each square and fill.

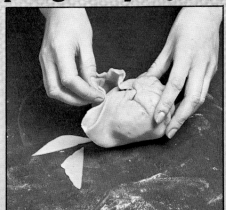

3 Damp the edges of each pastry square then gather up the edges neatly to the top of the apple.

4 Mould the pastry round the fruit, then press the seams firmly together to seal.

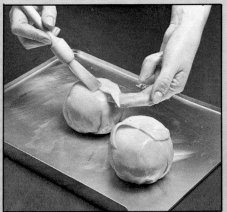

6 Mark a leaf pattern on triangular trimmings. Seal on to dumpling with a little beaten egg.

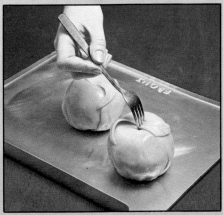

7 Prick the top of each dumpling with a fork to make holes for the steam to escape.

8 Brush with beaten egg and sprinkle with sugar to give the pastry a sweet glaze when cooked.

Light as air

Master the art of flaky pastry making and you will graduate to dishes which you have always left to the experts. The light-as-air layers of thin buttery pastry which melts in the mouth can be used in a wide variety of dishes. Pie toppings, tarts and tartlets are covered in detail here.

N ow that you have mastered the art of making shortcrust pastry, this will give you confidence to tackle a new type of pastry—flaky pastry.

Flaky pastry is made in such a way that air and fat are trapped between layers. Upon baking this trapped air expands, the fats melt, separating the layers, and the pastry lifts into flakes to form a crisp, tender pastry.

Flaky pastry, rough puff and puff pastry are all types of flaked pastry. At first glance all these pastries seem to be exactly the same and it is only when it comes to how and when each one is used that the differences will

become apparent. Here we discuss flaky pastry.

All these pastries are made by the successful application of the same principles. They rise in the same way and a number of the handling procedures are the same. The end results, however, are subtly different because of the way the layers of pastry are built up, and the proportions of fat used may also vary.

Flaky pastry
Flaky pastry, discussed in detail here, is a reasonably easy type of flaked pastry to make. For general

everyday cooking it is certainly the most useful pastry of the three and can happily be used for many sweet and savoury dishes. It is ideal for topping pies and making delicious tarts and results are just that bit more distinguished than those made with shortcrust.

Rough puff
Rough puff falls somewhere between flaky pastry and puff. It is quicker and easier to make than puff pastry, slightly lighter, though similar in texture and appearance to flaky pastry. Rough puff can be used

where flaky pastry is specified. It is an excellent choice when intricate or delicate shapes are required.

Puff pastry

Regarded as the finest of all the flaked pastries, puff is sadly reputed to be the most difficult to make. It is undoubtedly time-consuming to make, but its even, layered rising produces the crispest texture of all and the most flaky effect. It is just the thing to choose for a really good, light-as-air pastry for vol-au-vents, bouchées and mille-feuilles—the French name means a thousand leaves, which gives you some idea as to just how light this pastry can be.

INGREDIENTS FOR FLAKY PASTRY

Air, water, fat and flour are the vital ingredients for successful flaky pastry. Combined, they give a well-made flaky pastry its characteristics—lightness and richness.

Never, ever attempt to guess the proportions when making flaky pastry: exact weighing of the ingredients is absolutely essential. The chemistry must be just right if the end product is to be perfect.

Equally as important is the light handling of the pastry to incorporate the all-important air.

Flour

It is essential to use plain flour. White, strong, plain flour is even better. The raising agents in self-raising flour are unwanted and would, if used, break up the long strands of gluten in the flour which are necessary to produce the flaky layered results. The stronger the flour the better, as a strong flour contains more gluten, which has the elastic qualities that encourage the trapping of air in the dough.

Fat

Traditional English flaky pastry is made with equal quantities of butter and lard. All butter or margarine can be used or a mixture of margarine and lard. Never use all lard or a soft or whipped margarine. Soft margarines make the dough difficult to handle and will produce a 'tough' pastry.

Fats must be added to flaky pastry in the correct way. The method of adding fat plays an important part in the aerating operation. During bak-

ing, the fats melt, leaving empty spaces where the steam and air expand lifting the pastry layers above them.

Take great care to use the correct proportions. If you used too much fat the pastry would be difficult to mix, while if you used too little fat it would be tough and inedible.

Chilling the fat. It is absolutely essential that the fats used are firm and chilled before use. Warm or soft fats would be flattened and dispersed by the rolling. Chilled fat is needed to stay in position between the pastry to help build up the essential layers of trapped air. Pastry without these trapped layers of air will not be flaky but instead will be tough.

There is a second reason why soft fat should not be used: it would present problems when it came to rolling out, causing the dough to stick to the work surface and the rolling pin. Soft fat would make the pastry extremely messy to handle. The basic proportions could be altered because fat would certainly be lost. This, in turn, could tempt you to add more flour in a rescue attempt. Adding extra flour would only produce further toughening of the pastry.

Lemon juice and salt

A pinch of salt is always added to the dough. A little lemon juice makes the gluten in the flour more elastic. This elasticity is essential because the gluten has to stretch a great deal in order to rise and form the structure of the flaky layers.

EQUIPMENT

To make flaky pastry you will need the equipment for making, rolling out and baking as described on pages 136–139 for shortcrust. You will also need a round-bladed knife or small palette knife to cut in the fats and knock up the edges of the pastry for a secure edge.

A sharp knife is essential when cutting the pastry so that it does not drag when it is being cut or shaped. A clean cut pastry also ensures a better and more even rise.

Baking sheets, tins or trays do not need greasing because of the high fat content of the pastry which makes it self-greasing. Instead, sprinkle a little water on to a baking tray or sheet. This will be converted to steam in the hot oven and this steam

helps the pastry to rise.

MAKING FLAKY PASTRY

Making superb flaky pastry is not, as is often thought, a strict adherence to a vast set of complicated rules and regulations. The secret is more learning the art of correct handling. Heavy handling inevitably means a heavy pastry. Light, cool handling results in a pastry that is crisp, flaky and tender.

Keeping cool

You don't need a marble slab and icy cold hands when making flaky pastry—but, keep calm and cool both physically and mentally.

As with making all flaked pastries, a cool working atmosphere is obviously helpful. If the weather is hot or your kitchen is prone to reach heatwave proportions as soon as the oven is on, make the pastry early in the morning or in the evening when the temperature will be lower.

Chilling the equipment in the refrigerator and rinsing your hands under a cold tap make good sense. As already mentioned, it is absolutely essential to chill the fat.

Always give yourself plenty of time when making flaky pastry and try to avoid fitting it in between other jobs. It really does require all your attention for perfect results. Never try to hurry the processes along but allow a flexible hour and a half, especially if you are making flaky pastry for the first time.

Allow at least half an hour for the pastry to relax prior to shaping and baking. Wrap the pastry loosely in a polythene bag and place in a refrigerator.

If, at any time during the making, the pastry or fats get too warm, don't panic. Wrap the dough in a polythene bag and refrigerate for up to half an hour before starting again. Never carry on regardless, hoping for the best.

A light touch

Before you start pastry making, divide the specified quantity of fat into four equal portions. This is because the fat is added to the pastry in four stages by two different methods. Each method helps to introduce air into the pastry.

Put three portions of fat back in the refrigerator to keep chilled. The first portion of fat is then added to the total quantity of flour and salt in the mixing bowl. This fat is then rubbed in in the same way as when making shortcrust, letting the crumbs fall back into the bowl, which incorporates a certain amount of air.

Quickly and lightly add the lemon juice and water, mixing them in to give a fairly soft, pliable but not sticky dough. Turn the dough out on to a lightly floured board or working surface. The dough is then kneaded lightly (to strengthen the gluten) and make a smooth, crack-free dough.

Building up layers of fat

We now move on to the new technique, that of adding the remaining fats. The fats are added in three stages—by dotting the reserved quarters, one at a time, over the surface of the dough. The dough is then folded over it in such a way as to produce alternate layers of fat and dough, and the whole is rolled. This is repeated for each portion of fat.

Rolling the dough. Place the dough on to a lightly floured board. Using short, even and light strokes, roll the dough to an oblong, three times as long as it is wide, approximately 6 mm [¼"] thick. Use a round-bladed knife or small palette knife to mark the pastry into three equal sections.

Cutting the fat. Then cut up the first of the remaining quarters of fat (this will be one-quarter of the total amount of butter and one-quarter of the total amount of lard used). Cut the fat into small pieces. Dot the pieces of fat on the top two-thirds of the pastry to within 12 mm [½"] of the edge.

Folding the dough. The dough must now be folded to produce alternate layers of dough and fat. Start by lifting the fatless section of dough carefully with your hand and fold it over the centre section of dough. Do not handle the pastry excessively or pull it about clumsily with hot hands as this could make the dough sticky and unmanageable. Just fold it over like the flap of an envelope. The outside edge should reach the marked line running through the centre of the portion dotted with fat. Line the edge of the dough flush with the marked line.

Now lift the top section of dough

carefully with your hands. Fold it over the top of the other sections, taking care to keep the edges straight. Brush off any surplus flour from around the pastry.

Sealing the edges. The edges of the layers must now be sealed by lightly pressing down with a rolling pin. To do this give the dough a half turn, so that the folds are now at the

Step-by-step to making flaky pastry

MAKES 225 G [½ LB] PASTRY
225 g [½ lb] plain flour
2.5 ml [½ teaspoon] salt
75 g [3 oz] lard
75 g [3 oz] butter or margarine
10 ml [2 teaspoons] lemon juice
approximately 75 ml
[7 tablespoons] chilled water

1 Divide each fat into four equal pieces and place one portion of each on four separate plates. Place three plates in the refrigerator.

2 Sift flour and salt into mixing bowl. Cut in the first quarter of fats and rub fats into flour. Add lemon juice and water to make a soft pliable dough.

4 Roll out dough to an oblong, with short, light strokes. Using a round-bladed knife, lightly mark dough into three equal sections.

5 Cut another quarter of remaining fats into fairly small pieces and dot alternately over top of two marked sections of dough.

6 Fold the fatless section of dough across the centre section, making sure edges of dough are straight. Brush off surplus flour.

8 Lightly seal the three raw edges with a rolling pin and press dough at intervals to distribute the air. Relax in refrigerator.

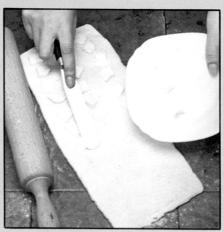

9 Repeat the process with the second quarter of fats from the refrigerator. Fold and roll to seal. Relax briefly if time allows.

10 Repeat the process with the remaining fats. Fold and roll to seal.

3 Turn out dough on to a lightly floured surface and knead lightly. Pat dough into a rectangular shape and lightly dust a rolling pin with flour.

Carefully fold top section over the centre section, again making sure that the edges of the dough are straight. Brush off any flour.

1 Relax the dough, covered in polythene, in the refrigerator for 30 minutes before use.

sides. Lightly seal the three raw edges with a rolling pin and press pastry parcel in about 3 places to distribute the air. The pastry may be relaxed at this point.

Re-rolling. The pastry is re-rolled to make new layers. A light hand is necessary on the rolling pin because heavy rolling will break up the air pockets and expel the precious air. Rolling must be consistent and even because uneven rolling would distort the shape of the rectangle. This would mean that the fat would become unevenly distributed and the resulting pastry would be patchy.

Making new layers. The process of dotting on fat, folding and rolling is repeated twice more, using the two remaining quarters of fats, relaxing the pastry after the second rolling. Do not over-roll or some of the precious air will be lost. An even better pastry will result if the pastry can be relaxed in between each rolling if time allows. The resting period makes the pastry easier to handle and also gives a more flaky texture.

Relaxing the dough. Cover the pastry loosely in a polythene bag and place in a refrigerator for a minimum of 30 minutes to firm and relax. After the resting period, roll the pastry into an oblong shape and fold into two. Use as required.

SHAPING AND GLAZING

Once the pastry is in the refrigerator relaxing, you can justifiably feel pretty happy with yourself, knowing that the major part of the job is over. All that is required is the final rolling and shaping. Described here are pie toppings, tarts and tartlets, using flaky pastry. For other pastry shapes and interesting decorative ideas, see pages 159–167. As flaky pastry is a soft dough, it tends to stretch easily, so it is necessary to always make sure that you and your baking equipment are all well organized beforehand.

Have baking trays, sheets or tins (which need no greasing as the pastry is self-greasing) close at hand. This will avoid carrying the cut shape(s) unnecessary distances.

Always roll the pastry with short, light strokes. When cutting the pastry, a sharp knife is essential. Make clean decisive cuts which avoid dragging or stretching the pastry unduly. A clean cut will ensure that

the pastry rises with maximum expansion.

Use a palette knife or fish slice for moving the smaller-sized pastry shapes. For pie toppings and larger shapes, gently roll the pastry over a rolling pin and carefully lift and unroll over the pie or on to a baking tray or sheet. Single-crust pies using flaky pastry are topped in exactly the same way as for shortcrust.

Ease the pastry into the correct shape once it is in position.

Glazing

To give an attractive glossy, appearance to flaky pastry, it has to be glazed. Eggs are always used. Savoury dishes can be brushed over with beaten egg, or beaten egg with a little milk added. For sweet dishes, beat egg white with a little caster sugar and brush over the pie.

OVEN TEMPERATURES AND TIMING

The final step in producing a light, crisp, flaky pastry is the baking. To obtain the best rise and flaky texture, the pastry must be cooked in a hot oven. The impact of high heat causes the fats between the layers to melt. This leaves empty spaces where the steam and air expand to lift the layers of pastry and quickly set the pastry into its final shape.

If the oven temperature is too low or if the pastry is put into an oven that has not reached the correct temperature, the fat will melt before the starch in the flour has had time to absorb it. As a result, the pastry will not rise and you will be left with a dry, tough pastry—and a very greasy oven!

If the oven temperature is too high, the surface of the pastry will form into a hard crust. This will stop the pastry from rising, because it has become too heavy.

Unless you have a fan-assisted oven, place the dish or tin containing the pastry just above the centre shelf for even rising and do not be tempted to open the oven door during the first fifteen minutes of baking. Sudden draughts of cold air will cause the pastry to collapse.

Flaky pastry by itself with no filling will be cooked after 25 minutes. Baking time must be adjusted for filled pies, especially for those with a raw filling which must cook with the pastry. If there is a filling which requires longer cooking, the oven temperature is reduced after the first 25 minutes' cooking time to prevent the pastry from overcooking. If the pastry top looks like over-browning, place a piece of greaseproof paper over the pastry and continue baking for the specified cooking time.

Never on any account bake flaky pastry in an oven with food which is likely to give off a lot of steam as it cooks. The excess moisture it gives off will make the pastry soggy and flat. Do not put pastry on top of hot fillings, but pre-cook and cool any fillings requiring long cooking.

Eat savoury pies immediately. If a pie is left for a long period, even in a warming drawer, it will toughen the pastry. If the pastry is to be eaten cold, you must cool the pie or tart uncovered, slowly in a draught-free place, otherwise it will lose its delicious flakiness.

STORAGE

Cooked flaky pastry soon loses its freshness, so do not store it for longer than three days. Place in an air-tight container, away from moist food or wrap it in cling film or foil, to preserve its crispness.

Uncooked flaky pastry, wrapped to exclude the air, can be stored in a refrigerator or very cool place for up to one week. Flaky pastry may be stored in a freezer, cooked for up to 3 months and uncooked for up to 6 months.

FLAKY CHOCOLATE TART

The crispy and light-as-air flaky pastry perfectly complements the deliciously rich and tasty chocolate filling.

SERVES 6
225 g [½ lb] flaky pastry

For the filling:
**50 g [2 oz] plain dessert
  chocolate
2 small eggs
50 g [2 oz] butter
50 g [2 oz] caster sugar
pinch of ground cinnamon
50 g [2 oz] ground almonds**

**50 g [2 oz] plain cake crumbs
pinch of salt**

1 Position the oven shelf just above centre and heat oven to 200°C [400°F] gas mark 6.

2 Line a 20 cm [8"] flan tin with the flaky pastry. Chill the pastry for fifteen minutes.

3 Line the pastry with a circle of greaseproof paper or kitchen foil and fill with baking beans.

4 Bake for ten minutes. Remove lining and beans and bake for a further 3–5 minutes until pastry is just set. Remove the tin from the oven and reduce oven temperature to 180°C [350°F] gas mark 4.

5 Break up the chocolate and place in a basin over a saucepan of hot, but not boiling water. Heat, stirring occasionally, until chocolate has melted.

6 Separate the eggs. Cream butter and sugar together in a large bowl until light and fluffy. Beat yolks together and add to butter mixture, a little at a time, beating well after each addition.

7 Beat melted chocolate into butter mixture, until all the chocolate has been incorporated.

8 Stir in ground cinnamon, almonds and cake crumbs. Mix together.

9 Add a pinch of salt to the egg whites and whisk until stiff, but not dry. Carefully fold egg whites into chocolate mixture.

10 Scrape the mixture into pastry case, using a spatula.

11 Bake for about 20 minutes. Remove from tin and serve hot with custard, or cold with thin cream.

Variations
● For a celebration tart, stir in 15 ml [1 tablespoon] Grand Marnier or your favourite liqueur with the chocolate.
● For a fruity variation, stir 25 g [1 oz] sultanas into the creamed chocolate mixture and substitute ground walnuts for the almonds.
● For milk chocolate lovers, use milk chocolate in place of the plain chocolate, omit the ground cin-

namon, and use biscuit crumbs in place of cake crumbs.

STICKY COCONUT TART

Sticky tarts are part of the heritage of British baking and their popularity has remained constant throughout the years. The tart turns an appetizing golden brown during cooking, concealing a deliciously sweet, soft centre.

SERVES 6
175 g [6 oz] flaky pastry

For the filling:
**225 g [½ lb] caster sugar
90 g [3½ oz] desiccated
  coconut
2 medium-sized eggs
10 ml [2 teaspoons] lemon juice**

1 Position the oven shelf to just above centre and heat oven to 200°C [400°F] gas mark 6.

2 Line a 17.5 cm [7"] flan tin with the flaky pastry. Chill the pastry for fifteen minutes.

Flaky chocolate tart is a success every time. Drizzle with glacé icing and sprinkle with almonds and cherries.

3 Line pastry with a circle of greaseproof paper or foil and fill with baking beans.

4 Bake for 10 minutes. Remove from the oven, remove lining and beans and return to oven for a further 10 minutes.

5 Meanwhile, start preparing the filling. Place sugar and coconut in a bowl and mix together.

6 Beat eggs and lemon juice together and stir into sugar mixture. Beat for one minute.

7 Remove the pastry case from the oven and reduce the temperature to 150°C [300°F] gas mark 2.

8 Pour the sugar and coconut mixture into tart case and return to oven for a further 45 minutes, until the top is golden brown and slightly puffed.

9 Serve immediately with thin cream.

Variations

●For a sticky syrup tart, substitute 100 g [¼ lb] golden syrup for the sugar and sprinkle base of tart with 25 g [1 oz] plain cake or fresh white breadcrumbs. Use only 50 g [2 oz] desiccated coconut.

●Lay wafer-thin slices of poached cooking apple over the base of tart. Sprinkle with a little lemon juice and a pinch of ground cinnamon before spreading over topping.

●Use soft brown sugar instead of caster sugar. Use 65 g [2½ oz] desiccated coconut and 25 g [1 oz] finely chopped walnuts.

STEAK, KIDNEY AND MUSHROOM PIE

◪◪◪ *Both the pastry and the filling benefit from being prepared in advance, ready to assemble and bake when required. It is essential that the filling is completely cold before it is topped with the pastry, otherwise the pastry will not rise successfully and might be soggy.*

SERVES 4
225 g [½lb] flaky pastry

For the filling:
700 g [1½ lb] stewing steak
225 g [½ lb] ox kidney
100 g [¼ lb] button mushrooms
30 ml [2 tablespoons] plain flour
2.5 ml [½ teaspoon] salt
freshly ground black pepper
30 ml [2 tablespoons] oil
275 ml [½ pt] beef stock
beaten egg to glaze

1 Discard fat and gristle from steak, cut into 5 cm [2"] cubes. Wash kidney, skin, remove core and cut into small pieces.

2 Prepare mushrooms by wiping the caps and removing earthy stalk ends.

3 Place the flour in a polythene bag, season and add the steak and kidney pieces in batches. Shake the bag to coat the meats in flour.

4 Heat the oil in a medium-sized saucepan, add the meats, in batches if necessary, and fry until evenly browned.

5 Allow saucepan to cool slightly before pouring in beef stock. Bring to the boil, cover and simmer for 2 hours or until meats are tender.

6 Add the mushrooms whole and cook for a further 10 minutes. Remove saucepan from heat, check seasonings and leave until completely cold.

7 When cold transfer the meat to an 850 ml [1½ pt] pie dish and reserve.

8 Heat oven to 220°C [425°F] gas mark 7.

9 Roll out pastry to 6 mm [¼"] thick and 4 cm [1½"] larger all round than pie dish.

10 Cut a strip the same width as the rim of the dish from the edge of the rolled out pastry. Damp the rim of the dish and seal the pastry strip on it.

11 Damp the pastry rim, carefully roll the pastry around the rolling pin and lift into position. Press lightly

to seal. Trim off surplus pastry and reserve.

12 Knock up edge to seal it securely and flute pastry at intervals of 8 mm [⅓"].

13 Insert a knife under the pastry on either side of the pie and raise the pastry slightly to make steam vents.

14 Roll out pastry trimmings and cut into four diamond shapes. Mark 'veins' on to shapes with the back of a knife to represent leaves.

15 Brush the underside of leaves with a little egg glaze and arrange on top of the pie.

16 Brush surface of pie with a little beaten egg to glaze.

17 Bake in heated oven for 30–35 minutes until pastry is well risen and golden brown. Serve.

Variations

●For chicken and vegetable pie, cut 450 g [1 lb] cooked chicken into pieces and place in a bowl with 100 g [¼ lb] cubed cooked ham. Add a small can of condensed chicken soup, 45 ml [3 tablespoons] water and a medium-sized packet of frozen mixed vegetables, just thawed. Add a dash of salt and pepper and mix together. Continue as directed from step 7.

●Substitute 900 g [2 lb] boneless lamb for the steak and kidney. Layer the cold cooked lamb mixture in a pie dish with 225 g [½ lb] sliced cooking apple and a sprinkling of ground nutmeg and cinnamon.

CHICKEN AND WALNUT PIE

This is a pie with a difference. The filling can be made in double quantity with half served as a casserole and the other half transferred into this pie and baked. The filling will re-heat while the pastry is cooking.

Because the meat is on the bone, a larger dish than usual is needed and the pastry may need a pie funnel in the centre to support it during cooking.

SERVES 4–6
900 g [2 lb] chicken drumsticks
30 ml [2 tablespoons] dry sherry
25 g [1 oz] caster or soft brown sugar
45 ml [3 tablespoons] oil
100 g [¼ lb] button mushrooms
225 g [½ lb] canned water chestnuts
550 ml [1 pt] chicken stock
25 g [1 oz] butter
50 g [2 oz] halved walnuts
225 g [½ lb] flaky pastry
beaten egg to glaze

1 Wipe chicken drumsticks and place in a shallow dish. Pour sherry over chicken and sprinkle with sugar.

2 Turn chicken in marinade and

cover. Leave to soak for 1½–2 hours, turning from time to time.

3 Heat the oil in a heavy-based frying-pan, add the chicken drumsticks and fry until evenly browned.

4 Meanwhile, wipe the mushroom caps and trim earthy stalks. Drain the water chestnuts and cut into halves if large.

5 Place chestnuts and mushrooms in a large casserole and lay the drumsticks on top.

6 Pour the chicken juices and the stock over the chicken, cover and cook in centre of oven for 1½–2 hours, until chicken is just tender.

7 Leave the casserole until completely cold. Transfer the chicken and gravy to a suitable pie dish, putting a pie funnel in the centre if necessary.

8 Dot chicken mixture with small pieces of butter and add walnuts.

9 Heat oven to 220°C [425°F] gas mark 7.

10 Roll out pastry to 6 mm [¼"] thick and 4 cm [1½"] larger all round than the pie dish. Cut a strip of pastry the same width as the rim of the pie dish from rolled-out pastry edge.

11 Damp the rim of the pie dish and seal the pastry strip on to it.

12 Stamp out rounds from the remaining pastry using a 5 cm [2"] plain round pastry cutter.

13 Place the pastry circles, overlapping, on top of the chicken, starting from rim of pie dish. Cover the chicken mixture completely with pastry circles. Place in refrigerator for 15 minutes to rest.

14 Brush the pastry with beaten egg

to glaze and bake in centre of oven for 25–30 minutes, until pastry is risen and golden brown. Serve.

Variations

● Try a Cornish cutlet pie. Braise 700 g [1½ lb] small lamb chops with sliced potatoes, root vegetables and thinly sliced onions. When completely cold, layer in a large pie dish, and sprinkle each layer with a little dry mustard and a good shake of Worcestershire sauce. Cover the meat with a layer of skinned, sliced tomatoes and top with pastry.

● For pigeon pie, first joint a brace (two) of pigeons. Season and braise the pigeon joints with 225 g [½ lb] mushrooms, 1 small onion, finely sliced, and a rich beef stock to which you can add a glass of good claret. When cold top with pastry and bake.

Filling pies for hearty appetites, traditional steak and kidney and mushroom pie and chicken and walnut pie.

CHANTILLY FRUIT TARTLETS

Make the tartlet cases in advance to assemble just before eating so that the filling has no time to penetrate the buttery crispness of the flaky pastry. Choose the fruit toppings which need no cooking to suit the season. If using canned fruits, drain well and gently pat dry with kitchen paper.

MAKES 12
175 g [6 oz] flaky pastry

For the filling:
25 g [1 oz] ratafia biscuits
30 ml [2 tablespoons]
  redcurrant jelly
225 g [½ lb] soft fruit,
  strawberries, raspberries,
  cherries etc
150 ml [¼ pt] thick cream
few drops vanilla extract

1 Place a shelf just above centre of the oven and heat to 220°C [425°F] gas mark 7.

2 Roll out the pastry to 6 mm [¼"] thick. Using a 7.5 cm [3"] round cutter, cut out twelve circles to fit a 12-hole or two 6-hole tartlet tins.

3 If necessary, re-roll pastry by layering trimmings one on top of the other. Roll and cut out the desired number of pastry circles.

4 Carefully line tartlet tin(s) with pastry circles and place the tin(s) in the refrigerator to rest for 15 minutes.

5 Cut circles of greaseproof paper or foil slightly larger than tins. Place linings on the pastry and fill with baking beans.

6 Bake blind for 10 minutes. Remove linings and beans and return to oven for a further 10 minutes.

7 Remove from oven and leave in tin(s) to cool for 3 minutes.

8 Using a small palette knife or round-bladed knife, carefully remove pastry cases from tins, place on a wire rack and leave to cool.

9 Put the ratafia biscuits in a polythene bag and crush finely with a rolling pin.

10 Place the redcurrant jelly in a bowl and beat with a wooden spoon. Sieve jelly into a small saucepan and heat gently (without boiling) until jelly melts. Remove from heat. Prepare the chosen fruit.

11 Put the cream and a few drops of vanilla extract in a bowl. Whip until the cream just holds its shape then fold in the biscuit crumbs.

12 Pipe or spoon the cream mixture into tartlet cases. Arrange the fruit on top of cream.

13 Brush melted jelly over fruit and serve immediately.

Rise and shine

Pastry making is fun so, roll up your sleeves and learn how to make rough puff pastry. You will never believe how easy it is to make a flaked pastry until you try rough puff.

Rough puff pastry rises in layers of flakes when cooked, like the flaky pastry, discussed on pages 149–158. Rough puff is, however, easier and quicker to make than flaky pastry. Both pastries contain exactly the same proportions of ingredients, but the methods of preparation differ.

Rough puff is just the right pastry to choose when you are looking for something that is that extra bit special—but don't have too much time to spare on the actual preparation.

Rough puff pastry is generally accepted as being best for dishes where the pastry is to be shaped and decorated. Rough puff will hold its shape with ease when cooked and is therefore suitable for intricate decorations. It can be cut into shapes which can then be used to make pie toppings. Serve little puffed shapes with soup, or spread or sandwich them with pâté for a party.

HIGH RISE PASTRY

As with all flaked pastries, the basic aim with rough puff is to introduce as much air as possible, to enable the pastry to rise in flaky layers. Fat is added to produce cavities which fill with air when the fat melts during baking. Water also evaporates during baking and the resulting steam lifts and stretches the dough to produce the well-known flaky texture.

The main difference between flaky pastry and puff pastry is in the way that the fat is added. When making flaky pastry the dough, at the outset, contains all the flour and water but only a small proportion of the fat. More fat is added subsequently. With rough puff pastry, all the fat is added to the flour at the beginning. In this respect it resembles shortcrust. The manner in which the fat is added, however, is different. Unlike shortcrust, the fat, once added, is not rubbed in.

A second difference between rough puff and flaky pastry is that rough puff is never kneaded. Flaky pastry is lightly kneaded at the beginning when it contains only one-

quarter of the fat to be used. Kneading is not practical for rough puff pastry, because all the fat is added at the beginning.

The similarity between rough puff and flaky pastry is the way in which both are rolled and folded several times. It is this repeated folding which distributes the fats evenly through the flour then the dough, trapping air and creating the layers which are characteristic of both types of pastry.

INGREDIENTS

The ingredients for rough puff pastry are the same as those given for flaky pastry, used in the same proportions of three parts fat to four parts flour.

As with flaky pastry, plain flour, preferably strong plain flour, is necessary when making rough puff pastry. Do not use self-raising flour because the raising agents present in it will inevitably break up the long strands of gluten in the flour. The elasticity of the gluten is an important factor as it is essential that the gluten (protein) can hold the bubbles of gas in the air. Salt is always added to the flour.

The same fats are used for rough puff as for flaky pastry—equal quantities of butter and lard, margarine and lard or all butter or all margarine. Whipped or soft margarines should never be used, as they will make the dough far too difficult to handle and the resulting layers, if any, would be tough.

As with flaky pastry, lemon juice is added with the chilled water to improve the elasticity of the gluten in the flour.

MAKING ROUGH PUFF
Preparing ingredients and equipment

Have all your ingredients and equipment ready before you start, because you should avoid stopping once you have started. The process of making rough puff relies to a certain extent on working with cold ingredients and equipment, quickly and efficiently. All sorts of problems can occur if you allow the fats to become soft and sticky, as a result to stopping half-way through pastry making to look for a particular piece of equipment.

Using chilled fat
The success of rough puff pastry lies

in the fats being hard before you start. With rough puff pastry care should be taken that the fats are used straight from the refrigerator and as hard as possible before adding to the flour. Before you start, weigh the fats then cut them into walnut-sized pieces and place them on a plate. Return to the refrigerator to keep well chilled. Without hard fats, rough puff pastry would have none of the melt-in-the-mouth flaky layers that are associated with this type of pastry.

Sifting the flour
The trapping of the air is started when the flour and salt are sifted together into a bowl. This simple process is the start of the aerating procedure. As the flour is lifted and allowed to fall through the sieve, air is trapped. Once the flour has been sifted into the bowl, it is essential not to stir it as some of the precious air would be lost. This would also mean your time and effort in sifting would be wasted.

Adding the fat
Rough puff pastry, like all the flaked pastries, depends on successfully distributing the fats through the flour. It is the way in which the fats are added to the flour that makes rough puff differ from other flaked pastries. With rough puff the fats are first cut into walnut-sized pieces and then added to the sifted flour and salt, all in one go. The fats are then tossed very lightly to coat them with flour.

Adding the liquid
Once the fats have been added to the flour, the next step is to add the water.

Use chilled water. Measure it and put it in a refrigerator. Do this when you are cutting up the fats.

Measure the water carefully, and never be tempted to add more than the stated amount. Too much liquid would give you a totally unmanageable dough. More seriously it would result in a pastry that would harden on baking showing no layers of flaky rising.

As with flaky pastry, lemon juice is added with the water.

The correct way to mix in the liquid is with a round-bladed or palette knife. Again a light hand is required so that none of the pieces of fat is broken down. More of a folding action is needed, so that the ingredients are bound together rather than stirred, creamed or rubbed-in.

MAKES 225 G [½ LB] PASTRY
75 g [3 oz] lard
75 g [3 oz] margarine
225 g [½ lb] plain flour
2.5 ml [½ teaspoon] salt
90 ml [6 tablespoons] chilled water
10 ml [2 teaspoons] lemon juice

4 Turn the dough out on to a lightly floured board or surface and shape by gently patting with the fingertips. Do not knead.

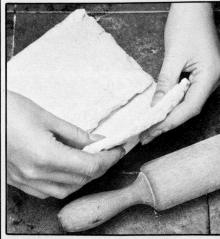

8 Fold the furthest section towards you so that it covers the other two. Seal the pastry edges lightly with the rolling pin or finger.

Step-by-step to rough puff pastry

1 Cut fats into walnut-sized pieces and place on a plate. Place plate in the refrigerator to keep fats chilled.

2 Sift flour and salt into a chilled bowl. Add chilled fats to flour and toss lightly with palette or round-bladed knife to coat fats in flour.

3 Add water and lemon juice to bowl and carefully gather mixture together with the fingertips to form a soft, pliable dough.

5 Using light short strokes, roll dough to a rectangle 37.5 × 12.5 cm [15 × 5"]. Do not over-flour board or rolling pin.

6 Place dough on board with length facing away from you. Lightly mark three equal sections across pastry with back of a knife.

7 Fold the section of dough nearest to you over the centre, using both hands. Place the edge straight on the marked line.

9 Give the dough a half turn so that the edges are top and bottom. Roll the pastry to its original size and repeat folding and sealing.

10 Place pastry on a plate and cover with a polythene bag. Place in refrigerator to relax for 30 minutes.

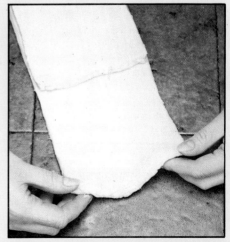

11 Repeat rolling, folding and sealing twice more. If the pastry is still mottled, roll and fold a fifth time. Relax for 30 minutes.

Forming the dough

Once the liquids are incorporated, the dough is ready to be quickly drawn together with the fingertips. It should be stressed at this point that the dough, once it has started to bind together, should not be kneaded into shape. All that is required is to gather it together with the fingertips to simply form one mass.

Turn the dough out on to a lightly floured board or surface. Avoid overflouring the surface or even adding more flour to the dough even if it appears to be sticky. With as little handling as possible, pat the dough into a neat rectangle.

If at this stage the dough is sticky, place it on a lightly floured plate, cover with a polythene bag and place in the refrigerator until the fats have hardened (this will take about 20 minutes).

Rolling the dough

As with the preparation of the dough, the rolling and folding procedures require a light touch. It is essential to use the rolling pin with light even strokes. Pressing and stretching the pastry will result in an uneven rise when the pastry is baked. If the pastry is stretched during the rolling process it may look as if it is suffering no harm. However, stretched pastry will shrink when it is baked. This could prove disastrous, particularly if you are using the pastry as a pie topping or covering.

Using short, even strokes, roll the pastry into a long rectangle approximately 37.5 × 12.5 cm [15 × 5″].

During this first rolling, take extra care to see that the side edges of the pastry are as neat and even as possible. Make sure, also, that the pastry is free of surplus flour. If there is any, brush if off gently with a pastry brush. The pastry at this point should have a mottled look. This shows that the fats are evenly distributed and your pastry is coming along successfully.

What is happening at this stage is that the pieces of fat have formed mounds in the dough and it is these mounds of fat that melt to form cavities when the dough is baked. It is in these cavities that the vital air is trapped. As the dough is subsequently re-rolled several times, these raised knobs of fat are distributed through the dough, therefore building up more and more potential cavities of air. This further explains the need for the fats to be hard. If they were soft at this stage, the fats would be easily squashed, expelling any of the air that may have been built up. Squashy fats would also prevent more pockets of air from forming.

Folding and sealing the dough

Once the dough has been rolled to the required length it needs to be folded. Lightly flour your hands and place the pastry with the length facing away from you. Using a round-bladed knife or palette knife, lightly mark the dough into three equal sections, crossways.

Lift the bottom section of the dough nearest to you and lay it over the centre section reaching the marked line. Do not press it down, just lay it on top, making sure that the raw edges are neatly aligned and not wavy.

Lift the top section of dough in both hands and carefully fold it towards you, laying it over the two layers. Again, make sure that the edges are aligned and not wavy.

To seal the raw edges, lightly press down with the rolling pin or the side of your little finger approximately three times across the dough. The dough is now ready for a second rolling.

Rolling and refolding

Give the dough a half turn, so that the raw edges are top and bottom. Using the rolling pin, very lightly press the dough down and away from you. Repeat the first rolling process again, until the dough reaches the same dimensions. Fold the pastry rectangle exactly as described before. Finish by sealing the edges with the rolling pin or your finger.

Relaxing the dough

By now, the dough will be in need of a rest, as it has been rolled and folded twice. To relax the dough, simply place it on a lightly floured plate and cover with a polythene bag. Place the plate in the refrigerator for at least 30 minutes. This resting time ensures that the fats firm up, because they will undoubtedly have softened during the rolling and folding. It also allows the gluten in the flour time to relax and gather its strength ready to be rolled and folded again.

Repeating the process

After this relaxing period, the rolling and folding processes are repeated

twice so that the dough is rolled and folded four times altogether.

By the end of the fourth rolling and folding, the pastry should be smooth. If for some reason it is still mottled, re-roll once more and relax for a further 30 minutes. Should the fifth rolling and folding not prove necessary, then further resting of the dough will not be necessary and this means that the pastry is ready for use.

MAKING IN ADVANCE

If you are making the pastry in advance, make it up to the final rolling stage and relax in the refrigerator until required. If you do this, however, the longer period in the refrigerator will make it cooler and therefore harder than you require. It will need to stand at room temperature for at least 30 minutes before use, so remember to remove it from the refrigerator and allow this extra amount of time before baking.

USING ROUGH PUFF PASTRY

When you are making an extra special pastry, it follows that it deserves to be shown at its best in the finished dish. Rough puff is ideal for intricate or shaped pastries, or to add a touch of glamour to a pie topping. It is the perfect choice when you are baking for a special celebration meal—or you simply want to try your hand at something different! All that is needed is a little time and patience.

Fleurons (half moons) of pastry look very attractive when served floating on a creamed soup. They are excellent and unusual, particularly when spread with pâté or a savoury mixture, to be served as nibbles at parties. They may be sandwiched with a savoury mix and can be made small, as snacks for a stand-up party or larger for a light lunch. The fillings may be put in before cooking or the pastry may be cooked, cooled and then sandwiched afterwards.

Fancy cutters

Pastry cutters come in an exciting variety of shapes and sizes nowadays as well as the standard round ones in graded sizes. Interesting shapes can add glamour to pastry—or just increase the fun—and will show off the risen glory of rough puff to its best advantage.

It is important that metal cutters are used for rough puff pastry because a clean, decisive cut is needed. A plastic cutter could drag the pastry. This in turn could seal the edges of the pastry which would stop the pastry from rising.

Making fleurons

If you do not own fancy shapes but have plain round or crinkle cutters, various exciting shapes can still be made by using them imaginatively. Fleuron shapes can be cut from pastry using a round cutter.

To make fleurons, roll the pastry and start working at the edge of the pastry nearest to you. Cut into the pastry, using only half of the round cutter furthest away. Work up the pastry making pairs of semi-circular cuts with the cutter.

Using shapes for pie toppings

The way in which you intend to use your cut shapes will determine what step you should take next.

Shapes of rough puff make ex-

Try your hand at making some attractive pastry shapes from rough puff pastry.

quisite pie toppings. Heart-shapes can be used in overlapping rings. Fleurons can be used on top of a pie. Arrange them radiating from the centre, all facing the same way and overlapping neatly. Alternatively, arrange them in concentric rings. During baking the pastry will rise to give a starry look to the top of the pie.

Shapes to be served plain

Place shapes which are to be served as tiny savouries on a baking sheet or tray. Brush lightly with a little beaten egg and sprinkle with seeds, chopped nuts or other suitable flavouring. Try poppy or sesame seeds, a little finely grated hard cheese or some finely chopped walnuts.

Shapes to be served with a topping

If the shapes are to be served as a base for a party savoury, first lay the uncooked shapes on a baking tray or sheet. Using the back of a round-bladed knife, lightly mark the shapes in a criss-cross pattern. Glaze the shapes and bake. The cross gives the topping something to grip on to and makes it more secure. Allow the shapes to cool completely before spreading on the topping, unless the topping is a hot one.

Using pastry trimmings

When you are using rough puff pastry, there are always pastry trimmings that can be turned into something special with very little effort. You do not need a pastry cutter; a sharp knife will do to cut the pastry into diamond shapes, squares or oblongs.

Making cheese fingers is a particularly delicious way of using rough puff trimmings. Roll the trimmings very thinly and divide the pastry into two equal-sized pieces. Cover one half of the pastry with a thin layer of grated hard cheese. Lay the remaining half of the pastry over the cheese. Carefully roll out the pastry again so that the cheese is sandwiched between the two layers of pastry. Use a sharp knife to cut the pastry into fingers and brush each finger with beaten egg, making sure not to brush the cut sides of the pastry.

Transfer to a baking sheet and bake in a hot oven 200°C [400°F] gas mark 6 for approximately ten minutes. Serve the cheese fingers hot or cold.

Making triple cheese sandwiches. For a real treat, roll out the pastry trimmings thinly and, using a small fancy cutter, cut out as many small shapes as possible. Re-roll if necessary and cut until it is all used up. Divide the total amount of pastry shapes into three equal piles.

Brush each shape lightly with beaten egg. Sprinkle two-thirds of the pastry shapes with finely grated, hard cheese mixed with a pinch of mixed herbs. Place half of the cheese-topped pastry shapes on a baking sheet or tray. Top each one with another cheese-topped pastry shape. Finally, top each shape with a plain pastry shape and press down lightly with the fingertips to secure. Bake in a hot oven, 200°C [400°F] gas mark 6, for 10 minutes until pastry is evenly risen and golden brown.

OVEN TEMPERATURES AND TIMING

Rough puff pastry, like all flaked pastries, requires a hot oven—200–220°C [400–425°F] gas mark 6–7. Place the shelf a little above the centre of the oven. If the pastry is placed in the oven before it has reached the required temperature, the pastry will not rise, so always pre-heat the oven. If this is not done, the fats will melt before the starch in the flour has had time to absorb the fat. The result will be that the pastry layers will not be formed.

Rough puff generally takes 20–25 minutes to cook, obviously depending on the size. If it is to be used as a pie topping, the filling should not take very much longer to reheat or to cook beneath it. If the filling does need a little longer, and you fear that the pastry could over-brown and perhaps burn, place a piece of greaseproof paper or foil over the crust. This will prevent the pastry from discolouring. If you pre-cook the filling you can avoid prolonged cooking which will result in a tough pastry with a dry taste.

STORAGE

Like flaky pastry, cooked rough puff will soon lose its freshness if stored for long periods of time. Up to three days is the maximum, stored in an airtight container or wrapped in cling film or foil to preserve as much of the crispy texture as possible.

Rough puff pastry will freeze like flaky pastry—for 6 months if uncooked, or for 3 months if cooked.

PEACH AND BANANA PUFFS

These delicious pastries may be served hot with a sweet white sauce, as a cold dessert with ice-cream or simply on their own for tea. For a special treat, poach the fruit in white wine instead of water. If using canned peaches, omit the poaching and use the thickened syrup as the sauce for serving with the puffs.

MAKES 8 INDIVIDUAL
PASTRIES
225 g [½ lb] rough puff pastry
250 ml [½ pt] dry white wine, or syrup from canned peaches (both optional)
45 ml [3 tablespoons] lemon juice
5 ml [1 teaspoon] ground allspice
40 g [1½ oz] soft brown sugar
4 small fresh peaches or 8 canned peach halves, drained
1 medium-sized banana
beaten egg white
caster sugar

1 If using fresh fruit, pour the wine, or the same quantity of water, into a sauté pan or large saucepan. Add 30 ml [2 tablespoons] lemon juice, ground allspice and sugar.

2 Stir once then bring to the boil. Simmer for approximately 2 minutes until sugar has completely dissolved.

3 Skin, halve and remove stones from fresh peaches.

4 Remove the pan from the heat and add fresh peach halves. Reduce the heat, cover and simmer gently for 10–15 minutes, until the peaches are just tender.

5 Uncover the pan and set aside until the fruit is completely cold.

6 Using a slotted or perforated spoon, carefully lift the peaches out of the liquid and pat them dry on kitchen paper. Reserve the poaching liquid.

7 If using canned peaches, drain them, reserving the syrup.

8 Position the shelf just above the centre and heat the oven to 200°C [400°F] gas mark 6.

9 Using a sharp knife, cut the pastry into two equal-sized pieces. Roll out each piece of pastry to 3 mm [⅛"] thick.

10 Using a 7.5 cm [3"] fluted cutter cut out eight circles from one piece of the pastry.

11 Using a 10 cm [4"] fluted cutter cut out eight circles from other pieces of pastry.

12 Layer the trimmings on top of each other and roll out to 3 mm [⅛"] thick.

13 Using a very small fancy cutter, cut out 24 fancy shapes from the trimmings and reserve.

14 Peel the banana and cut into 24 thin slices. Place the slices in a bowl and add the remaining lemon juice. Toss them to coat with lemon juice.

15 Place the eight smaller pastry circles on a baking sheet or tray and brush edges with a little beaten egg white.

16 Place 3 slices of banana, over-

lapping in the centre of each pastry circle. Place a peach half, cavity side downwards, on top of the banana.

17 Cover each peach with a larger circle of pastry. Press the edges together to seal.

18 Brush the top surface of each pie with a little beaten egg white. Arrange three fancy pastry shapes on top of each one.

19 Brush the decorations with egg white and sprinkle lids with a little caster sugar.

20 Bake for 20–25 minutes, until pastry is puffed and golden brown.

21 Transfer the puffs to a wire cake-rack. Serve hot with the poaching liquid thickened with arrowroot, or cold with cream.

Variations
● Use apricots instead of peaches and add a little Amaretti (almond liqueur) to poaching liquid or syrup.
● Place a small ball of marzipan in each peach cavity before baking.

CHEESE D'ARTOIS
Layers of rough puff pastry are sandwiched with cheese and lightly seasoned. The pastry can be cut into straws or, if you have some small fancy cutters, into fancy shapes for party-time eating. For something a little more substantial, cut larger portions and serve with a green salad for high tea.

MAKES 10 FINGERS
75 g [6 oz] rough puff pastry

For the filling:
25 g [1 oz] butter
50 g [2 oz] Cheddar cheese
pinch of cayenne pepper
pinch of salt
beaten egg to glaze

1 Position the oven shelf just above the centre and heat oven to 200°C [400°F] gas mark 6.

2 Roll out pastry to a long thin rectangle 20 × 25 cm [8 × 10"]. Using a sharp knife, cut pastry into two rectangles.

3 Carefully roll one piece of pastry over the rolling pin and transfer to a baking sheet or tray. Unroll pastry on sheet and ease back into rectangle shape.

Scrumptious peach and banana puffs: melt-in-the-mouth pastry with a fruity surprise filling.

4 Melt butter in a small saucepan over a low heat.

5 Grate the cheese. Remove pan from heat and stir in cheese and seasonings.

6 Spread the cheese and butter mixture over the pastry rectangle on the sheet to cover it evenly.

7 Brush remaining pastry rectangle with beaten egg and lay it, egg-side downward, on cheese mixture.

8 Gently press pastry down with the palm of the hand to secure it in position.

9 Using a long, sharp knife, cut pastry into 12 mm [½"] fingers, cutting through pastry cleanly and decisively.

10 Alternatively, cut pastry across width into 2.5 cm [1"] fingers, then cut each finger diagonally, to form diamond shapes.

11 Place pastry in refrigerator for 20 minutes to relax.

12 Bake for 15–25 minutes until pastry is golden brown.

13 Using a fish slice, transfer the cheese shapes to a wire tray and leave until cold.

MINCE PIES
You don't have to wait for Christmas to come to make a batch of mince pies. Made with rough puff pastry these traditional pies turn tea-time into a special occasion and will prove irresistible for the sweet-toothed members of the family. Make and bake them in advance to reheat or serve cold. You will need a 12-hole tartlet tin or two 6-hole tins.

MAKES 12 PIES
225 g [½ lb] rough puff pastry

For the filling:
350 g [¾ lb] mincemeat
beaten egg to glaze
caster sugar

1 Position the shelf just above the centre and heat the oven to 220°C [425°F] gas mark 7. Roll out the pastry to 3 mm [⅛"] thick.

Traditional tea-time treats, Eccles cakes, made with light-as-air pastry and a fruity filling, and decorative mince pies.

2 Using a fluted cutter the same size as the hollows of the tartlet tin, cut out the lids for the tarts.

3 Using a small fancy star-shaped cutter, cut star shapes out of centre of each pastry circle.

4 Using a cutter 2.5 cm [1"] larger than the first, cut out as many bases as you can from the remaining pastry.

5 Layer the pastry trimmings one on top of the other and re-roll. Stamp out the remaining number of rounds needed.

6 Line the tartlet tin hollows with the larger rounds, moulding them to fit.

7 Place a heaped teaspoonful of mincemeat in each hollow.

8 Brush the edges of each lid with cold water and place them, damp side down, over the fillings. Press the edges of the lids to seal.

9 Place the pies in the refrigerator for 20 minutes to relax.

10 Brush the pies with beaten egg to glaze and sprinkle lightly with caster sugar.

11 Bake the pies for 20–25 minutes.

12 Remove from the oven and leave them in the tin for a few minutes.

13 Remove the pies from the tin, using a palette knife if necessary. If serving cold, put them on a wire rack to cool.

Variations

● Sprinkle pastry base with a little ground almonds and sprinkle over a little rum or brandy before filling with mincemeat.
● Serve the mince pies with a cube of Stilton or a blob of cream cheese on top.
● Instead of using all mincemeat to fill the tarts, use half mincemeat, a quarter chopped walnuts and a quarter of stewed apple.

ECCLES CAKES

The secret of good Eccles cakes is not to skimp on the filling—make sure there is plenty of the delicious fruit in the middle to complement the buttery pastry. Serve them hot as a special pudding with lashings of custard or cool with thick cream at tea-time. They can quite happily be made in advance and re-heated just before serving.

MAKES 16 CAKES
225 g [½ lb] rough puff pastry

For the filling:
25 g [1 oz] butter or margarine
15 ml [1 tablespoon] light, soft brown sugar
100 g [¼ lb] currants
50 g [2 oz] mixed peel
2.5 ml [½ teaspoon] mixed spice

For the glaze:
milk
caster sugar

1 Position the shelf just above the centre and heat oven to 220°C [425°F] gas mark 7.

refrigerator for 20 minutes to relax the pastry.

10 Using a sharp knife make three diagonal slits across the top of each cake. Brush with milk and sprinkle with a little caster sugar.

11 Bake the cakes for 20–25 minutes until cakes are puffed and golden brown.

Variations
● Substitute mincemeat for the filling.
● Make cherry Eccles by omitting the mixed peel and substituting 50 g [2 oz] chopped glacé cherries. Soak the currants in 30 ml [2 tablespoons] cherry brandy before using.
● Omit 25 g [1 oz] currants and replace with 25 g [1 oz] chopped walnuts. Use ground cinnamon instead of mixed spice.

CHEESE AND PRAWN JALOUSIE

A jalousie really shows off rough puff pastry at its best—decorative and light as air. A jalousie can have a sweet or savoury filling and is suitable served at supper or a summer lunch or as part of a picnic or buffet. Cut into slices and serve hot or cold, garnished with parsley sprigs, sliced tomatoes and a few prawns.

SERVES 6
225 g [½ lb] rough puff pastry

For the filling:
50 g [2 oz] prawns
25 g [1 oz] red pepper
275 g [10 oz] full fat soft cheese
30 ml [2 tablespoons] thick cream
pinch of salt
pinch of paprika
pinch of dry mustard
10 ml [2 teaspoons] chopped chives
2 hard-boiled eggs

1 Position the shelf just above the centre and heat the oven to 200°C [400°F] gas mark 6.

2 Roll out the pastry to a long thin rectangle, 20 × 25 cm [8 × 10"]. Cut the pastry in half to make two rectangles.

3 Carefully roll one piece of pastry over the rolling pin and transfer it to a baking sheet or tray. Unroll the pastry on to the baking sheet or tray and ease back into shape.

4 Carefully fold remaining rectangle of pastry in half lengthwise. Using a sharp knife cut diagonal slits right through the double layer of pastry on the folded edge to within 12 mm [½"] of the raw edge. Place in the refrigerator while preparing the filling.

5 Chop prawns and red pepper coarsely. Place all filling ingredients in a bowl with the exception of the hard-boiled eggs. Mix together to combine.

6 Brush edges of the pastry on the baking sheet or tray with water to dampen.

7 Peel and slice the hard-boiled eggs and arrange the egg slices on the pastry to within 2.5 cm [1"] of the pastry edges. Spread prawn filling over the egg slices.

8 Carefully lift slit pastry on to one half of the filling and unfold. Ease it into shape to cover filling. The filling should just be visible through the decorative slits in the pastry.

9 Firmly press the pastry edges together to seal. Knock up and flute the edges in exactly the same way as you would for a single-crust pie.

10 Brush the jalousie with beaten egg, taking care not to brush between the slits.

11 Bake for 20 minutes, until the pastry is risen and golden brown.

12 Leave the jalousie to cool on the baking sheet or tray for 5 minutes. Then transfer to a wire rack to cool. Alternatively, transfer to a serving dish and serve hot.

Variations
● Use chopped tongue in place of the prawns and 50 g [2 oz] mushrooms in place of the red pepper.
● A very simple, yet effective variation is to add a pinch of curry powder to the seasonings, so that its flavour is just detectable.
● Add 50 g [2 oz] finely chopped walnuts to the filling mixture.

2 Roll out pastry to 3 mm [⅛"] thick. Using a 8.5 cm [3½"] plain cutter, cut out 16 circles.

3 If necessary, layer the pastry trimmings one on top of the other and re-roll. Stamp the remaining number of rounds needed.

4 Very lightly roll the pastry circles with a rolling pin to make them slightly larger.

5 Place butter or margarine in a small saucepan and add remaining filling ingredients. Heat over a low heat until butter has melted, then stir to mix together.

6 Dampen pastry edges with a little milk and place a heaped teaspoon of the filling in the centre of each circle.

7 Using your fingertips, gather the pastry edges up over the filling and pinch together to seal.

8 Turn the cakes over so that the joins are underneath and gently flatten each cake with the palm of your hand.

9 Place cakes on a rinsed baking sheet or tray and place in the

Soft choux shuffle

Choux pastry is unlike any other pastry. Light, crisp and deliciously delicate, choux pastry is not a true pastry but is used to make scrumptious eclairs, and the queen of desserts—profiteroles.

This unusual pastry, like so many others, originated in France. The French first used the pastry to make delicate buns and they gave them the name 'choux', French for cabbages, because the little buns were irregular in shape, resembling cabbages.

Choux pastry is not a true pastry, because the method used to make it is unlike other pastries, although the ingredients are much the same. Basically choux is a thick sauce, called a panada. The reason that it has been accepted in baking terminology as a pastry is that choux is used mainly as a container for either sweet or savoury mixtures. It can more accurately be defined as a type of fancy cake rather than a traditional pastry.

Tradition dictates that the pastry is only flavoured with vanilla. However, there are some interesting flavour variations. Described here is the basic method of making choux pastry plus some mouthwatering recipes

for sweet buns, desserts and cakes for you to try.

INGREDIENTS

With the exception of eggs, the basic ingredients required to make choux pastry are the same as for most of the other pastries.

Flour: plain flour gives good results but the best flour to use is a strong plain flour. A high percentage of gluten is needed because, like bread, the pastry is required to rise and it is the gluten that assists this rising.

Self-raising flour is unsuitable, because the raising agents upset the balance and inhibit the rising of the pastry during baking.

Fats: butter or margarine can be used for choux pastry. Butter has no advantage over margarine; they both produce pastry with a good colour and a crisp, golden finish. Soft margarine should not be used because it has too high a water content. Lard is

not successful because it does not give a good colour or flavour—both absolutely necessary for good choux pastry.

Eggs: eggs add colour and flavour; they also help to incorporate air as they are beaten into the pastry. Always use medium-sized eggs for the correct proportions.

Liquid: a high proportion of liquid is used to make choux pastry and it is always water. Milk or even a proportion of milk has no practical advantage and should never be used. The liquid plays an important role in the pastry rising and is included instead of any raising agent (other than eggs). The liquid turns into steam during cooking and this puffs up the pastry to two or three times its original size.

Salt: a pinch of salt is used to bring out the flavour of the other ingredients. Even though you may choose to use salted butter, it is still advisable to add a pinch of salt.

EQUIPMENT

Because choux pastry is made by a method quite different from other pastries, the equipment you will need is also different. For a start you can forget about rolling pins and large mixing bowls.

Instead you will need a saucepan, a double thickness of greaseproof paper, a wooden spoon or an electric hand-held whisk to mix the pastry and a piping bag or metal spoons for shaping the pastry.

Scales are essential for accurate weighing of all the ingredients; unbalanced proportions will result in a soggy pastry that will not rise during baking and will definitely not produce a light and well puffed pastry.

A small, non-stick saucepan is the second on the list of priorities because, like the melting method of making cakes, this pastry is made in a saucepan. You do not need a heavy-based pan because there is no prolonged cooking of ingredients that are likely to burn or stick. Obviously a non-stick pan is the best choice, but an ordinary saucepan will serve just the same purpose. A non-stick pan is definitely out if you intend to use a hand-held electric whisk for mixing the ingredients together.

Greaseproof paper is used to hold the flour before adding it to the mixture. A double thickness of greaseproof about 20 cm [8"] square will be large enough. A sheet of greaseproof paper is by far the most convenient receptacle for the flour, because it is essential to add the flour to the mixture all in one go. The action is quicker and more efficient when the greaseproof paper is lifted and the flour can be shot straight into the saucepan.

A wooden spoon is necessary to beat the pastry in the saucepan.

An electric whisk is an added bonus in that it speeds up the method of making the pastry and saves effort.

Spoons, small or large, may be used for shaping the mixture if you do not own a piping bag. Drop the spoonfuls of the mixture on to the baking tray, scraping one spoon out with a second spoon.

A medium-sized piping bag is essential if you are making a decorative shape such as an oblong. A greaseproof paper piping bag will not do because the mixture is far too stiff for the paper to withstand. Éclairs, for instance, really need to be piped through a plain tube, while fancy shaped, small buns can be piped through a fancy nozzle.

A baking sheet is needed for baking the pastry—and to make choux in the traditional French cabbage shape, you will also need a roasting tin to act as a lid (see strawberry choux buns).

Sundry items include a sieve for the flour and salt and a measuring jug for the liquid. If you are piping the pastry for éclairs you are going to need a round-bladed knife to cut off the éclairs neatly as the pastry leaves the bag.

GETTING ORGANIZED

It is extremely important when making choux pastry that you plan in advance. It is not a pastry that can safely be left half-way through the making—this will have a detrimental effect on the end result. Assemble all the ingredients before you start so there will be no delays.

Preparing the baking sheet

Choux is baked on a baking sheet. Brush this lightly with the melted fat or oil and lightly sift flour over. There is a second reason for using flour, other than the obvious one of stopping the pastry from sticking to the baking surface. A flour covered tray can very easily be marked with lines, using the end of a wooden spoon, to show you where to begin and stop piping.

Step-by-step to choux pastry

FOR SERVINGS, SEE CHART
65 g [2½ oz] plain flour
2 medium-sized eggs
50 g [2 oz] butter or
** margarine**
a pinch of salt
150 ml [¼ pt] water
few drops vanilla extract

1 Sift flour on to a piece of greaseproof paper. Place eggs in a basin and whisk lightly together.

OR draw the pan off the heat and add the flour; whisk with a hand-held electric whisk until smooth.

4 Return pan to a low heat and beat vigorously for 1-2 minutes until the mixture forms a smooth ball.

Setting the oven

It is vital that choux pastry is made, shaped and baked directly, without any waiting. It is therefore extremely important that the oven should be ready for it. Position the oven shelves towards the top of the oven, where it will be hottest. Set the oven to 200°C [400°F] gas mark 6. Switch oven on at least fifteen minutes before you start making the pastry.

MAKING THE CHOUX PASTRY
Preparing the flour and eggs

Begin by sifting the flour on to a double thickness of greaseproof paper. Break the eggs into a bowl and beat them with a wooden spoon just to amalgamate them. Keep them in reserve ready for use.

Melting the fat

Place the measured fat, salt and water into a small saucepan over a moderate heat. Stir with a wooden spoon from time to time, until the fat has melted and the liquid comes just to the boil. This is definitely a time not to stray from the cooker because the moment the water comes to the boil and the fat has melted, you must remove the saucepan from the heat. Left to boil, some of the water would certainly evaporate, changing the basic proportions—it could result in insufficient liquid.

Adding the flour

Place the saucepan on a wooden board or a steady surface for the next step, and work quickly, adding the flour immediately. Pick up the greaseproof paper by two sides and shoot the flour on to the paste. Hold the handle of the saucepan in one hand and the wooden spoon in the other. Beat the flour into the melted mixture quickly until all the flour is absorbed by the liquid. If you are using a hand-held electric whisk, follow the same procedure, whisking the mixture. During the beating the starch grains in the flour burst to absorb the fat, a process known as gelatinization. When the pastry is ready it will be smooth with a texture similar to that of thick mashed potato.

Beating the paste

Return the saucepan to a low heat and beat vigorously, until a smooth ball is formed which leaves the side of the pan without sticking. This process should take no longer than two minutes at the most. Overbeating once the mixture has formed a smooth ball will cause the fat and flour to separate; there is no way to overcome this, so do not be tempted to keep beating. You can now compliment yourself, because you are safely half-way through the process—and all that remains is to add the eggs and shape the choux before baking.

Adding the eggs

Remove the pan from the heat. Place on a steady surface. Allow to cool for two minutes. Again, holding the handle of the saucepan in one hand and the wooden spoon or hand-held electric whisk in the other, add the egg a little at a time. Beat well after each addition until all the eggs are incorporated in the mixture. It is essential that you do not start to add the eggs while the mixture is hot, because this will curdle the eggs, while the protein in the egg will set. Always make sure that the mixture has had time to cool slightly before you add any of the egg.

Beating the eggs into the mixture also means that you are beating in air, which assists the pastry to rise. When all the eggs have been incorporated, the paste should be just stiff enough to stand in soft peaks when lifted with either the wooden spoon or the whisk. Finally, flavour the pastry with a few drops of vanilla extract.

Place butter, salt and water in a saucepan over a moderate heat. Bring slowly to the boil, stirring.

3 Quickly draw the pan off the heat and tip in all of the flour. Beat with a wooden spoon until smooth.

Draw pan off heat; allow to cool for 2 minutes. Beat in eggs a little at a time until incorporated.

6 Beat in vanilla extract. Spoon or pipe the mixture on to prepared baking sheet.

SHAPING CHOUX PASTRY

Choux pastry is easy to shape as the mixture is stiff and holds its form. It is ideal for piping into plain or fancy shapes, using a nylon piping bag and a plain tube or fancy nozzle.

With a piping bag and tubes or nozzles you can make éclair shapes, smooth-sided buns, rosettes and star shapes. To make éclairs, which are smooth sided and usually 7.5 cm [3"] long (unbaked) you will need a 12 mm [½"] plain piping tube. For small, even-sized, smooth or fancy shaped buns, for example, those used for profiteroles, you will need a 12 mm [½"] plain or star-shaped tube.

If you do not own a piping bag, you can make bun shapes by using different-sized spoons. Simply drop a heaped teaspoon or tablespoon of the mixture on to a prepared baking tray. Use a second spoon to scrape the mixture off the first spoon. Space the smaller buns 2.5 cm [1"] apart and the larger buns 5 cm [2"] apart, to allow for expansion during baking. It is rather important that the pastry is well spaced rather than being piped or dropped so that it touches (unless, of course, the recipe demands it).

BAKING CHOUX PASTRY

When choux pastry is put into a hot oven at 200°C [400°F] gas mark 6, the air beaten into the pastry expands quickly, the water turns to steam and the pastry puffs up and out rapidly. This fast expansion is essential; the outer structure of the paste then sets by the coagulation of the eggs and the complete gelatinization of the starch. If the choux is covered with a roasting tin while being baked it rises even more. An example of this technique is given in the recipe for strawberry choux buns.

Baking time

The baking time for choux pastry is a lengthy one. At first the higher temperature of 200°C [400°F] gas mark 6 is used to expand and then set the pastry; 20 minutes are required at this temperature. The oven temperature is then lowered to 190°C [375°F] gas mark 5 to ensure that the pastry shell is quite firm and dried out. A further 10-15 minutes are needed to cook the choux without fear of overbrowning. If the correct oven temperatures and timing are not followed to the letter, the pastry will be soft and collapse as soon as it is removed from the oven.

On no account be tempted to open the oven door, especially during the first 15 minutes of baking time. If you do so, the pastry will sink and there is very little chance that it will recover.

Releasing the steam

Immediately the pastry comes out of the oven, make a small slit in the side of the pastry shape with the end of a pointed knife. This allows the steam inside the pastry to escape and ensures that the pastry remains crisp as it cools. If the pastry were simply left to cool, the steam inside the pastry shape would make the inside soggy and indigestible.

Because of the nature of the pastry, there is still a good chance that the very centre of the pastry will be uncooked. Do not worry about this; another 'trick of the trade' is to scrape out and discard any uncooked pastry from the centre with the end of a teaspoon, working through the slit opening. If you are going to add a filling, it may be easier to cut open the pastry shapes to remove any uncooked pastry.

STORING AND FREEZING

Choux pastry is at its best the day it is made. It can, however, be stored satisfactorily baked, but unfilled or decorated, in an airtight container for up to three days. To freeze, bake the pastry in the required shape. Freeze it with or without a filling, but do not decorate it. Place the baked cooled pastry in a polythene freezer container or bag, foil or heavy-duty freezer wrap and store in the freezer for up to 6 months. Decorate as soon as the pastry has thawed.

FINISHING TOUCHES

Sweet choux pastries are usually given both a filling and a topping—although there are the odd exceptions to this rule.

Because the pastry is a rather special one, it is well worth the trouble to finish off choux cakes with special fillings and toppings. It is also a good idea to put the finishing touches as close to serving time as possible, so that the pastries are served at their best. If the pastry were to be completed too far in advance, it is certain to lose some of its crispness and become disappointingly soggy because of exposure to air and contact with the filling.

Step-by-step shapi

1 Lightly brush a baking tray with melted fat or oil. Sift the greased surface with flour. Heat oven to 200°C [400°F] gas mark 6. Make pastry. Allow to cool slightly.

5 For buns, use a plain tube or fancy nozzle and fill the piping bag. Hold the bag vertically; press out the required amount for small or large bun shapes.

7 Bake at the top of oven. Reduce oven temperature to 190°C [375°F] gas mark 5 and cook until well puffed and browned, for timings see chart.

d baking choux pastry

Using the handle of a wooden spoon, draw guidelines on prepared tray. For ring shapes, mark around a plate or pastry cutter of the required size.

3 For finger shapes for éclairs, fill a piping bag fitted with a 12 mm [½"] tube. Hold at a 45° angle to the marked surface just above the tray; press the bag.

4 Pipe the pastry across the tray, following marked lines. At the line end, raise the nozzle; use a wet, round-bladed knife to cut off the pastry cleanly.

R use a teaspoon or tablespoon to drop the pastry on to the tray, using the pastry straight from the saucepan. Scrape the spoon clean with a second spoon.

6 To make choux rings 20 cm [8"] diameter, first mark the baking tray. Fit piping bag with either a plain or fancy nozzle. Hold at a 45° angle and pipe in a circle.

OR pipe plain or fancy ball shapes so that they just touch each other to form a crown, following a circle which you have previously marked on the tray.

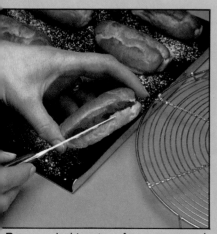

Remove baking tray from oven and using a sharp knife, slit the side of each bun, finger or ring to allow steam to escape and prevent pastry becoming soggy.

9 Transfer pastry to a wire rack. When cool, store in an airtight tin. Before serving, fill with one of the mixtures suggested in this course.

10 To ice éclairs, make a glacé icing, flavouring it as wished. Dip the top of the filled éclair in the icing. Allow excess to drip off. Leave on a wire rack to set icing.

FILLINGS

Whipped cream

Whipped cream is the quickest and the most popular filling for choux pastries. Use thick cream; whip it until it stands in soft peaks and then spoon or pipe into the pastry to form a filling. For variety, the cream can be flavoured by the addition of a little flavouring extract such as vanilla, or even a liqueur.

Lightening the cream makes it go further and cuts down the expense. Whip thick cream until it stands in soft peaks, then fold in whisked egg white (allowing one whisked egg white per 150 ml [$\frac{1}{4}$ pt] cream). This cream may be flavoured as for whipped cream.

Crème pâtissière

French pastry cream or crème pâtissière (also called confectioner's custard) can be substituted for fresh cream and is the traditional filling of small choux buns to make profiteroles. The quantity needed for different types of pastries is given in the chart. This will store in the refrigerator, covered with cling film or a disc of greaseproof paper, for at least 2 days.

Flavourings

Any of the following can be added to 425 ml [$\frac{3}{4}$ pt] pastry cream as made in the step-by-step instructions.
● Use 2.5 ml [$\frac{1}{2}$ teaspoon] vanilla extract.
● Melt 50 g [2 oz] plain or milk chocolate and stir into the hot pastry cream following the egg white.
● For coffee, use 10 ml [2 teaspoons] coffee essence or the same amount of strong black coffee.
● For orange or lemon, use the grated zest of one small orange or lemon.
● For rum, use 15 ml [1 tablespoon] rum.
● Mix together equal quantities of your favourite fruit purée and pastry cream.

Crème au beurre

This filling (literally 'butter cream') makes a delicious filling for choux pastry. Use it in the same quantities as crème pâtissière.

Ice-cream

Ice-cream, either plain or flavoured, makes an excellent filling for the larger buns or rings. If using ice-cream, fill the pastry with the ice-cream immediately before serving.

Type	Size to pipe using 12mm [$\frac{1}{2}$"] plain tube	Spoon size	Space between each	Bak she
Éclairs makes 16	7.5 cm [3"] long	15 ml [1 tablespoon]	2.5 cm [1"]	
Choux buns makes 12	5 cm [2"] diameter 2.5 cm [1"] high	15 ml [1 tablespoon]	5 cm [2"]	
Profiteroles makes 30	2.5 cm [1"] diameter 1.2 cm [$\frac{1}{2}$"] high	7.5 ml [$\frac{1}{2}$ tablespoon]	2.5 cm [1"]	
Rings (i.e. Paris-Brest) makes 3	20 cm [8"] diameter	75 ml [5 tablespoons]	—	

Step-by-step crème pâtissière

Crème pâtissière, sometimes called confectioner's custard, is a useful substitute for fresh cream. It is particularly suited to choux buns.

MAKES 425 ML [$\frac{3}{4}$ PT] PASTRY CREAM
25 g [1 oz] plain flour
10 ml [2 teaspoons] cornflour
275 ml [$\frac{1}{2}$ pt] milk
2 medium-sized egg yolks
50 g [2 oz] caster sugar
1 medium-sized egg white
few drops of vanilla extract (optional)

1 Sift flour and cornflour into a bowl Add a quarter of the milk and bea together until smooth.

4 Put the bowl over a saucepan of water over low heat. Stir continuously until the mixture thickens to a thick custard.

5 Remove bowl from heat and allo to cool. Meanwhile, put the eg white in a bowl and whisk unt stiff.

For choux pastry made with 65 g [2½ oz] flour

Oven temperatures and times	Cream filling	Sauce	Icing
200°C [400°F] gas mark 6 for 20 minutes, then: 190°C [375°F] gas mark 5 for 15 minutes	Thick cream: 150 ml [¼ pt] or Crème pâtissière: 425 ml [¾ pt]	—	150 ml [¼ pt]
As éclairs	Thick cream: 150 ml [¼ pt] or Crème pâtissière: 425 ml [¾ pt]	—	150 ml [¼ pt]
200°C [400°F] gas mark 6 for 15 minutes, then: 190°C [375°F] gas mark 5 for 10 minutes	Thick cream: 150 ml [¼ pt] or Crème pâtissière 425 ml [¾ pt]	150 ml [¼ pt]	—
As éclairs	Thick cream: 275 ml [½ pt] or Crème pâtissière: 575 ml [1 pt]	—	150 ml [¼ pt]

2 Place the yolks and sugar in a small bowl and mix together to form a smooth paste. Stir into flour mixture.

3 Put remaining milk in a saucepan and bring to the boil. Pour it on to the egg mixture, stirring continuously.

6 Fold the egg white into the cooled pastry cream and return the bowl to a low heat. Lightly stir the cream for 2 minutes.

7 To flavour, fold vanilla extract, melted chocolate or coffee into the hot cream; or, when cold, fold in an equal amount of fruit purée.

Fruit and nuts
Soft fruit, such as raspberries, strawberries and redcurrants, make delicious additions with cream or ice-cream. Fruit purées and chestnut purées can also be used with cream or crème pâtissière.

TOPPINGS
It is the toppings that add that final glamorous touch to choux pastry. A finger of choux pastry, for example, is immediately transformed into a delicious chocolate éclair when it is filled and chocolate topped.

Icing sugar is the simplest of all toppings, as it can be lightly sifted over the pastry.

Glacé icing (icing sugar and water) is a good choice for topping choux pastry because it looks extremely attractive dribbled over a choux finger or bun. It has the further advantage that, before it sets, it can be scattered with chopped or flaked nuts, grated chocolate, chopped glacé cherries or chopped crystalized fruit. It is also a very useful medium for sticking profiteroles together.

Chocolate icing is a must when making éclairs; that very professional shiny icing is very simple to reproduce in your kitchen. Dissolve 25 g [1 oz] caster sugar in 75 ml [5 tablespoons] water and bring to the boil. Boil steadily for 2 minutes without stirring. Meanwhile, melt 75 g [3 oz] plain chocolate in a bowl over hot water. Add the sugar syrup to the melted chocolate until the icing coats the back of a wooden spoon. Then cover the tops of the éclairs with the warm icing.

Caramel topping: this sets over the top of the choux to form a crisp golden surface. Put 175 g [6 oz] granulated sugar with 75 ml [5 tablespoons] water in a small heavy-based saucepan and put over low heat until the sugar has melted. Increase the heat to high and cook for about 4 minutes until the sugar has turned to a deep golden caramel. Little round choux are then coated in much the same way as éclairs (see step-by-step pictures), but with the following exception. The sugar is extremely hot, so protect your fingers by putting the choux on a skewer to dip it. If the caramel sets before all the choux are coated, add 15 ml [1 tablespoon] water to the sugar and reheat gently over low heat until the sugar is workable again.

SOME FAMOUS CHOUX PASTRIES

Most famous of all choux pastry shapes is the cream-filled, chocolate-coated choux finger known as an éclair.

A small spoonful of about 5 ml [1 teaspoon] size of choux paste, dropped on to a baking tray, or a similar quantity piped from a 12 mm [½"] tube will give you a tiny puff about the size of a walnut when baked. These are best known in the pudding called profiteroles (see recipe). Cream-filled and iced, four of these are sufficient for a portion.

Croquembouche is another pyramid dessert. The puffs can be filled with orange-flavoured pastry cream and each puff is three-quarters submerged in the caramel so that it is both glazed on the outside and will stick to the one next to it. This makes a lovely party centre-piece if decorated with orange segments. It is, however, extremely difficult to serve neatly. Try making individual pyramids of 4 puffs for each portion.

These small cream puffs are sometimes used to decorate other gâteau the best-known of these being gâteaux St Honoré. This splendid concoction has a circle of shortcrust as its base with a cream-filled ring of choux on top. The centre of the circle is filled with pastry cream and the top covered with little cream-filled puffs, dipped in caramel.

Choux buns can be blobbed on to the baking sheet in 15 ml [1 tablespoon] drops or the same quantity piped with either plain or fancy nozzles. They are usually named for the filling; for example, choux Montmorency is filled with crème pâtissière and cherries, and choux à la normande with apple purée and a third of its weight of crème pâtissière.

Tiny cream puffs can be placed on top of larger ones, and chocolate icing poured over the two, like a nun's habit, to form a simple religieuse.

A special method of producing a particularly puffed-up choux, which does indeed justify the name of cabbage, is given in the recipe for strawberry choux buns. The principle is that the baking tray of buns is covered, in order to trap and conserve steam, which causes the maximum expansion of the choux. This craggy type of puff usually has icing sugar sifted over it, as the surface is too irregular for glacé icing.

A Paris-Brest is a celebrated gâteau made in the form of a ring. For this you need a single baked choux ring, with a 20 cm [8"] diameter when raw. There are several versions, but a ring split and filled with praline crème pâtissière and then topped with coffee glacé icing or sprinkled with icing sugar and chopped almonds makes a lovely party dessert.

PROFITEROLES

Nothing can compete with this extravagant dinner party dessert and you will be hard put to find a guest who is not delighted to round off a meal with a portion of these delicious little choux buns filled with thick cream and then coated in a chocolate sauce.

Traditionally, they are served in a pyramid so that the chocolate sauce can dribble down. If you find that you cannot cope with such an arrangement, serve them in individual dessert dishes, allowing approximately four buns per serving.

SERVES 6
425 ml [¾ pt] whipped cream
basic quantity of choux
    pastry (see step-by-step
    instructions)

For the chocolate sauce:
150 ml [¼ pt] strong black
    coffee

Profiteroles filled with whipped cream and topped with chocolate sauce are a dessert to remember.

100 g [¼ lb] plain chocolate
25 g [1 oz] caster sugar

1 Heat oven to 200°C [400°F] gas mark 6. Lightly brush two baking sheets with melted fat or oil.

2 Make the pastry as shown in step-by-step to choux.

3 Place the choux pastry in a large piping bag fitted with a 12 mm [½"] medium-sized plain tube.

4 Pipe approximately 30 buns on to baking sheets, making sure that the pastry shapes are spaced at least 2.5 cm [1"] apart.

5 Alternatively, use a teaspoon and drop the mixture neatly on to the prepared baking sheets, smoothing the shapes into balls.

6 Bake buns in the top of heated oven for 15 minutes. Reduce oven temperature to 190°C [375°F] gas mark 5 and bake for a further 10 minutes.

7 Remove the buns from oven and make a small slit along the side of each bun. Remove any uncooked pastry from the centre of each bun with the end of a teaspoon if this is necessary.

8 Leave buns to cool completely on a wire rack.

9 Using a teaspoon, carefully fill each bun with the lightly whipped cream. Arrange the filled buns in a pyramid shape on a decorative serving dish.

10 Place the coffee in a small saucepan and heat to boiling, remove from the heat.

11 Melt the chocolate by breaking it into small pieces and placing in a small bowl over a pan of hot, but not boiling water, stirring from time to time.

12 Remove from the heat and place the bowl containing the chocolate on a steady surface. Stir in the coffee a little at a time until it is entirely incorporated.

13 Return the chocolate mixture to the small saucepan with the sugar and stir over a low heat until the

sauce thinly coats the back of a wooden spoon.

14 Allow the sauce to cool slightly then drizzle over the arrangement of buns so that each bun is thinly coated with the sauce. Leave to set before serving.

Variation
● Serve with a fruit sauce rather than a chocolate one. Purée the drained contents of a can of fruit (apricots, raspberries, etc) then thicken the purée with 10 ml [2 teaspoons] arrowroot. Stir in 15 ml [1 tablespoon] sherry or some of your favourite liqueur.

CHOCOLATE ECLAIRS
The all time favourite made from choux pastry must be chocolate éclairs, those light-as-air fingers of pastry, traditionally filled with thick whipped cream and coated with a delicious chocolate or coffee icing.

MAKES 16 ÉCLAIRS
choux pastry based on 65 g [2½ oz] flour (see step-by-step instructions)
150 ml [¼ pt] thick cream
15 ml [1 tablespoon] milk

For the chocolate icing:
25 g [1 oz] caster sugar
75 ml [5 tablespoons] water
75 g [3 oz] plain chocolate

1 Heat oven to 200°C [400°F] gas mark 6. Lightly brush a baking tray with melted fat or oil and then dust very lightly with a small quantity of flour.

2 Make choux pastry as directed in the step-by-step instructions given on pages 170–171.

3 Using the handle of a wooden spoon, mark 16 lines across the prepared baking tray, 7.5 cm [3"] long and approximately 2.5 cm [1"] apart.

4 Put the choux pastry in a medium-sized piping bag fitted with a 12 mm [½"] plain piping tube.

5 Using the marked lines on the baking tray as a guide, pipe the pastry into finger shapes. Cut off the pastry with a round-bladed knife.

6 Bake in top of oven for 20 minutes. Reduce oven temperature to 190°C [375°F] gas mark 5 and bake for a further 15 minutes.

7 Remove the baking tray from oven. With a small sharp knife, make a small slit along the side of each éclair, about 4 cm [1½"] long.

8 Scrape out any uncooked pastry from the centre of each éclair, if this is necessary, with the handle of a teaspoon. Transfer the éclairs to a wire rack and leave to cool.

9 When the éclairs are completely cold, enlarge the slit to approximately two-thirds of the length of each éclair.

10 Put the cream and milk in a bowl and whisk until cream just holds its shape. Place the cream in a medium-sized nylon piping bag fitted with a small star nozzle and fill each bun. Alternatively, use a teaspoon to fill the inside of each bun with the cream.

11 To make the chocolate icing, dissolve the caster sugar in 75 ml [5 tablespoons] water and bring to the boil. Boil steadily for 2 minutes without stirring.

12 Meanwhile, melt the chocolate in a bowl over hot water.

13 Add the sugar syrup to the melted chocolate and stir in.

14 Coat the top of each éclair following the step-by-step instructions and leave until icing is set.

Variations
● Flavour the cream with rum, omitting the milk. Substitute milk chocolate for plain chocolate to make the icing.
● For a special decorative effect, use both plain and milk chocolate. Cover the éclairs with plain chocolate, then melt 25 g [1 oz] of milk chocolate and place in a greaseproof paper piping bag fitted with a small plain tube. Pipe the milk chocolate in a zig-zag design over the plain chocolate and sprinkle each éclair with a few toasted almonds.
● Instead of filling the cold éclairs with thick cream use crème pâtissière and coat the tops of the éclairs with a complementary filling.

STRAWBERRY CHOUX BUNS

▨▨▨ *This special-occasion recipe is a good example of how to shape choux pastry without using any fancy equipment. It also demonstrates another baking trick. You may have wondered how bakers manage to produce those wonderfully 'craggy' choux buns. The answer is by a rather different baking procedure. The pastry is dropped on to the baking tray and then a baking or roasting tin is inverted over the buns on the tray. The tin rim should stand inside the baking tray, so that there is a close fit; the idea is to keep in as much as possible of the steam produced during cooking. It is important not to remove the tin from the tray during the cooking time or the choux will definitely collapse. Because more of the steam is retained, these buns will rise much more; they have the traditional appearance the French had in mind when they named the pastry. If you find this baking method complicated, these choux buns can also be baked by the method described in the step-by-steps.*

MAKES 12 BUNS
425 ml [¾ pt] crème pâtissière
grated zest of 1 small orange
choux pastry based on 65 g
   [2½ oz] flour
100 g [¼ lb] fresh strawberries
25 g [1 oz] icing sugar

1 Make pastry cream following the step-by-step instructions and stir in the grated orange zest. Reserve.

2 Heat oven to 200°C [400°F] gas mark 6. Lightly brush a large baking tray with melted fat or oil. Make the choux pastry following the step-by-step instructions.

3 Take a tablespoon of the mixture at a time and place it on the prepared baking tray, easing the mixture from the tablespoon with a second spoon.

4 Make sure that the pastry shapes are at least 5 cm [2"] apart.

5 Place a roasting tin over the baking tray so that it fits snugly. If it is uneven, place a metal weight on top of the tin. If you wish, you may leave the pastry shapes uncovered.

6 Bake the buns in the top of heated oven for 20 minutes. Reduce the oven temperature to 190°C [375°F] gas mark 5 and bake for a further 15 minutes.

7 Remove the baking tray from oven and remove the tin from on top. Cut each bun into two horizontally. Remove any uncooked pastry with a teaspoon from the inside of the buns. Place the buns on a wire rack to cool.

8 Wash and hull the strawberries and cut the larger ones in half if necessary.

9 When cold, use a teaspoon to fill the bottom half of each bun with the orange-flavoured pastry cream.

10 Divide the strawberries between the buns, placing them on top of the pastry cream.

11 Place the 'top' of each bun on to the strawberry and cream filling and press down gently to secure.

12 Place the filled buns on a wire rack and dust the top of each bun lightly with a little sifted icing sugar.

Variations
●Flavour the pastry cream with rum as well as the orange zest. Omit the strawberries and replace with 25 g [1 oz] sultanas. Coat the top of each bun with chocolate glacé icing and sprinkle liberally with chopped pistachio nuts.
●Omit the pastry cream and strawberries. Fill each bun with spoonfuls of strawberry ice-cream and coat the top of each bun with plain glacé icing. Sprinkle with chopped hazelnuts.

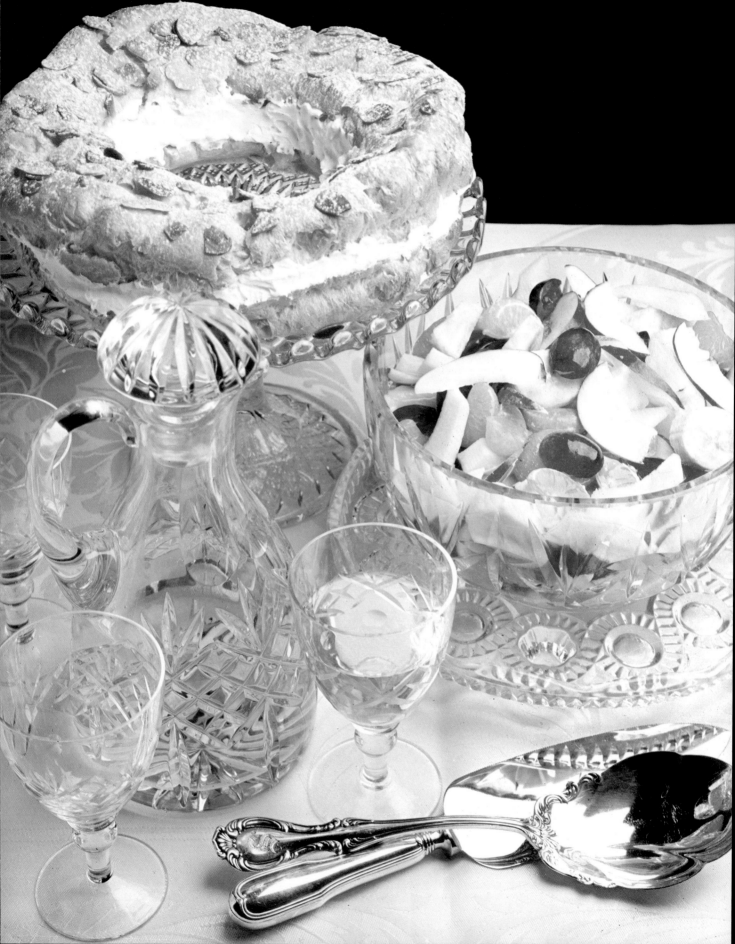

Star recipe

★

SCOTTISH SHORTBREAD

Shortbread, crisp, buttery and delicious, is one of the national dishes of Scotland. In Scotland, it is often made in attractive wooden moulds which are printed with a thistle or perhaps a game bird. The traditional shape for shortbread is known as a 'petticoat tail'—a triangular slice with a pretty, fluted edge. You can, however, cut biscuits using conventional biscuit cutters if wished. Rice flour is used in shortbread, because it gives lighter, crisper results but if you cannot obtain this, use all plain flour instead. In making shortbread, the sugar is added before the butter as the mixture is too dense to add sugar after the butter has been rubbed in.

As well as being served as a biscuit, shortbread can be used as a base for ice cream or creamy desserts with fruit purée.

SERVES 6–8
100 g [¼ lb] plain flour
50 g [2 oz] rice flour
pinch of salt
50 g [2 oz] caster sugar
100 g [¼ lb] butter
caster sugar to dredge

1 Heat the oven to 160°C [325°F] gas mark 3. Lightly grease a baking tray and dust rice flour in a mould or 17.5 cm [7"] sandwich tin.

2 Sift the two flours and the salt into a large bowl. Stir in the sugar with a round-bladed or palette knife.

3 Cut the fat into the flour, until the mixture resembles very large breadcrumbs and clings together.

4 Knead the mixture into a smooth crack-free ball. If the dough becomes sticky cover with foil and refrigerate for 10 minutes.

5 Press the shortbread into a short-bread mould with the palm of your hand. Alternatively, press into a 17.5 cm [7"] sandwich tin.

6 If using a mould, holding the mould close to the prepared baking tray, tap the base and the shortbread will come out.

7 If using a tin, flute the edge of the round, using your fingers or the handle of a teaspoon so that the edge looks frilly.

8 Mark round into portions on top, using a sharp knife. Do not cut straight through to the base.

9 Bake in centre of the oven for three-quarters of an hour until very pale golden in colour and firm to touch.

10 Cool shortbread on baking tray for 10 minutes. Transfer on to a wire cake rack. Dredge with caster sugar and cut into slices.

Star recipe

FROSTED PLUM TRICORNS

▽ *Crisp pastry encasing a surprise*
▲ *filling of plums and cream makes*
these decorative parcels an impressive
dessert. Yet they are economical to
make as only one plum is needed for
each parcel and not a scrap of pastry is
wasted because the shapes are cut
from the main body of the pastry.
Choose firm, good-sized plums for the
filling.

SERVES 4
175 g [6 oz] shortcrust pastry
8 plums
40 ml [8 teaspoons] caster sugar
150 ml [¼ pt] cream

For the glaze:
milk
caster sugar

TRICORNS

Tricorns are pyramid-shaped
pastry parcels with a fruit filling.

Tricorns are extremely decorative, but rather tricky to
make so the fruit must be able to
sit firm, leaving you both hands
free to shape the pastry. Suitable fruit include fresh plums,
apricots, greengages and bananas. Canned or soft fruit is not
firm enough.

To prepare stoned fruit,
wash, halve and stone the fruit.
Peel and quarter bananas. Fill
cavities of stoned fruit with
caster sugar (and some spice if
liked) before sandwiching the
two halves together.

1 Heat oven to 200°C [400°F] gas
mark 6. Then prepare the fruit. Cut
right round each plum, split in half
and remove the stones.

2 Fill the cavity of each plum with
5 ml [1 teaspoon] caster sugar.
Sandwich the halves together and
set the plums aside.

3 Roll the pastry out on a lightly
floured board to a rectangle 30 ×
26 cm [12 × 10"]. Cut in half
lengthways.

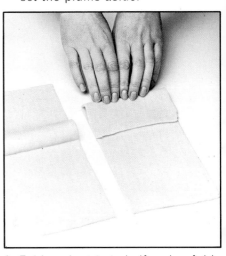

4 Fold each strip in half and unfold.
Then fold both ends of each strip
to the centre crease and unfold
back to original position.

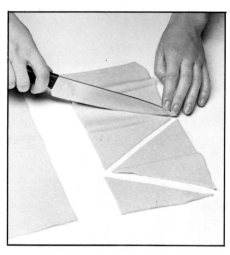

5 Cut each strip into 3 equal triangles by cutting diagonally up and down, using the crease mark as your guide.

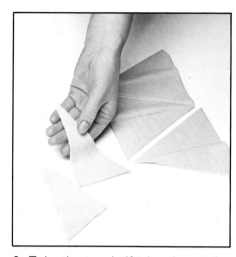

6 Take the two half triangles at the ends of each strip and put them together to make another 2 equal triangles.

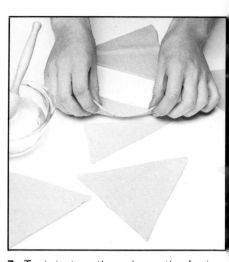

7 To join together, damp the facing edges, overlap them slightly and press seam firmly to seal. Repeat for second triangle.

8 Make the guidelines for shaping the tricorns. Take each triangle, fold each point to its opposite side and unfold after each fold.

9 Brush the outside tricorn edges with cold water. Stand a prepared plum upright in the centre of each pastry triangle.

10 Bring each corner of pastry up to meet at the top of the plum to make a pyramid shape. Seal the seams firmly together.

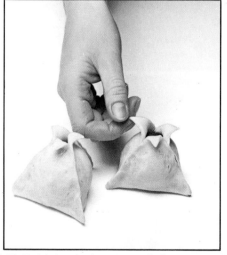

11 Fold back the tips of the pastry, making a hole for the steam to escape. Carefully transfer tricorns on to an ungreased baking tray.

12 Brush sides with milk and sprinkle with sugar to give the pastry a sweet glaze. Bake above centre of oven for 30 minutes.

13 Just before serving, dribble a little cream into the steam vent to fill the tricorns and sprinkle lavishly with caster sugar.

Recipe Index